LAMBERT FLORIN
Photographer and Fact Chaser Extraordinary

It is not enough for Lambert Florin to accept awards year after year for superior photography and to lecture to many groups on his travels around the western states and Canada. He must go digging for rocks ("ites" in the mountains and deserts, "ates" on the beaches). He must study birds and flowers to add to his prodigious knowledge. And he must continue to produce books for an appreciative public always wanting one more. This is the restless, tireless Mr. Florin who lives in Portland and knows more about ghost towns, old cemeteries, churches and how to get to them than Rand, McNally and the AAA put together.

HISTORIC WESTERN CHURCHES

HISTORIC WESTERN CHURCHES

by

LAMBERT FLORIN

Marysville, Montana Methodist Episcopal and Roman Catholic Churches are located companionably on adjacent street corners. Town located not far north of Helena was once filled with thousands of miners, hangers on. Main mine workings and mill owned was Thomas Cruse who donated land for churches in Marysville and Helena. Larger city's Catholic Church of the Sacred Heart was built in style of 14th century German Gothic at cost of one million dollars.

SUPERIOR PUBLISHING COMPANY • SEATTLE

FIRST EDITION

FRAYN PRINTING COMPANY ⬦ SEATTLE, WASHINGTON

Historic Western Churches
Is Dedicated to

**David C. Mason, M.D., whose help
and encouragement have made
this book possible**

Manhattan, Nevada's Catholic Church was constructed at Belmont when that town was a roaring, sin-packed mining camp and seat of Nye County. When Belmont faded, church structure was hauled fourteen miles to then burgeoning Manhattan. Feat seems almost impossible considering narrow road of alternating sand and steep, narrow mountain stretches. Now, Manhattan, too, is ghost town and once much needed church stands in splendid isolation above present huddle of shacks in remaining town.

Campanario photographed from mission gardens west of church is close approximation of original as shown in 1853 drawings. Collapse took place before any photo record. Bells were lost for many years, reassembled with difficulty when campanario was rebuilt.

FOREWORD

Since 1955 the author has spent several weeks each summer taking pictures and collecting material for books about ghost towns and old mining camp cemeteries. He has combed the hustings from near the Arctic Circle to well below the Rio Grande, from the Pacific Ocean to the Dakotas. Some 450 old camps, more or less ghostly, all historic, have been at least partly documented in photographs and historical data.

In many of these places early day churches still stand, some forlornly empty and deserted, some still in service. Wherever they seemed to arouse public interest, architecturally, historically or both, they have been photographed and added to the record.

This bit of background will help explain the seemingly arbitrary choice of documented churches, and why some of the pictures will seem familiar to the reader of the author's other books in the *Western Ghost Town* series, *Boot Hill* and *Tales the Western Tombstone Tell*. Yet many of the photos have been made especially for this book.

Also it will be noted that although there are in this country at least 200 distinct religious denominations, the churches here represent only a very small portion of them. Most early western churches were founded by those few denominations active in the 1700s and 1800s which included members with sufficient zeal and fortitude to try to proselytize the Indians or to organize church groups among a largely transient and ungodly population. Many early churches were founded "spontaneously" when there were enough members of the same faith. For these and other reasons we find few old churches representing relatively obscure faiths.

Our country is often spoken of as a "melting pot" of many different races and nationalities. Yet it is interesting to note that much of the Old West was settled by distinct groups that remained unmerged to a large degree, at least in a religious sense. In our great Southwest, including New Mexico, Arizona and Southern California, the church structure is predominately Catholic due to the fact that the area was opened up by Spanish explorers who dedicated the land as "New Spain" and bestowed their own religious beliefs on the natives. By the same token, in Canadian British Columbia almost all settlers were British and the churches they established were mainly Anglican.

No such generalities can be applied to the large expanse between, that is the Pacific Northwest and Rocky Mountain states. Here the denominations were more varied, almost every town having several different churches. There were exceptions of course. The Tualatin Plains Presbyterian Church was the only one in the settlement, being founded and still maintained by a tight group of Scots from the same county in the "Old Country." In Idaho City the Catholic Church served a congregation of Irish as long as they were employed in the mines. Puget Island in the Columbia River has long supported but one church, Lutheran, since its population is made up of Scandinavian fishermen.

Frank S. Mead dedicates his fine, definitive book *Handbook of Denominations,* "To those in the Church who see that the great truths we hold in common are more important to God than all the little fences and barriers which divide us." Although denominations have proliferated endlessly, all have a common aim, worship of a supreme, all powerful being, although His name might not be the same to all. At least one sect, Baha'i, seeks to unite all faiths, including Buddhism and others of Oriental origin.

Today the trend is toward unity, though the way is rocky. Modification of rigid doctrine emphasizes the oneness of man and God. Anyone feeling that little progress has thus far been accomplished might do well to take another look at relations between denominations during the period as late as the settling of our West. Acrimonious dissension reached a tragic height after the massacre of Marcus Whitman, his wife and many members of the Methodist Mission at Waiilatpu near the present Walla Walla, Washington.

A much lighter episode occurred in the Willamette Valley of Oregon. When Methodist Missionary Jason Lee arrived to establish his church for the Indians most of the few white settlers were French Canadians, ordinarily of Catholic persuasion. Among them were several couples anxious to be married. In the emergency they were willing to settle for the ceremonies performed by Rev. Lee. Soon after came the arrival of Fr. Blanchet who would establish the Catholic mission of St. Paul nearby. Naturally, the French Canadians moved over to his camp, and Fr. Blanchet was informed about the Methodist marriages. He laid down the dogma that these couples were not married, that they were living in sin, and promptly remarried them "properly." The incident infuriated Rev. Lee.

The original Methodist mission on the Willamette has long since rotted away. So has the first Catholic log church built near by. Eroding factors of time have leveled most of these earliest missions and churches, particularly in the moist northwest regions. Rot, fire and vandalism have all taken their toll, earthquakes have destroyed some, damaged others. But an astonishingly large number of religious relics have survived, a sprinkling from the 1850s, many from the 60s and in increasing numbers of later establishment. A number in the arid Southwest date from a period very much earlier.

In this book we attempt to picture and tell the story of some of these. Insofar as possible, those selected to appear here represent a cross section of the physical religious structures that took shape in a period when "God Came West."

Lambert Florin

CONTENTS

9

Historic Methodist Episcopal Church, Bodie, Calif., built about 1881.

10

CALIFORNIA

Gold, silver and six-guns

Last earthly journey for those who died in Bodie was short—from town to morgue (center) to cemetery (foreground). Good Methodists made detour to little church (behind morgue). Frequent epidemics of pneumonia affected many able-bodied workers exposed to freezing temperatures when soaked with sweat below ground.

When ground was frozen hard burials were delayed. Newspapers took undertaker to task for leaving "12 bodies at a time unburied." He countered, "I don't remember more than seven." When snow melted water compounded difficulties. Press reported, "At Bodie the ground is so wet they have to bail out freshly dug graves and then pile rocks on the coffin to keep it from floating out. At some of these burials the preacher is at a loss as to whether to read the funeral or baptismal service." (More photos, story see *Boothill*).

Angels in the

WHAT WERE CHURCHES doing in Bodie, that infamous cesspool in iniquity, the "city that God forgot"? The simple answer is not much. In fact it was not until 1878, nineteen years after William Bodey found his first gold nuggets here, that hope began to rise in some quarters for a church and five years after that before it got one.

A local newspaper voiced the need. In November, 1878, it was reported, "The need of a church is becoming more urgent every day. Mr. Walker called upon the clergy of the place to establish a house of worship. He told several of them that the recurring deaths from pneumonia were producing a beneficial effect in the way of directing the inhabitants toward the consideration of the probabilities in the hereafter."

And in December there was another item on the subject. "We have no church but Miners' Union Hall answers that need and a variety of other purposes. On Saturday afternoon, for instance, the hall was occupied for a 'Grand Testimonial'

Interior of M.E. Church shows much deterioration about 1955.

Flesh Pots

and a complimentary banquet to Billy Costello the champion lightweight of the Pacific Coast, matched to fight Harry Maynard for $1000 a side . . . At ten o'clock Sunday morning, the Rev. Father Cassin of the Roman Catholic Church said Mass in the same place but dismissed his congregation in time to allow Rev. G. B. Hinkle of the Methodist Episcopal Church to preach to his little flock. At 2 p.m. the same platform was occupied by an amateur minstrel performance on which occasion there were not a few of the dead and buried jokes of the past generation perpetrated on the present one."

During the next few years the newspaper carried bits of information in its quest for a church building and regular services as in one issue the following March: "Bodie in its boasted progress and improvement has evidently forgotten what she needs the most, that is, a church; a big one with a spire as tall as our expectation. It ought to make the very boulders blush when made known that the entire Mono County never has had even the semblance of a church building. . . . Bodie is probably the only city of 8,000 inhabitants in the world that has no church. It is also the only place where Pinafore was never sung until last night . . . A church sociable will be given by the ladies of Rev. Hinkle's Society tomorrow evening. The best of music and other entertainment is down on the program. Oysters, lemonade, candies, fruits and popcorn balls for refreshments . . . Let everybody attend."

The first public awareness that the town would at last have an edifice of its own came in April, 1880, when the newspaper announced, "Rev. Mr. Hinkle will soon commence the erection of a Methodist Church on Green Street above Fuller, an excellent location."

In 1880 the Bodie *Weekly Standard News* and *Free Press* were printing regular "Church News" columns on Saturdays. "Bodie to have church. Subscriptions started for the use of Rev. Warrington of the M. E. Church." On Saturday, June 14, 1884 the *Bodie Evening Miner* gave the notice, "Methodist Episcopal Church—T. P. Bradshaw Pastor, Sabbath Services 10:30 A.M. Sunday School 7:30 P.M.—Song, service and preaching.

Prayer meeting every Thursday at 7:30. *Seats Free*. All cordially invited." And a second notice —"St. John's Catholic Church—Father Melvin, Mass every Sunday morning at half past ten o'clock. Sunday school at 1:30. Vespers in the evenings at 7:30. *Seats free*. You are cordially welcomed."

Two years later in 1886 with both M. E. and Catholic Churches at last erected, one of the papers sought to clear up a misunderstanding as to how funds were obtained for construction. "The Methodists finally built a church on Green Street, but it is supposed that as the saloon and gambling element was very much depleted, the funds were secured by popular subscription and not from a tax on these establishments as suggested by one of our more facetious newspaper correspondents. The Catholics also constructed a church, St. John the Baptist, on Wood Street."

That Catholic Church had the same difficulties in funding. It was around 1878 that the Bishop of the Diocese sent out young John B. Cassin, just out of the seminary and newly ordained to establish and build a church in the hell-raising camp.

Rev. Warrington of the Methodist Church received many letters from worried mothers concerned about the spiritual welfare of sons seeking their fortunes in Bodie. Preserved is one answering letter meant to console the writer, in part reading, "I do not wonder that you consider your son to have 'entered into a sea of sin,' lashed by the tempest of lust and passion. Such dissipation as is indulged here has never been written about in books. Let me give you a resume of what has happened this week. On Monday morning a man was lynched for shooting another in cold blood. On Friday two men grappled with each other, each holding fast with left hands while emptying their guns into each other's stomachs. One dropped dead and the other is expected to breathe his last at any moment." The minister felt however that the woman's son was not in any danger of a similar fate "except by his own choosing."

The young priest made the trip in the same rough-shod stagecoach that carried all passengers. The weather was bitter cold and Fr. Cassin wore a heavy woolen muffler around his neck. Conversation between one of the male travelers and a flashily dressed woman gradually identified the man as a gambler and the woman as a prostitute, both intending to enter business in Bodie. The two began an exchange of experiences in other mining camps, the language used being uninhibited in the extreme. Fr. Cassin suffered in silence for a time, then quietly removed his muffler. Stunned silence then prevailed in the coach.

Although easily surviving this experience, Father Cassin later seemed unequal to the task of building his church. Expected to don the hat of architect, builder and fund raiser the priest was often seen walking around the lot selected in a confused manner. At last a kind-hearted carpen-

Miners' union hall (center building) in group of false-fronts is most solid remnant remaining on more than mile-long Bodie street. Gaps indicate where small structures have fallen to decay, fires destroying most of town. Inside of hall is long auditorium, once lined with chairs on sides, stage at far end used for union meetings, carnivals, plays, dances, exhibitions, Sunday services for Methodists and Catholics, now filled with thousands of artifacts connected with Bodie's early days, including white cross once surmounting Catholic Church of St. John the Baptist, salvaged from destroying blaze.

Magnificent Mono County Courthouse is most conspicuous feature in hundreds of square miles of high mountain country. Structure represents one more link with Bodie, also in Mono County. Funds for construction, $31,000, were largely accumulated from taxable property in then flourishing mining camp. Almost since completion of structure in 1881, California bear flag has been flown along with national emblem. Huge celebration dedicated new courthouse on March 26, 1881. Next month Bridgeport's largest saloon, Loose's, was moved to a spot strategically convenient to new Courthouse. Cannon was made in Standard Machine Shop in Bodie, a gift from that town's most prominent citizen, James Stuart Cain. Cain was father-in-law of late Ella Cain, Bridgeport, long-time friend of author.

Typical scene in Bodie today shows line of once elegant residences with Methodist Church in background.

ter took over, drawing plans that were adequate and supervising erection on the rocky hillside site. With the building in more expert hands the priest took to soliciting in the gambling dens and saloons. He even screwed up the courage to invade the cribs along Maiden Lane.

Fr. Cassin administered the faith in Bodie for five years, the most hectic in his life as he afterwards related to a new congregation in the far more sedate Santa Rosa. Called upon to administer the last rites to a man shot in a saloon brawl, the priest bent down over the bleeding man sprawled on the floor. At that moment the near-dying victim spied his slayer among the spectators. With his last reserve of strength he whipped out his gun and sent a bullet whizzing past the ears of the priest.

His old church in Bodie burned to the ground some time around 1928. Legend says the historic structure had fallen victim to arson. It was true a man attempted to buy the long unused building for a paltry sum, just for the lumber. Refused, he was not seen again, the fire occurring shortly after that incident. The church was completely destroyed but for the large white cross on the steeple which fell to the ground out of the flames' reach. This lone surviving relic is treasured today in the museum housed in the same Miners' Union Hall where Fr. Cassin had first said Mass in Bodie.

The story of the wide-open camp has been covered in many ways, in many articles and books. It can only be touched on briefly here, beginning with that hot day in July, 1859, when a short, middle-aged man with graying mustache and hair led his burro along a rock flank on the east slope of the High Sierra. Something in the sand caught his attention and the man, William Bodey, stopped to examine the area more closely. After some surface scratching he is said to have exclaimed to the burro, "Say, old Peter, this sure looks like paydirt at last. If it is you and I know we sure came a hell of a ways to find it."

Bodey waited to allow his trailing companions Doyle, Garraty and half-Cherokee "Black" Taylor to catch up with him. The quartette camped there for the night, but before cooking supper washed out some of the dirt they scraped up. When a bright string of gold nuggets coiled around the bottom of the first pan, the men knew they had it made. They quickly established a permanent camp near the spring and built a little cabin.

The next winter was a bad one, as winters at that altitude of well over 8,000 feet always are.

Bodey and Taylor (the other two had moved on), ran out of supplies and trekked down to Mono Lake for more. On the way back they were overtaken by a severe blizzard. Bodey became lost and was buried in the snow, his body not discovered until next spring. Taylor made it back to the cabin, but later wandered on to other camps. Some years later he was attacked and killed by a band of hostile Indians, though first accounting for ten of them. These incidents strongly contributed to the long standing superstition that all discoverers of rich gold deposits were doomed to a violent end.

During the several months between Bodey's discovery and his death several other men had made camps in the vicinity, the tiny nucleus of a gold camp that would attract thousands of people, return millions in gold and attain a reputation unequalled for wickedness. The town was named Bodie after William Bodey the discoverer, the difference in spelling accounted for in several varying stories.

By the year 1878 Bodie was a lively place as noted in the press. "There was a good humored albeit boisterous crowd out to see the races Sunday . . . The faro banks are doing their share of the business, stud horse poker draws the best house . . . A costly barroom mirror was demolished in Bodie last night by a stray pistol shot which missed the bar keeper . . . A wildcat and bull terrier dog will make the fur fly at $100 a side at Upper Dance House tomorrow night . . . The mining superintendent dared a hurdy girl out of a saloon to fight him a few evenings ago and got a black eye for his temerity . . . The reprehensible habit of some rowdies who ride untamed mustangs down our streets, endangering the necks of innocent mustangs is to be discouraged . . . Main Street has more saloons along a given length than any other thoroughfare in the world."

These samples of entertaining episodes reflect the lighter side of life in Bodie, alternating items deal with the sadistic, murderously violent interludes that give substance to Bodie's bad reputation. "The Bad Man From Bodie" was a household phrase. Equally well known was the story concerning the little daughter of the minister of nearby Bridgeport's church. Having been told that her father was being transferred to the church at Bodie she ended her prayers that night with, "Good bye, God, we are going to Bodie." When the tale reached the town, the Bodie press was quick to react. The correct version, one paper said should have been, "Good, by God, we are going to Bodie."

Pioneer structure in Bridgeport that served Louis Wedertz family many years as combination home, store, became church in appearance and fact when gothic windows and low-steepled tower were added. Latter serves as entry, with entire remaining area converted into nave with small sanctuary and altar placed at far end. George Delury Jr., custodian, is proud of fact that father, George Sr., served as Justice of Peace in famous Bodie for many years. When Bodie became ghost town, father moved to Bridgeport as County Clerk. When he retired, son George inherited job, serving until retirement in April, 1965. Church served Baptists, Methodists and Presbyterians for many years, present emphasis on regular Presbyterian services with Rev. Edward Brown of Lee Vining as Pastor.

From Beans to Bibles

UNION BRIDGEPORT, it was known in the days of 1908 but when Bodie was booming it was store and home for Louis Wedertz and family. In later days when his son Frank built a new home for the aging parents, he presented the building to the town of Bridgeport to be remodeled for use primarily as a Protestant church, available to any faith.

The town of Bridgeport is linked in history with the far more spectacular and notorious Bodie. Its situation unique, set in the center of a grassy expanse once known only as "Big Meadow" at nearly 7,000 feet in elevation, the town has as backdrop the fantastic outline of some of the most scenic sections of the High Sierra where are located the only glaciers in the range. Game and fish abound in nearby forest and streams. Summers are mild, pleasant, winters bitter cold with heavy snows.

The first white man to set foot in the mountain-girt meadow was George Byron Day, where about 1855 he arrived with the first wagon train party headed by William Whitney, who later wrote, "We came across the plains at the invita-

tion of a man named Green who accompanied us. We ran the first wagon train that ever went up the East Walker River Canyon, ten miles of terror in the river and over boulders in a very swift current. We came into a valley beautiful as Paradise with the purest water and richest grass I ever saw. Now our stock was at last happy and would grow fast. We were surrounded by high mountains. We built a log house for Mr. Green on the east side and then went over to the west side to locate a ranch for ourselves." In 1863 when much of California was devastated by severe drought the Big Meadow offered abundant forage for thousands of cattle driven to the high places.

After the first log cabins were erected for emergency shelter, the most urgent need was for lumber. So a sawmill was erected as almost the first business venture, then a blacksmith shop to shoe the oxen. The first white women to live in the valley were Mrs. Vaughn and Mrs. Parsons who worked as cooks at the sawmill.

The settlement was located in Mono County as was, some contended, big, booming Aurora not many miles away (see Ghost Town Shadows). Naturally the county seat was fixed at Aurora but to satisfy those who believed Aurora was in Nevada, the county seat of Esmeralda County, Nevada, was there too. The two seats of government were discreetly placed at opposite ends of the street for less voter confusion at election time. It was said many townspeople took advantage of the situation to vote in counties of two states.

When in 1864 news came that Aurora was officially four miles east of the state line in Nevada, California's Mono County relocated the seat, this time safely within the boundary in Big Meadow rather than the first-considered Monoville near the inland "dead sea", Mono Lake. When a modest two-story frame structure was erected to serve as courthouse across the East Walker River from the main settlement, a connecting bridge was built and the whole area called Bridgeport.

A prominent pioneer family here was founded in 1879 by immigrant Louis Wedertz. In Hanover, Germany, to evade army draft, he stowed away in a packing case on the docks and narrowly escaped drowning when the case was pushed into the water. Landing safely in New Orleans, Louis met and married his wife Dorothy. They went to San Francisco via Panama and then on to Aurora. Finding mining not to his taste, young Wedertz and bride moved to Bridgeport on a land claim. They built a combination store and restaurant, raised a family of five daughters and three sons, one of whom was Frank, donor of the old store and home.

Previously the community had attended services offered by an itinerant priest who carried his paraphernalia from town to town over the widespread, primitive area, serving such places as Lee Vining and Mammoth. It was not until 1962 that a Catholic church was built in Bridgeport, serving the town itself and remote outlying settlements in the high mountain places.

In Sonora's old cemetery are many graves dating back to early 1850s. Some display elaborate wrought iron enclosures.

Piety Hill Was Church Rich

ALTHOUGH GOLD CAMPS along California's Sierra foothills numbered into the hundreds, each distinct in some particular, Sonora is remembered for at least three individual features. It was founded by Mexicans from the state of Sonora and almost came to revolution when racially intolerant Americans arrived. Secondly, among mines classed as "pocket type," the Big Bonanza in the heart of town was the richest of any in the Mother Lode. And, where other camps boasted of a church or two, Sonora's Piety Hill proudly showed five.

The group of Mexicans who pushed north from the slightly earlier Wood's Hole diggings called the place Sonoran Camp and worked the mines peaceably for several months. In the spring of 1849 the first whites arrived, a group of nineteen men including twelve Americans. They soon installed a crude form of law and order, elected R. S. Ham as alcalde and all went reasonably well until the fall of that year. By that time some fifteen hundred Mexicans, Chileans and Peruvians had poured into Sonora and neighboring Tuolumne camps and before winter settled in the population numbered more than five thousand. It was said, "You couldn't get a mule through the crowds unless you held his ears back."

And in the crowds there were many trigger-happy rascals, almost every night seeing blood shed in the narrow alleys back of the numerous saloons. Rather than risk a civil war of violence, the authorities levied a heavy tax on all "foreign-

Often termed "most beautiful in Mother Lode," St. James Episcopal Church in Sonora was designed by Rev. John Gassman of San Francisco. When he came to gold camp to view finished structure he was so enthusiastic about the way constructors had carried out his plans he sent back to Bishop Kip for permission to remain as pastor. Structure was built on potentially gold-rich land, several mines within stone's throw having yielded millions in nearly pure yellow metal (More photos, story see *Ghost Town Album*).

18

ers." The levy proved so burdensome that in a few weeks most non-Americans moved on to other camps, reducing the population to almost half. The mass exodus however included many of the big spenders and with a business depression feared, the tax was lifted. Many exiles returned and so did prosperity.

Just prior to this the Chileans discovered gold on Piety Hill, less than three hundred feet from the St. James Episcopal Church and a short distance from four others. Forced to sell out, the South Americans accepted a pittance from three American partners who worked the mine in routine fashion for several years until they broke through the "roof" of a pocket of almost solid gold. In one day they readied a shipment to the San Francisco mint worth $160,000. Within a week they shoveled out half a million and after extracting as much more they sold out and left the Mother Lode for the "palaces of joy" in San Francisco. The metal taken from Big Bonanza, San Guiseppe and Golden Gate in or near Sonora was known the world over for its peculiar "fineness," a purity instantly recognized in the mint.

Although the first buildings along Washington, Sonora's main street, were of brush and canvas, they were soon replaced by lumber structures. In 1852 a disastrous fire consumed all of these and an enterprising group established a brick yard and kiln nearby so more durable replacements could be made. But for a new Episcopal Church members wanted a wooden Gothic structure similar to the ones back East whence many had come. Accordingly, gold-rich men donated three lots at the head of Washington Street for the site, giving sufficient space for fire safety. Plans for the classic structure were drawn by Rev. John Gassman of San Francisco and by the spring of 1859 enough donations were received to warrant the start of construction.

Most famous of Hornitos badmen was Joaquin Murieta. According to well-founded tradition, bandit made headquarters here, escaped from favorite saloon through underground passage when danger threatened. When author visited Hornitos in 1961 he found definite evidence of tunnel, pictured here, opening less evident in 1968 (More photos, story see *Boot Hill*).

Church Faces Violent Past

As Hornitos faded into limbo Catherine's Church became extension of Mariposa Diocese with irregular services. Then came long periods of complete abandonment. By 1935 church was badly deteriorated and efforts for restoration began. Sagging beams were shored up on stone foundations and on each side four buttresses braced walls. Conjecture is that the stones were salvaged from section of the miles of fences built by Chinese in early days, these having utilized most loose rocks. Improvements did not include wiring for electricity, but picturesque old "coal oil" lamps with tin reflectors seem far more fitting to old church.

HORNITOS IS FULL OF GHOSTS, a few residents keeping vigil with them. The post office still functions, the tavern too, both facing the still distinct plaza. St. Catherine's Church stands on a nearby hill top among those strange little ovens that are actually tombs, looking back on the riotous mining camp days.

Fr. Francis Walsh of St. Joseph's in Mariposa says, "St. Catherine's Church is in my parish but is no longer used except at Easter and Christmas when we have special services. The church was never wired for electricity so it is still lit only by the old original kerosene lamps, one at each side of the altar and a larger one hanging near the choir loft. Each has a tin reflector but sheds very little light . . . I said Mass there last Christmas in near darkness, feeling transported back to the old mining days. Everything is exactly as it was then."

The old days of violence began a few miles from the southern terminus of California's Mother Lode where a noticeable outcropping of snowy white quartz occurred. As early as the summer of 1848 some Mexican prospectors found gold in the glittering rocks and settled there. In November of the same year came Kentuckian Col. Thorn with wife and Negro slaves. He built an imposing adobe store-home, the front and tall chimney of brick which was said to have been freighted around the Horn.

Even before his arrival the Quartzburg settlement was notorious for flagrant vice and as the camp grew so did gambling, prostitution, murder and assorted wickedness. Says one historian, "Seldom have so many variations of murder, fornication, adultery and incest been represented in one group."

To the very religious Col. Thorn all this was intolerable and he organized a Vigilante Committee to clean up his town. In the dead of a cold winter night members went through the camp routing out of bed all those on Thorn's black list. Forty-odd Mexican men and women straggled out into the thin, blowing snow, most in night clothes, none with any personal belongings or funds.

The forlorn band walked some three or four

miles when the women gave out, almost frozen. At this spot were several small stone cairns resembling the outdoor ovens used by Mexicans and termed "hornitos." Reyes Montano, notorious murderer and acknowledged leader, started a fire in one of them. Then lifting off the flat slab on top, he recoiled at seeing human bones inside. The hornitos were actually tombs. Another fire was built a short distance away and the exiles spent the night in some degree of comfort.

Daylight revealed several ranches in the neighborhood and one of the outcasts made quick use of his accomplishments as a horse thief. The smell of roasting horse flesh soon filled the air and spirits rose. The group put up ramadas of brush and struggled through the winter.

In the warmer weather one man jumped in the small stream near the camp to take a bath and saw something that changed everything—a sizeable nugget of shining gold. The entire party splashed in and gathered a handful. A woman carried the gold to Thorn's store for food and supplies, Thorn no doubt allowing the sight of gold to overcome his scruples. It is also assumed

he spread the news that the metal was even more plentiful at the new site than at Quartzburg.

In no time at all the little camp ground near the tombs grew into Hornitos, arranged around a central plaza. Each of the erstwhile outlaws grew rich, the men by mining, women by the occupation they knew best, with customers well able to pay.

With the naturally tremendous influx of outsiders came many honest, hard working miners, some with families, and the need for a church became acute. Construction of St. Catherine's Catholic Church began about 1863 and was finished in a year or two.

By this time Quartzburg's gold was almost gone and in a few years the place was deserted. Adobe buildings slowly melted away, even the stately structure built by Col. Thorne collapsing into heaps of rubble. The bricks were taken by Hornitos residents for their buildings and Quartzburg became a true ghost town, marked only by a few mounds of adobe, watched over by the church on the hill.

Few inches of surface soil barely cover solid, rocky underlay, making digging of conventional graves difficult and in old days nearly impossible. Original Mexican settlers scraped off soil, laid row of flat rocks, placed simple coffin on this and surrounded it with other stones. Such burial structures generally termed "grottos" among Spanish speaking people were here called "hornitos" because of resemblance to commonly used outdoor bake ovens. Several of originals remain, in vandalized condition. Those shown here, enclosed in and protected by the Catholic cemetery fence, remain from early 1870s. At left lower background is approximate site of exile-founders campground.

Copper in the Midst of Gold

AT THE END of the Civil War in April, 1865, the prosperity of Copperopolis was shattered and the last measure of reverence given to the town's Congregational Church. On the Sunday following Pres. Lincoln's death in Ford's Theater soldier members of the Union Blues formed parade ranks in front of the armory at the south end of Copperopolis and proceeded with slow, measured steps to the church at the other end of the main street to file into the brick edifice for memorial service to the slain president.

For a few exciting years the camp was a definite anomaly. Although situated in the middle of California's famous gold belt its people mined for copper and took out many tons of the red metal.

The excitement started about 1860 when two big copper mines were located, Union and Quail Hill. Ore assayed 30% copper and was worth $120 per ton at the mine. The population grew to 10,000 in 1863 and ox teams hauled ore to the value of $1,600,000 over private toll roads. Ambitious promoters began the construction of the Stockton-Copperopolis Railroad.

All the while the bloody Civil War was raging. There were many southern sympathizers in this central part of California and they were vociferous in demanding that the name of the Union mine be changed to Confederate. But rebel voices were silenced when Pres. Lincoln sent a regiment of soldiers to Copperopolis to make sure the copper produced was properly channeled to the north and that no sabotage occurred. At this time the price of copper reached the staggering high of 55¢ a pound, but with the war at an end, Pres. Lincoln dead, the good times of Copperopolis ended and the Congregational Church passed with it into history.

Sun-drenched brick edifice was built and dedicated as First Congregational Church of Copperopolis, foundations of meta-andesite rock heavily laced with copper. Two years after consecration in 1863 it was scene of memorial services for assassinated Pres. Abraham Lincoln. End of Civil War was also end of economic boom in copper, leaving town in doldrums. Though there have been some small resurgences, Copperopolis has been near ghost ever since. With lack of sufficient number of Congregational members for maintenance, church was sold to I.O.O.F. Lodge for meeting hall. When these too dwindled away structure was turned over to community for any purpose desired.

San Diego mission as it looked in 1927 when author photographed it with simple box camera. Facade appears much the same in photos made in 1950-62 period when occupied by U.S. Army. Soldiers tore out interior furnishings, added second floor. At that time ramshackle adobe structures filled space in front, campanario, bell tower had collapsed. When this photo was made, interior of church was hollow shell without roof and walls in state of collapse. Plans for restoration had then been under way since 1915.

CALIFORNIA'S SERIES OF MISSIONS, extending from San Diego in the south to Sonoma in the north, is of great historical worth. Original plans did not include all twenty-one. Two were to be established at points located and explored by Spanish ships, at San Diego and Monterey, and a third somewhere between them to break the long land journey. Each mission would be connected with a garrisoned presidio and so would God and the military bring religion to the natives and at the same time protect this northern outpost of New Spain from threatened encroachment by the Russians.

San Diego, discovered by Juan Rodriguez Cabrillo in 1542, was the first colonizing objective of two Spanish expeditions sent out from Mexico in 1769. One went overland, the other on two ships, *San Carlos* and *San Antonio*. The packets arrived in the bay first, crews of both suffering badly from scurvy, and a camp was made at the mouth of the San Diego River. Originally numbering ninety, scurvy and accident had reduced the miserable crew to thirty before the land party arrived. The latter was intact but all members were near starvation and thoroughly exhausted.

Southern California, at the time of Spanish settlement, had a larger population of natives per square mile than any other area in the country. Blessed with a salubrious climate and an ample supply of natural foodstuffs it was only natural for them to live a life of what the Spanish scornfully termed "indolent sloth." Their diet was made up of whatever was at hand. Called "Diggers" because of their easy utilization of wild onions and many other plentiful bulbs and roots. Cress in the river shallows, acorns, snared rabbits and birds formed a balanced diet. The Spanish, looking down their noses at this kind of simple food, died like flies from scurvy caused by lack of green stuffs in the diet.

While the natives several times swarmed over the ships at anchor near the shore, raiding for hardware and ripping up the sails, they refused to touch stored food supplies, having some faint suspicion that it was salt pork and sea-biscuit that was killing the members of the settlement.

The two debilitated Spanish contingents considered problems and plans. Governor Portola, commanding the sea party, elected to lead his sorry remnant northward in search of Monterey Bay. Father Junipero Serra, in charge of the overland group, would stay to found the first mission—San Diego de Alcala.

With his aiding padres and soldiers, Serra selected as the site the crown of the prominent hill just south of the river and in full view of San Diego Bay and harbor entrance beside Point Loma. Here was erected a chapel of brush from the river bed and on July 16, 1769, was founded the first mission in California. As the soldiers started building an adobe presidio, the *San Antonio* was sent south to San Blas in Baja, California, for badly needed supplies and medicines.

Nineteen more men died of scurvy before the return of Portola from the north and two Spaniards succumbed to wounds from Indian arrows in one of several attacks by the savages. Not one Indian had so far been converted and when it became obvious the whole project might soon fail, Portola laid down his decision. If the relief ship failed to return by St. Joseph's Day, March 19, all would attempt to return to civilization. Father Serra privately made up his mind that he would not return under any circumstances, that if his close friend Fr. Crespi would stay with him, he would remain and take his chances with the Indians and starvation.

Seven months after the *San Antonio* had departed, and on the evening before St. Joseph's Day, the vessel was sighted off Point Loma, but it did not enter the Bay. Its captain was headed for Monterey, planning to stop at San Diego on the way back, perhaps months later. About the time the ship was out of sight of the anxious watchers on shore, it lost an anchor and was forced to return to San Diego Bay. Portola, on sighting the San Antonio as it passed by had allowed a period of grace and all survivors were on hand to welcome the vessel. The infant San Diego Mission was saved. Today the hill south of the river is the green landscaped Presidio Hill Park. A rough brick cross against the sky and hummocks of

a's First

melted adobe on the ground are evidence of the first efforts of Crown and Cross in California.

By 1774 it was clearly evident the hill site was unsuitable for a permanent mission. The early selection was strategic, as any ship entering the harbor could be sighted immediately, but now the Indians, at last coming in to be baptized and converted, were continually in trouble with soldiers at the garrison. While the dusky, squat Digger maidens would hardly be termed seductive under ordinary circumstances, soldiers long separated from Spanish senoritas were easily enticed. Beyond this, the hilltop site was too small for agricultural purposes. So the mission was moved six miles up and across the San Diego River to the present site.

Restoration was completed in 1931. Walls were rebuilt, some original adobes incorporated and many roofing tiles replaced, although entire new roof was necessary. While securing structure's future, restoration offered little air of antiquity—plaster glaringly white, for example.

25

Handsome statue in mission garden is thought to represent patron saint, San Diego de Alcala.

Most important consideration in choosing location for missions was good, arable land with vailable water for irrigation. At San Diego, Padres immediately planted date palms among other food crops. Snapshot dater 1927 shows original group of trees. They were then surrounded by fruiting cati and gnarled olives. All were later destroyed to make room for new highway passing front door of mission.

Dedicated As Cannons Boomed

SAN CARLOS MISSION was the second one of those established by Fr. Serra. It was founded at Monterey Bay near the presidio set up to prevent further southward movement by the Russians. The dedication in 1770 was a gala, joyous affair but the booming cannon meant to impress the Indians only sent them scurrying into the hills.

As at San Diego padres found Indians and soldiers did not mix well so in a year's time San Carlos Mission was moved to a site near the "Rio Carmelo," two gun shots from the sea. Carmelite priests had visited the area with Sebastian Viscaino in 1602 and noting a strong resemblance to the landscape around Mount Carmel, they named the site after the birthplace of their order.

Fr. Serra put a crew to work cutting timbers for construction of the first church, a dwelling and storehouses. Five soldiers who accompanied the party from Monterey helped build their quarters and palisade surrounding the establishment.

In 1791 a new church was built of stone, designed by architect Manuel Ruiz, brought from overseas. Since then the building has gone through several changes, passed through periods of neglect and near ruin. Modern restoration was done in the 1930s under the able supervision of Harry Downie. As it stands today San Carlos Borromeo de Carmelo is regarded by many as the most beautiful and romantic in the entire Serra series.

Campanario of San Carlos Mission is plastered with swallows' nests. Birds are identical with more famed cousins appearing each St. Joseph's Day at Capistrano.

Fountain style conforms to that in other mission gardens. Designed originally from Moorish-Spanish, form now shows influence of primitive Indian artisans. Spectacular star window centering facade invariably calls for second look. Is it lop-sided? Possibly designer intended feature placed on side rather than balanced on one tip. Although his bones rest inside, Fr. Serra never saw this part of his church. It was erected around his grave.

Ornate reredos is third since stone church was built. Original one was ruined when roof collapsed during one period of neglect. Second one displayed same arch and figures centered in it, lacked other ornamentation. Altar is at bottom of photo and graves of padres just beneath.

Sarcophagus sculptured by Jo Mora shows reclining figure of Fr. Serra with sorrowing, life-long friend Fr. Crespi bending over him.

Considered loveliest of California missions, San Carlos stands in area famed for scenic beauty. In early days exposed to far flung views of Monterey cypress, Carmel River and blue Pacific, mission is now surrounded by expensive homes, hotels. Edifice has passed through seven stages of building, dating from initial wooden chapel. Well cared for semi-tropical gardens fill forecourt, predominant bloom here masses of orange California poppies.

Body of Fr. Serra was buried in preferred location at left of altar in then existing adobe church. Next to his lie graves of lifelong associate Fr. Crespi (at left) and right, Fr. Laseun who carried on Serra's work. During nearly 100-year period of neglect of San Carlos (and other missions following secularization) graves lay in ruined church exposed to weather and encroachment of weeds. Twice since stone church was built on same site. In 1856 and 1882 rumors that Serra's body no longer lay in original grave forced exhumation. Twice Serra's bones were removed, identified and replaced. Then in 1943 church authorities started proceedings for canonization of revered mission founder. Proceedings required that Fr. Serra's remains be once again brought out of grave for even further identification. Founder Fr. Serra made headquarters at Carmel, living under simplest conditions. In these restored quarters in 1784, wearied, 70-year old leader called to him close friend Fr. Palou. "Please assist me to die" he whispered. When news of death spread, presidio guns at Monterey boomed, mission bells tolled.

Romance i

San Juan Capistrano, most handsome, beautiful of all California mission churches, stood only six years, two more than were required to build it. Much sandstone was used in construction, supply quarry six miles away. Carretas, burros, oxen and Indians transported materials. Constructed in cruciform, chancel, sanctuary, were of solid stone, walls south of transepts of adobe.

When earthquake struck, adobe easily crumbled, allowing stone roof to collapse upon kneeling Indians. Many of those in front were able to join priest in solid sanctuary, escaping carnage. Ruins are softened by exuberant growth of vines, shrubs. Gaunt, leafless stubs at right are poinsettias trimmed back for dormant season in early summer. Christmas time sees them in blaze of red throughout mission gardens.

he Ruins

HE MISSION of San Juan Capistrano, famed in legend and romantic tales of bells, love and tragedy actually has a real history more dramatic than any fancied myth. Contrary to the difficult struggles suffered by other foundling missions, San Juan enjoyed peace and prosperity from the start. Soon outgrowing the original tiny adobe church, a new church was begun in 1796. Completed nine years later the magnificent structure stood as a monument to show what could be accomplished by primitive Indians under harmonious direction of Spanish stonemasons and architect. Over the front entrance stood a bell tower lifting its belfry 120 feet in the air. The gilded cross it bore could be seen for ten miles.

Only six years later, while the nave was filled with praying Indians, the tower began to sway, wildly jangling the bells. In moments the walls fell in, allowing the massive domes overhead to crash down in a jumble of heavy rocks. Forty worshipping natives were killed outright in the earthquake with many more severely injured. The two Indian boys who had climbed the tower to assume the great honor of ringing the bells for Mass were killed. The great stone church was in ruins, never to be repaired.

In 1775 Fr. Lasuen set up a cross on the spot selected for a new mission honoring St. John of Capistrano, Italy. The location was within sight of the ocean-pointing headland later made famous by Richard Henry Dana in his *Two Years Before The Mast*. After dedicating the ground surrounding the cross Lasuen and his helpers started construction of a simple chapel. After eight days of work there came word from San Diego that Indians had attacked the mission there, killing Fr. Luis Jayme and burning the buildings. Fearing a general attack the priests at the barely founded Capistrano Mission buried the bells and went to San Diego where they sought safety in the presidio on the hill. A year later, Fr. Serra, heading a second party to Capistrano, found the cross still standing intact. Bells were rescued from the rubble, hung in a tree and work was started on another church. This was considerably larger than originally planned and

Cloistered walkway is south-facing section of quadrangle enclosing mission complex. Original "Serra's Church" is at far end, to left.

much more solidly constructed So well was it built it still stands on the grounds today, surviving the disastrous quake of 1812. It is the only structure still standing in which Fr. Serra officiated at Mass and is considered the oldest church in California.

"Father Serra's Church" stands near the southeast corner of what was an extensive quadrangle, parts of which remain. The establishment was large enough to at least temporarily house all neophyte Indians who herded the cattle and sheep and cultivated the fertile fields during the day. Extending south from the southwest corner was a line of buildings quartering the soldiers, these well separated from Indian sleeping rooms in the main square. How effective the separation was here and at other missions may be surmised by the fact that large numbers of Indians died of venereal diseases unknown before arrival of soldiers and sailors.

The magnificent new stone church destroyed by that fatal earthquake in 1812 might otherwise have stood as a splendid museum piece but it could not have been long a viable mission unit in any event. When deep lying faults centering in the Santa Barbara Channel readjusted themselves, shattering many nearby missions, a worse disaster was already brewing, a cataclysm that would crush all of them.

The province of New Spain was already in ferment with a general movement to secede from the mother land and it became the independent Republic of Mexico in 1824. A few years later the new country issued the fatal decree of seculariza-

Bells were originally hung in campanile surmounting front of stone church. They crashed to ground when earthquake shattered tower, were replaced in this campanario in 1813. Small pair at left was cast in 1796, others in 1804. Throughout history of Mission San Juan Capistrano these bells have been subjects of song, legend.

Life-size figure carved in wood represents St. Francis de Assisi, patron saint of Franciscan Order, one of many works of art preserved on grounds and in buildings of San Juan Capistrano.

tion for the missions. All church lands and property other than the church building itself reverted to the government to be converted from mission to pueblo. Cut off were such sources of support as the selling of thousands of cow-hides, the shipping of them so graphically described by Dana. Some missions struggled on for a time, but the blow would be mortal sooner or later. A century of neglect would slowly spread ruin over the chain of settlements established by the Spanish Crown and Sword.

Old statue in mission garden represents founder Fr. Serra comforting Indian lad. White "doves" are persistent, gentle, readily taking food from hands of visitors. One of many mission legends claims any bird born of "foreign" color turns white immediately. Certain it is that birds of other colors mysteriously disappear over night.

Grounds of mission are mass of luxuriant, colorful, semi-tropical flowers. Shown here is rampant Bougainvillea vine supported by ruined arch. South American import is at home here; varies in color from old deep magenta purple thru newer crimson lake, blooming almost year around.

Oldest adobe house in California, built in 1794, contemporary with early mission days, stands in good condition in what was Indian village of San Juan Capistrano. Built and since occupied by Rios family, well cared for structure is smothered by flowers, shrubs, trees; old grapefruit in foreground. Caught taking pictures, Dr. Mason and author were invited inside to view rooms still furnished with original furniture brought around Horn—huge, canopied bedsteads, spindle-backed chairs in everyday use.

Mission fo

Arched entrance to mission cemetery is located just east of main door to church, essentially same as when constructed. Massive-leaved agaves flank sides.

Gates to cemetery gardens bear colorful designs, seemingly authentic relic of mission days. Actually they were painted by Walt Disney artists as background setting for Zorro episodes. They do follow genuine style of early mission period.

More than twenty California missions were extended to nearby fertile or populous areas, these sub-missions termed assistencias. One of these was San Antonio de Padua, likely name saint of founder, Fr. Antonio Peryi, Mission President of San Luis Rey de Francia, some miles down San Luis River. Assistencia flourished from start, at one time swarming with more than a thousand neophytes. After secularization establishment affectionately called "Pala" decayed, but a most complete dissolution came with American occupancy, private owners utterly ignoring historical value of chapel and grounds. In 1903 Landmarks Club purchased property and began restoration.

Campanario shown here is detached from chapel, retains original bells. In 1904 many service clubs formed El Camino Real Assn. to indicate old padres route from one mission to next. Ceremonies of opening included placing of first 100 lb. cast iron bell in front of Plaza Church in Los Angeles. By 1913, 450 were placed, by 1921 most had been vandalized or stolen. Year 1959 saw resumption of effort by many organizations including Auto Club to restore, replace bells. Short crook and name plate identifies this bell as original.

Digger Indians

AFTER THE DEATH of Fr. Serra at Mission Carlos Borromeo de Carmelo, his place as Father Presidents was ably taken by Fr. Fermin Francisco de Lasuen. It was Fr. Lasuen who, on June 13, 1798, led solemn ceremonies that founded Mission San Louis Rey de Francia.

The site was idyllic, on the summit of a slight eminence four miles from the sea and just above the San Luis Rey River. A crude adobe chapel was quickly erected and planning begun for a more solid church, the first substantial building being completed in 1802 under plans and supervision of Fr. Antonio Peryi. This was soon found inadequate for the increasing family of Indian neophytes.

Foundations for the third and present building were laid in 1811, completion on the Feast Day of St. Francis de Assisi, Oct. 4, 1815. Built of adobe faced with fire brick, the edifice was at once massive and resistant to weather. Its beautifully proportioned facade (upper part actually an espadana, Spanish type of false front), the graceful doorway, massive bell tower and colorful gardens impressed Duhaut Cilly who visited the church in 1827. He wrote "The buildings are drawn on a large and ample plan, wholly the idea of Fr. Peryi. He directed the execution of it in which he was ably assisted by a very skillful man." The "man" referred to had also aided in construction of the mission at Santa Barbara as is evident on comparison. The imposing white

Church of Mission San Luis Rey de Francia shared with that of San Juan Capistrano floor plan in cruciform; the only California missions so designed. All are remarkable examples of self-sufficiency in construction of native materials. Walls of San Luis have thick inner core of unusually shaped adobe bricks, 8x8x24 inches in size, laid diagonally. Brick and tile lavishly used were fired in mission kiln. Facade would seem to have once supported additional tower to match existing one.

structure must have made a tremendous impression on all who saw it standing in the lovely valley otherwise unmarked by human habitation.

Father Peryi was placed in charge of the mission, Indian neophytes, surrounding gardens and orchards. Under his able supervision the establishment prospered for over thirty years. By 1811 over three hundred neophytes were enrolled. Many horses, cattle and sheep roamed the adjacent pastures and carefully cultivated gardens, irrigated from the river, provided ample food for all.

While some missionaries had difficulty adjusting to the ways of a primitive race composed of Digger Indians, Fr. Peryi ranked high among the understanding ones. He was successful because he inspired love and cooperation among a people coming under a way of life utterly different from their previous indolent, carefree ways. Revolting under too much restraint at some other missions, natives at San Luis Rey were consistently industrious and peaceable.

With secularization, the Spanish Fr. Peryi was forced to leave the mission and his beloved Indians. Planning to flee from San Diego by ship, the padre arranged to leave at night in order to avoid the sorrow of parting from his Indian charges. As his ship was weighing anchor the beloved priest shoved off from the beach in the vessel's long boat. Somehow learning of his departure a large band of Indians took fast ponies and got to San Diego Bay just in time to receive the priest's blessings as he held his arms wide in benediction. For many years afterward the Indians placed flowers and burned candles before Fr. Peryi's picture, neglecting established saints in favor of this man personally known and loved.

Under secularization the Indians gradually scattered and the buildings began to decay with neglect. Troops and civilians held bull fights in the garden court and caroused in the living quarters. The church and main buildings were later sold to the United States Government and in the spring of 1893 they were restored and rededicated as a Franciscan college. Although in good condition today the old mission shows loss of charm in modern improvements.

Most of original Pauma Indians, dispossessed when Americans took away property, moved elsewhere, leaving behind only those buried in Pala Cemetery. Later, Palatinguas from Warner's Ranch and others resettled area, now worship in little chapel nearby. Cemetery is one of few remaining where Indians annually celebrate All Saints Eve, October 31. Cemetery then is crowded with Indians, the women tending lighted candles on each grave, men standing apart along church wall, watching. Scene is one of extreme beauty. Shown here at left are feathery, pendant branches of pepper tree, descendant of those introduced by Peruvian sailors at mother mission. Terra cotta saint carrying Cross and Bible is one of pair occuping niches at either side of main front door to church. Traces remain of once brilliant coloring.

First Church Bells Rang in 1861

MONG EUREKA'S EARLY RESIDENTS was W. E. Jewett of New Brunswick who arrived in Humboldt County with his parents at the age of two. Mr. Jewett spent most of his life in Eureka observing and recording events there right up to his death on the day after Christmas, 1966. Concluding his last newsletter to the *Humboldt Historian* Will Jewett wrote "God willing, I will again be writing in the next issue."

About Eureka's early churches Jewett wrote in the May, 1963, issue ". . . then there was the old Congregational Church, located at the corner of Fourth and G Streets, now a show window of Daly's Store . . . Of course I attended the Congregational Church. Morning service was at eleven, Sunday School at two in the afternoon, evening service at seven thirty, and weekly prayer meetings on Wednesday evenings. The room where we held prayer meeting was at the rear of the church and almost up against the old Centennial Hall. The Tenth Battalion had established a drum corps that practiced at the same hour we held prayers. Like as not, they would break into a long roll just when one of the brothers was saying his prayer. None of us could hear him, but trusted that the Lord could. Going to Church was in those days, a real factor in life, not merely an occasional diversion.

"In those early days the Episcopal Church, the Methodist Church, the Catholic Church and the Congregational Church all had bells in their belfries and none of them had the same tone, so one could tell which bell started ringing first. In the Congregational Church Mr. Allard, I think his initials were J. K., was the sexton and rang the bell. It was a monument in my life when he permitted me to ring that bell. Mr. Allard also took up the collection on Sundays and a contribution was always contributed by my father.

"In Sunday School each of us took as a collection gift five cents. Nickels had not in those early days come into use in this part of the country so what we took was a small silver five cent piece called, I believe, a 'half dime.' Well, one Sunday morning, going from our house toward H Street, I dropped my coin in the dust of the wagon road.

The others would not wait for further search. So I went that Sunday to church with no contribution. Day after day I searched for this coin, but just couldn't find it."

Little Will grew up, as the years went by, moved to San Francisco for a time, thence to Berkeley where he married. More years passed and he returned to Eureka with his wife and several children. There he bought a piece of land on which to build a home for his family. The lot included part of the old wagon road. "Of course we had to have a garden, so one evening after work I was spading the front yard, digging up the old road which had been packed hard by wagon travel over the years. Turning over one shovelful I noticed something white and picked it up. Yes, it was that old five cent piece I had lost so many years before."

Eureka today has many fine churches. One of the most picturesque is St. Bernard's Catholic, the structure having its beginnings in the early 1850s. At that time Eureka's few parishioners received blessings only occasionally when some hardy priest came along on muleback while traveling north from the gold camps along the Trinity River. First such recorded visit was by Fr. James Croke, a missionary from Oregon. He celebrated Mass, baptized infants, gave the sacrament, living meanwhile with the Shanahan family. In succession there followed Fr. Hugh Gallagher, Fr. Florian Schwenninger, Benedictine monk from the Tyrol and graduate of University of Innsbruck. It remained for Fr. Thomas Crinnion to actually organize the parish in 1858, but even he could spend little time there because of the acute shortage of priests.

Three years later the population of Eureka was large enough to sustain a church and on Nov. 2, 1861, the *Humboldt Times* recorded, "Work has commenced upon the building of a new Catholic church which is under contract to be enclosed within 90 days. It is to be 30 x 60 feet on the ground and a height and style to correspond." The work proceeded as weather permitted aided by a series of festivals to raise money for the furnishings. The Christmas party was a great success although the *Times* reported, "The hall was not large enough for any degree of comfort for the crowd attending."

Once established St. Bernard's stretched out to missions at Del Norte and Crescent City, preaching in either requiring a three-day trip for the priest. In 1875 Fr. Edward Kelly took over duties at church and missions. He lasted only a year, was replaced by Fr. John Nulty who soon complained that the coastal rains and winds were too much for him and was transferred to Gold Hill, Nevada (see Ghost Town Bonanza). Fr. Charles Lynch's stay was also short, he being followed by Fr. John Sheridan who arrived in 1883.

Fr. Sheridan began his tenure with vigor, immediately initiating plans to build a new church, the old one obviously inadequate for the several thousand Eureka people. He entered into a contract with local architect James Simpson, to draw up plans for a larger structure to cost $12,000. Building soon was under way, with completion and dedication on June of 1886. Consecration was by Bishop, after which Fr. Sheridan said the first Mass and Fr. Buchard preached a sermon based on a text from Matthew 16:18. In 1892 Fr. Sheridan died and was buried under the side altar dedicated to the Virgin Mary.

St. Bernard's Catholic Church in Eureka was named for famed Cistarian Abbot of Clairvaux, great church leader of 12th Century. Edifice of classic Gothic architecture seats more than 700. With completion of new church, old structure was used as hall for some years until new one was built.

Oldest known photo of Ferndale made in 1875. Almost hidden in trees at extreme upper left are spires of "Fern Dale's" old Shaw home, oldest in town, still carefully preserved. Later Congregational Church was built across street. Left of upper center are two halls facing each other, at left with Gothic windows Masonic Hall, actually used for other fraternal organizations as well. Here, before their own buildings were erected, several Protestant churches held services. This structure still stands in place. Across street is Centennial Hall where Catholics attended Mass regularly, later moved to another location. In lower center is large stable still under construction. L shaped structure behind was Ferndale Hotel. Photo courtesy Ronald Smith, Ferndale.

Plymouth Congregational Church in small community of Hayfork in wilds of Trinity Alps in Northern California was built under difficult conditions, overcome by generosity and hard work on part of congregation.

Author's modern photo shows much of Ferndale and includes such an assemblage of churches as is seldom seen in small towns. At left and most prominent is M. E. Church adjoining large cemetery in which is interred 120 year old John Bradbury. Others following sequence, some plainly visible, others partly so, some hidden—St. Mary's Episcopal, Our Saviour's Luthern, lacy spires of Catholic Church of the Assumption, Congregational, Assembly of God, St. Mark's Lutheran. Site of Adventist is not visible. In addition, such organizations as Salvation Army, etc. held services.

Many Churches, Much Color

THE GOOD CHURCH WOMEN of Ferndale were not all two-fisted in their attitudes toward blatant immorality in the town but enough of them were to form a "hatchet brigade" and storm one of the larger houses of ill repute. Or so the story goes. They were armed and carried cans of kerosene. They stomped up on the house porch and shouted in angry tones something like, "We order you filthy scum out of this town—so get out or we'll burn this rotten place to the ground!"

It is not written what the results of the skirmish were but the zeal displayed did extend to other activities of the church women in their effort to make Ferndale a better place in which to live. In 1878 the Ferndale *Enterprise* noted the town had three churches—the Methodist Episcopal with its own building, Congregational holding services in the Masonic Hall, Catholic holding Mass every other Sunday in Centennial Hall. But there were more to come.

The Rev. J. H. Strong was Methodist pastor in early 1878 which seems to have been not long after its church was erected, but a change came in October of that year, the Enterprise recording it November 1, 1878: "Gone—Rev. Strong and family left on steamer *Whitlaw* yesterday (Thursday) afternoon. His resignation of his pastoral charge here and his departure leaves but one pastor in our place, Rev. Dr. Jones. As Dr. Jones is our father (meaning his own father: Ed.) we cannot speak of him and his works as we otherwise would. However his abilities, popularity and high-toned conservative, independent course are well known here. A friend suggests we write about anything and everybody as we choose as they may merit and deserve. The suggestion may be a good one and we will try to be governed by it—when we have to show him off as a black crow."

The Methodists were strongly Evangelistic and held "protracted services" in the church, one report reading, "Eight united with the church last Sunday and many more have expressed their determination to lead a better life . . . Many have discarded their way of evil . . . may the good work go on."

Janitorial work in the church was done willing-ly by the women members but sometimes they registered mild complaints, as according to the *Enterprise* September 26, 1879: "The ladies of the M. E. Church went in a body and gave the church a thorough cleaning. We heard several times since that they did wish that the gentlemen would not expectorate tobacco juice on the floor. Gentlemen, surely you would not do such a thing, would you?"

In January of 1880 the M. E. Church had a narrow escape from destruction by fire. The nave was illuminated by two chandeliers supporting kerosene lamps. For purposes of cleaning chimneys, trimming wicks and filling fonts, the fixtures could be lowered by ropes running over pulleys. After one Tuesday evening prayer service the sexton began letting down the front chandelier to blow out the lamps. The rope broke, allowing the fixture to crash down on the pews, setting the place afire. Fortunately a number of worshipers had loitered to chat near the door. The *Enterprise* said they "were of sufficient number to suppress the flames, but the chandelier is a wreck."

In June of the same year the *Enterprise* reported "The Rev. Mr. Rhine will lecture on temperance next Tuesday evening in the M. E. Church. All are invited and especially the imbibers of ardent spirits. A rousing big time is anticipated."

The Methodist Church flourished for many years but foundered in the bitter ending of an experiment initiated in brotherly love. The Congregationalists had much enlarged their own edifice, but soon found it an over-extension. The church was so roomy as to dwarf its relatively tiny congregation and presented problems in heating and maintenance. The Methodist people, having some room to spare, invited their Congregational brothers to join them in worship. The offer was accepted and reciprocated. For a time the combined congregations jointly and alternately attended both churches.

All went well for a time; then internal friction between fundamentalists on both sides began to rear its ugly head. Worship services were conducted without friction, but at formal meetings tempers flared and they often ended with dissenters stalking furiously from the church. It was evident to all that the federation must end, as it did, but with some irony. Many Methodist members, more in sympathy with Congregationalist views, joined that church. Now the Congregationalists had sufficiently large membership to fill and maintain their own church, but the shrunken remnant of faithful Methodists could not. On a sad Sunday in 1961 the little group made its decision. Locking up their church they went to join with the M. E. congregation at nearby Fortuna. The Ferndale church has remained closed since.

The earliest assemblies of the Congregational adherents, as reported in the Ferndale paper, were held in the Masonic Hall. "Preaching every Sabbath at eleven a.m. Prayer meeting every Thursday evening at seven thirty." In October, it reported progress: "The work on the building of the Congregational Church is being rapidly pushed forward by McLeod and Colburn. The edifice when completed will be 35 x 54 feet . . . Topped by a cupola it will be 78 feet from base to top of the vane. The church will be a neat, modest and pretty one, which will speak volumes for the energy of Rev. G. M. Dexter, and for the liberality of the members and friends of the church." Completion of the structure was announced November 19, 1880.

By 1953 the Congregational Church, having outgrown itself, was remodeled and enlarged. "The nave and chancel cover an area larger than was originally occupied by the entire church." Every effort, the paper said, was made to retain the character of the original edifice. During the period of reconstruction the congregation met for services and prayer meeting in the Masonic Hall.

Old wooden headboard in Ferndale Cemetery adjoining M. E. Church gives John Bradbury's age as 120 years. Astounding life span is seemingly authenticated in *Enterprise* obituary of March 30, 1897. ". . . deceased was a native of Buckinghamshire, England . . . while the exact date of his birth is not known we learn that he was, beyond all doubt between 120 and 130 years of age." Further details delate how John and two brothers came to America "80 years ago," frst settling near a tiny community of three houses called Chicago, Illinois." "He decided not to invest his several hundred dollars in real estate, which had he done so he would now be several times a millionaire." He came to Humboldt County about 1867. "For the past 26 years he has lived with Mr. Nelson. He was even then well along in years and nearly blind . . . for eight or nine years he suffered with a sore leg . . . and during his last four weeks was helpless . . . deceased was a good man . . ." Historic headboard has never fallen victim to vandals, but is suffering from erosion, inscription slowly disappearing. Strong sidelighting here throws letters into relief.

Streets of Ferndale are lined with elaborately ornamented structures usually termed "Victorian." This one, depending heavily on turned spindles for effect was second hospital. Long-time director was Dr. H. J. Ring. Of recent years building has reverted to use as rooming house. Stone dog on right is one of pair guarding entrance walk.

The Episcopal Church did not apparently have a large enough congregation to hold services regularly, even after the handsome St. Mary's Church was built, so plain outside with ornate interior. Worship was conducted about once a month with the pastor traveling from Eureka. More regular meetings began sometime in the late 1950s, the minister now coming from Fortuna.

Richard T. Du Brau wrote in his book *"The Romance of Lutheranism in California,"* "St. Mark's Lutheran Church, Ferndale, was the mother church of a vast area which stretched from Sonoma to the Oregon border. The church was organized on April 26, 1906. From Ferndale missionaries spread out into various directions of Humboldt and Del Norte Counties, often reaching over into Trinity and down into Mendocino."

The Lutheran Church had started with slow strides, beginning in the early 1890s. Henry Christian Strube, "father of Lutheranism in Humboldt County," wrote to Jacob Buehler of the Missouri Synod requesting that "something be done for isolated Lutherans in the Eel River Valley." In June of 1893 Pastor J. H. Theiss arrived, conducting first services on the 13th. Thirty people attended, five children were baptized and Holy Communion celebrated. Theiss also conducted services in Eureka and neighboring communities.

The next missionary to the area was Frank C. Streufert who made several discouraging efforts to establish a regular church. At his last service in 1903 he asked that the forty people present sign a request to the Synod for a regular pastor. A number rose but sat down again when Streufert made it clear that they would be expected to promise regular contributions toward a salary. Only one person actually came forward, Carl Marcussen, a fifteen-year-old boy.

In 1850 B. C. (before churches) the Ferndale site was a bare flat delta of the Eel River, land deposited by a river usually peaceable but a raging, silt-laden torrent in times of flood. A minor Wiyot Indian village, Butsatswil, originally occupied the spot.

In 1850 the schooner *General Morgan,* owned by Samuel Brannan and commanded by J. Brannan, anchored off the Eel. The next day two boats came ashore, successfully breasting a strong current. The U. S. Revenue Cutter *Laura Virginia,* also waiting off the river mouth, sent in one boat but it capsized with the loss of one man, the others swept out to sea where they were rescued.

After burying the drowned man, the Brannan party explored the area, then attempted to return to the *General Morgan.* Unable to breach the heavy surf the men hauled their boat around the bluff to the north, launching it again in a bay protected by two long, narrow peninsulas. A few days later the *Laura Virginia* came into the bay, Capt. Hans Buhne mapping the harbor and naming it Humboldt after explorer Baron Von Humboldt. Buhne could not claim discovery, however, as in 1806 Capt. Jonathan Winship sailed his *O'Cain* into this shelter while hunting sea otter for American-Russian Fur Co.

One passenger on the *Laura Virginia* was Stephen William Shaw who was to be instrumental in founding Ferndale. In the summer of 1852, Shaw, his brother Seth Louis, and several others selected homestead land a few miles south of Humboldt Bay. The group spent weeks clearing away trees and dense stands of giant ferns covering the coveted farm land. They built a stout cabin on the Shaw claim, completing it on August 25.

All the settlers helping in the building project now moved in to spend the winter in communal fashion. Besides the Shaw brothers there were ten other pioneers who arrived in subsequent weeks. One of them, Seth Kinman, noted later, "We were a great crowd of us and we literally crowded the cabin chock full." Later he wrote in his diary it was one of the hardest winters he had ever known. Close confinement and too much togetherness caused every man to suffer from cabin fever. They had no beds and had to huddle together to keep warm, all but the Shaws scattering at the first sign of spring. Since they called their cabin Fern Dale, the community growing up around it took that name.

S. W. Shaw proved to be more artist than farmer and sold out but his brother Seth stayed on. In 1856 he finished a beautiful new home, an architectural gem in the style of Hawthorne's "House of Seven Gables." (After a period of neglect the house today has a new foundation which was badly needed. It serves as the residence of the Frank Fords.) The house was the forerunner of dozens of lacy homes and store buildings that constitute the "Victorian museum" that is Ferndale today.

Most of the source material for this area's history was pointed out to me by Ferndale high school student David Anderson. He has an added interest in fossils, old bottles and in seismic sciences, giving me details of the observations being made in the Ferndale region.

For many years the University of California's

Department of Sciences used a seismograph made by the German-Japanese firm, Bosch and Omori, Joseph Bognuda in charge of its operation. When it became obsolete, the delicate instrument was replaced by a more improved one, and Bognuda asked that the old one be presented to the village of Ferndale.

Why Ferndale? The community was founded on a spot centered in a veritable network of faults, split-offs of the notorious San Andreas fault. Two of these slightly less troublemakers, Russ and Little Salmon, surround Ferndale, both entering the ocean at this point, the village frequently shaken by the shift of one or the other. What more appropriate location could be selected for a still accurate, if out-moded, seismograph?

The instrument was placed in the old jail cell at the rear of the fire station. It was mounted on a cement pier stuck in the ground and is now under the protection of two residents, Ronald Smith and James Scalvini, who selected David Anderson for the actual custodian. One of his daily duties is to coat the tape with a film of soot over a smoking kerosene burner, the wide band then fitted to the revolving drum to receive the scratchings of the stylus. David displays tapes showing agitation marks, explaining them as made by heavy surf pounding on the beach some three miles away. "The only bother is in times of bad storms," he says. Although an antique, the machine is so sensitive as to record with accuracy vibrations caused by strong winds and the passing of heavy trucks . . . while refusing to be agitated by fire engines roaring out of the same building.

Mendocino Masonic Hall was finished just before building of first Presbyterian Church directly across street. Handsome three-story structure still stands as monument to early Mendocino's fraternal organizations. This striking sculpture, carved from single block of redwood surmounts tower high above street. Symbolism is mystery to non Masons.

First Service Held

VICTORIAN MENDOCINO, with its lacy houses and gracefully spired churches, is built on a peninsula that slopes gently down from mountains to end abruptly in sea-girt cliffs. The setting is idyllic except when swept by raging winter storms.

In 1851 such a gale tossed a small ship against the rocks, one heavily laden with costly silks, tea and Oriental art objects. Among those in San Francisco hearing the news was politician-lumberman Harry Meiggs. He had a hard head for business but was somewhat of a romancer, seeing himself now as salvaging the rich treasure trove —luxury items he could sell at high prices in a San Francisco booming with a gold rush.

Meiggs, whose mills and docks were at North Beach, organized and sent an expedition north from Bodega to search for the wreck. The treasure hunt was headed by Jerome Ford whose destiny would be to build a city and a church. The party was unable to find any signs of a broken ship but did find a bearded, ragged man who said he was the sole survivor of it. He gave his name as William Kasten and related how he had crawled exhausted from the pounding surf to be met by friendly Pomo Indians. They took him to the south side of the peninsula, to a gentle bay edged with white sand, and there he spent the winter. He took Ford and party up the river, then called Booldam, later Big River, and pointed out a solid phalanx of giant redwood trees extending from water to mountains.

Ford rushed back to tell Meiggs that he had found treasure, not in silks, but in an inexhaustible supply of timber for his mills. Meiggs sent heavy machinery on the *Ontario* to Big River and informed squatter Kasten he would erect a big sawmill and begin cutting timber.

Kasten agreed to the practicability of the idea but remarked, "Of course you can't take the land just like that. After all, I own everything here by squatter's rights." He named a price and Meiggs felt forced to accept it, buying the whole peninsula, which became the site of Mendocino, and a sizable belt of redwood running inland. As an added benefit he promised Kasten plenty of the first lumber cut for a fine house. This was the first house built in Mendocino and stands today on Albion Street.

Perhaps that winter with local Indians spoiled Kasten for white company for he sold out to William Kelly for $3,500. With several others, Kelly was in partnership with Meiggs, supplying most of the money for the first sawmill. Now owning a home and feeling his finances secure, Kelly married a girl from Prince Rupert where he had lived. Then suddenly Meiggs decamped for South America, taking his funds with him and sending the infant town into a depression.

On a Saturday evening in 1854, two Methodist preachers, Reverends Bateman and Preston, appeared at the Kelly home in search of shelter. Although under stress, Kelly fed the two and put them up for the night. Next morning one preached a service in the mill cookhouse, the other holding evening service. Their congregations numbered twelve; and thus did God come to Mendocino.

These and other ministers came and moved on, preaching at the Kelly home or wherever they could. Four years later one hundred and fifty people lived in Mendocino and a real house of worship was wanted, one with regular services by a resident preacher. It was well understood that while there was plenty of redwood for a church, the regular minister might be hard to come by, the town being reached only by ship or mountain trails.

Residents formed a building committee, electing J. B. Ford as chairman and William Heeser treasurer. The site selected was in the community center directly across the street from the new Masonic Temple with the fancy carving on top. Building commenced immediately and, when finished, the little church faced south, had an aisle down the middle with seats on either side and two pews east of the pulpit for the choir.

When the building was ready for painting, Methodist minister Rev. Robert Kellan arrived, with his boys ten and twelve. Recently widowed, he said that he would like to settle in this community away from the reminders of his dead wife.

n Cook House

Mr. Ford told him, "We will be glad to have you, of course, and we will need a minister. But the church must first be painted." Rev. Kellan took the hint, immediately going to work with brush and paint bucket. He also became the first minister to serve in Mendocino with any regularity. Trustees Peter Kelly, J. B. Ford and Dr. D. F. Lansing stated that, although Kellan was ordained as a Methodist, the church was to be open to any evangelical denomination.

The congregation, always open-minded about denominational affiliation, soon decided the time had come to settle on one. Among those present at the meeting of decision were a Methodist, a Congregationalist, an Episcopalian and a Baptist, but the oldest and most revered was Peter Kelly, ordained as an elder in the First Presbyterian Church of Charlottestown, Prince Edward Island. The outcome of the meeting was a unanimous vote for Mendocino's affiliation with the Presbytery of San Francisco and was received into that body in 1860.

First Presbyterian Church, built in classic New England style, faces Pacific Ocean without intervening buildings. Edifice originally fronted on highway entering city, present route now running past rear of church.

Founded in 1859 church could have been part of almost any denomination, original congregations representing most Protestant faiths. It became Presbyterian through leadership of Elder Peter Kelly who led flock into unity. Jerome Ford donated bell, purchased in Troy, N.Y. for $500 and shipped around Horn. Its clear tones have been heard countless times around the world in film *Johnny Belinda* which used Mendocino church and choir as background. Still faithful member joining church in 1917 is local historian Mrs. Nannie Escola.

Two years later the small church received a steeple and later a bell was placed in the belfry. The first funeral conducted was for Thomas R. Hall, a young soldier murdered at the gang mill in 1861. Two years later the church sanctuary was the scene of the funeral for Peter Kelly.

By 1865 Mendocino was booming. Redwood trees were falling by thousands to be cut into lumber in several mills along the coast. People were pouring in, houses and business places going up. When the church became inadequate a new and larger one was started, in October, 1867, and this, the present church, was completed the following May. It is built in English Gothic style with steep roofs. The windows have diamond-shaped lights with narrow borders of stained glass. There are two aisles in the nave with fifty-six pews seating two hundred and eighty people.

Charming Baptist Church is distinctive in architecture and history, built entirely of local redwood. Dedicated June 10, 1894, as Rev. Ross preached text from Ex. 25:8, chairs used instead of pews. Callas like those shown in photo grow as if native, needing little or no attention are seen everywhere in Mendocino, even on wild cliffs above ocean.

COLORADO

The roaring Rockies

Imposing, ruined facade of St. Aloysius Church at Morley is startling when unexpectedly sighted from highway. All buildings in coal camp were deliberately wrecked at close of mining operations to save taxes on usable structures. Tall plants in foreground are ubiquitous mullein. Woolly-foliaged, yellow flowered plant, seen nearly everywhere, was introduced from Europe.

And it Wasn't Built by Rockefeller

WHEN THE TRINIDAD *Chronicle-News* carried on June 1, 1918, the item that Rt. Rev. Bishop J. Henry Thien consecrated the Catholic Church at Morley, the news made hardly a ripple in the big, roistering, coal-minded city. But in nearby Morley many hearts were stirred. Not only did the Mexican miners and their large families now have their own place of worship; they felt proud that they had constructed and paid for it. It was about the only building in Morley not built by John D. Rockefeller.

Before the discovery of coal there, Morley was only a station stop on the Santa Fe Railroad as it went over the Raton Pass. It was named for Ray Morley, right-of-way man for the Santa Fe when that road built west from Kansas in an attempt to beat the Denver and Rio Grande Western into New Mexico and Colorado.

The Raton Pass was deemed the best route by both railroads but the site at the summit was controlled by "Uncle" Dick Wooten, one of the early pioneers on the Santa Fe Trail trade route. Uncle Dick, a legendary figure in the Denver-Central City area during the gold rush days, was most famous as purveyor of that potent concoction known as "Taos Lightning." Although he built and operated the toll road as a way over the pass from New Mexico to Colorado, many of his visitors had no wish to proceed farther in either direction. Uncle Dick is long gone but his house and tollgate still stand about three miles south of Morley.

Though Uncle Dick had no wish to have either railroad build over the pass, to ruin his profitable business, he was astute enough to recognize the inevitable. After much of what Judge Dean Mabry of Trinidad terms "cloak and dagger" activity, Wooten agreed to entertain representatives of both roads in a midnight session at his inn. Uncle Dick sat at the head of the table, Santa Fe men along one side, Denver and Rio Grande men on the other. In the middle was a large jug of Taos Lightning. When it was nearly empty, the Denver and Rio Grande people were *under* the conference table. Ray Morley for the Santa Fe road was still able to receive passage rights and congratulations from Uncle Dick.

Morley got his waiting grading crews to work under the feeble rays of lanterns; and Raton Pass became the right-of-way for the Santa Fe.

Although everyone was aware that there were tremendous deposits of coal beneath the small town of Morley, the development of them came later than in almost all of the area's veins, largely because of the lack of a railroad. Originally part of the Maxwell Land Grant (see *Boot Hill*), mining rights had been purchased by John D. Rockefeller. The magnate was in such public disrepute, because of his heavy-handed treatment of his miners in Colorado, that he was even verbally attacked on the floor of Congress. As a result, when he did start operations at Morley, he made every effort to counteract his bad reputation as a ruthless mine owner.

Morley became a luxurious town, so far as coal camps go. Streets were laid out with plenty of width. Houses were comfortable, substantially constructed of brick and concrete. Flower gardens were encouraged, with the company staging a contest each year for the showiest patch of blooms. (Groups of stately hollyhocks still persist among the ruins of the town). Rockefeller was willing to provide free electricity for porch lights, asking that they be left burning so that the town would appear more attractive at night, but he balked at free electricity inside the house. Although he piped running water into each residence he stopped short of flush toilets. Every house had its "Chick Sale" out in back. Although the tycoon did provide a store (to which the miners owed their souls and bodies), and a building to house a Y.M.C.A., he refused the men a church presumably because it would have to be of Catholic faith.

After long and fruitless pleading the workers got together to build their own church. Most of the materials were apparently scrounged from surplus company stock with rock and sand from surrounding mountainsides. Since the completed edifice, dedicated to St. Aloysius, was the result of their own efforts, the miners took deep pride in it, keeping it in good repair and landscaping the grounds with shrubs and flowers, the attendance at Masses nearly perfect.

When the Morley mines were closed down, the buildings were put under the wrecking ball to save taxes. The once proud church suffered the common fate, but the still standing white facade gleams conspicuously from the deeply scarred mountainside.

Saloon Closed Up . . . Church Moved In

VICTOR WAS TOO NEAR the larger and far more famous camp of Cripple Creek to have a separate identity, standing always in the shadow of its neighbor. Rivalry was kept at fever pitch all during the glory years of gold mining. Cripple Creek residents were fond of claiming that their town was on the slopes of Pike's Peak, which it almost was, that well-known landmark being in full view of the camp. Victor claimed that its Battle Mountain, while not being so famous, was the location of the Portland Mine that yielded more than $65,000,000 in gold from its 3,000 foot deep shaft. The side of Battle Mountain was almost covered by the 180 acres of mine buildings and dumps, making a scar that will long remain a hideous blight on the landscape. Thousands of people made a livelihood from the mines around Victor but almost everyone has either died or moved away.

Victor and Cripple Creek were periodically ravaged by disastrous fires and the rivals fought the common foe together. A large part of Cripple Creek was laid low in 1896, many hundreds of people made homeless. While they were huddling under blankets on the hillside out of reach of still smouldering ruins, a contingency arrived from Victor, wagons loaded with more bedding and plenty of food for all. A few years later when the same fate befell Victor, Cripple Creek was equally speedy in rendering aid.

As in other rough mining camps, religion had difficulty in getting a foothold, and once established, in staying. Many factors made the going hard, as old newspaper accounts brought out. The Victor *Daily Record,* said editorially on March 16, 1905, "The Gospel pursued in hot haste the immigration of the people. . . . In those days the Masons, Elks, Odd Fellows, the unions and churches would hold meetings in the same humble frame structures, but on different nights. . . . Obstacles to religion were work . . . the never ending toil on the Sabbath."

When it came to making a choice between observing the Sabbath and celebrating the Fourth of July, when they coincided, most Victorians preferred the parades, races and exploding blasting powder. The *Record* stood up with them. On July 3, 1897, it sarcastically referred to the notorious red light district of Cripple Creek when it said, "The goody-goody people of Cripple Creek mean to suppress all patriotic doings on the Fourth, (Sunday). Patriotism must be below par with our neighbors, for didn't she close up gambling on Fridays and reopen the games on the following Sunday? Are not the saloons, bagnios, and gambling halls running wide open on Sundays. Is it more a desecration of the Sabbath to have a drilling match than to go to a Meyer's Ave. debauch? Is it any worse to play baseball than faro or roulette? Oh, consistency, thy keepers are not the divines of Cripple."

One of the few faiths to maintain a firm hold during the years of Victor's ascendency was that of the First Church of Christ, Scientist. It was sometime around 1898 that the group organized and became a church, first services held September 19, 1901.

In 1909 one of the members noticed that a previously thriving saloon had closed its doors. The place had suffered from a "bad press" that had publicly emphasized a few too many violent episodes originating there. At any rate, failing patronage had caused it to be put up for sale, and the building looked good to the Scientists who as yet had no church edifice. The church bought the old saloon, and by 1908 had it remodeled and furnished at a cost of $7,908. Dedication was not celebrated until one Sabbath five years later when the debt was canceled.

In 1925 the congregation became noticeably small. Many mines were closing or curtailing operations with failing returns and increasing expenses, and Victor seemed headed for desertion. The several churches in town closed or operated on a monthly basis. The First Church of Christ, Scientist held on through the next several difficult years but in 1928 could not continue as a church, the by-laws of the Manual requiring a larger membership than it then had. According to the Mother Church in Boston, the Scientists remaining in Victor continued to meet until November 14, 1955.

Victor as a town is now a near ghost, especially in winter when the deep snows of almost 10,000-foot elevation lie deep in the deserted streets.

Battered relic in Victor (above) once served as church edifice for First Church of Christ, Scientist, and before that as rowdy, notorious saloon. Building still is in fairly good condition as are many other solid but empty structures in Victor (For more about Victor see *Ghost Town Album*).

Panoramic view of famed Cripple Creek (below) was made from road to neighboring Victor. Crowning small elevation are Catholic Church and Sisters of Mercy Hospital across street. Visiting priest still attends to church at intervals. Both structures, spared in several fires, served as sanctuaries for victims of all faiths.

Colorado Stalwart

T. JAMES Methodist Episcopal Church in Central City is likely the oldest Protestant Church in Colorado still serving a membership. As soon as the foundation and basement were completed a temporary roof was placed, allowing services to be held in the basement for several years while additional funds were being accumulated. Final completion was in 1872 with dedication ceremonies held that year.

In 1899 a pipe organ operated by water power was installed, the novel motivation proving satisfactory until 1932 when electricity replaced the water. The building's coal-burning furnace has been in use since 1897. In 1957 the congregation was considering replacement of the carpet installed in 1900.

Central City, termed the "Richest Square Mile on Earth," may have been the richest but could hardly be called "square." The town is composed of three main streets that claw their way steeply up Gregory Gulch, sinuously confined by canyon walls. Although long ago depleted of nuggets, having drowsed through a period of near-ghost-town status, Central City is again active in summer with the revived theater season in the famed old Opera House.

Traffic of any kind was for years practically non-existent but now the opening of the "season" sees one-way traffic for sleek automobiles, a single line crawling bumper to bumper, another slowly descending the parallel street. Much the same situation prevailed in 1859 with burros, mule teams and their drivers.

Colorado history was made in 1859 when Gregory found rich gold deposits in his gulch. Within a year the defile was clogged with thousands of eager prospectors, an almost "instant" population transferred from the earlier, more shallow diggings on Cherry Creek at Denver. Though gold mad, these men displayed another face when they organized St. James Methodist Episcopal Church that same year.

The *Miners' Register* reported on November 5, 1864, "Madam Wright, who has for so long been the nuisance of Eureka Street, whose crib is just below the new Methodist Church, was arrested for larceny last night . . . and was bound over to appear at the next term of the district court. . . . It is high time she was routed from the place she occupies on one of the most public and respectable streets of our city. Perhaps such creatures should be permitted to remain in a community but compelled to remove to some remote locality where their presence will not be so annoying."

"Dawn's early light" finds Central City's Eureka Street deserted except for man taking air in front of famed Teller House. Just above old hostelry is reactivated Opera House, above that Assay Office. Directly across street from laboratory where miners received good or bad news is St. James Methodist Episcopal Church, "oldest protestant church in Colorado still serving its membership"—Denver Post, June 23, 1957 (more photos, story *Ghost Town Trails*).

Methodist Church in Breckenridge was founded by Rev. William Houbert, one of Methodisms first representatives in Colorado. Assigned by his church to South Park Mission in early 1860s, he established church in Hamilton near Fairplay, then crossed Continental Divide to Breckenridge. Building shown here was erected in 1880 and still stands.

Most famous of Methodist preachers in Colorado's early mining era was John Lewis Dyer, affectionately known as Father Dyer. Arriving in mountain state at 49, Father Dyer enthusiastically undertook missions that would have killed many younger men. Starting with wild Buckskin Joe, he preached in streets and saloons, lacking regular church auditoriums. Though many of camps on his scheduled rounds were geographically close, they were separated by Continental Divide or rushing, unbridged rivers.

Regularly preaching at Buckskin Joe on Sunday mornings, he tramped to Montgomery for 2:30 services, climbed over snowy divide in time to conduct evening services at Breckenridge—distance of circuit, 20 miles. Between Sundays he reached eight other mining camps. A centrally located cabin in French Gulch served as something like home for ambulatory preacher.

Church Conference paid Father Dyer as four-month salary $43 out of collections. In order to subsist preacher squeezed small additional income as mail carrier, carpenter, assessor, prospector. Traveling equipment consisted of buffalo skin, blanket, crackers, coffee, sugar, bacon, dried apples, tin cup and old oyster can. Transportation was on horseback in summer, skis in winter (More story, photos see *Ghost Town Trails*).

Episcopal Church, one of the first religious structures in Buena Vista, Colo., was frame structure erected on stone foundation. Construction began in 1888 with consecration celebrated on Sept. 13 next year. From here a number of preaching stations were created in Granite, Lake County. Little brick Christ Church in Canyon City was part of mission field including Rosita, Ula, Silver Cliff and eventually Westcliffe. (More photos, story see *Western Ghost Towns*).

Buena Vista today with Episcopal Church still active is quiet, peaceful village, but in first hectic years it was one of most wicked, lawless in West. This area along Arkansas River was favorite hunting ground of Ute Indians. Prospectors came in with apparent lack of valuable metals in pleasant valley, moved on and land became sparsely settled by ranchers. With sudden boom of Leadville building of railroad through valley in 1879, land was bought up by W. M. Kasson and converted to townsite. For some time rails ended at Buena Vista, bringing greatest period of prosperity. Town became supply center for wildly expanding mining camps not yet connected. A tent city at first, buildings soon became more permanent, these mostly hotels, dancehalls, etc. and in came gamblers, bunco men, desperados of every description.

Sheldon Jackson Memorial Chapel, Fairplay, Colo. is striking exception to makeshift quarters in small, temporary mining camps in Colorado Rockies. Among several historic buildings in town on banks of South Platte near middle of South Park, is the white, graceful architectural monument to religious progress in early Colorado, brain child of Rev. Sheldon Jackson and 8 citizens who organized First Presbyterian Church of Fairplay, Aug 11, 1871. Just 2 years later Jackson preached dedicatory sermon in chapel.

Money ran out before bell was purchased but year after dedication, bonanza discoverer, Gen Graham, donated funds. Only bell in town, it rang also for schools and fires. During '30's church was known as Fairplay Community Church under guidance of Rev. J. N. Hillhouse. In '45 name was again changed to honor founder Sheldon Jackson.

The Pastor Got the Gate

IN THE EARLY DAYS of Trinidad's history the town had few Protestants of any denomination but by the early 1860s some Methodists, Presbyterians, Congregationalists and Lutherans had come in from the "States." By 1880 members of the latter faith who had been worshipping in homes and halls began to lay plans for a church of their own.

Could they have a building better than the ordinary pile of adobe? Could it be one with attractive Gothic touches? What about the Scotch stonecutter Charley Innes who had built so many stout coke ovens in smelters all over southern Colorado—could he build a church? Yes, Innes said, he could. He could make one as fancy as any of those in New England but he wouldn't copy any particular style. "I must have my own way about it," he said. "Your church will be different from any other you ever saw." Charley was right. When the building was finished everyone had to agree it was unique.

The congregation had displayed a certain uniqueness of its own when the time came to dedicate the cornerstone. The regular pastor being absent, members had no hesitation in inviting the rabbi of the local synagogue to officiate in his place. Returning to Trinidad before the actual ceremony was staged, the pastor was outraged, summarily canceling the invitation. On the day before the cornerstone was to be dedicated he was as emphatically fired. The Jewish rabbi presided at the cornerstone laying ceremonies of the Zion Church as scheduled.

Trinidad is one of the oldest cities in Colorado, even in the U. S., the first white settlers being Onate and his crew. Before that gold hunting expedition, the site of what would be Ciudad de Trinity was an ancient Indian ceremonial ground and later important because of its position on the Mountain Branch of the Santa Fe Trail at the foot of Raton Pass. Along the older streets have passed Mexican farmers and sheepherders, mountain men, trappers and fighting railroad construction men. With the discovery and mining of huge coal deposits close by, the town termed Trinity grew into a near metropolis. If a certain grimy, sooty pall settled ineradicably, the populace accepted it as a companion to prosperity. But there came a time when a new age brought diesel fuel and electric power. Trinidad reeled; so did her economy. Even her places of worship struggled to survive. Trinidad's Lutheran congregation shrank to a mere knot of worshipers rattling around in the nave of their unique church building.

Trinidad is located at an altitude of 6000 feet in the foothill chain of the wind-whipped Culebra Range and every winter tore at Zion Church until by 1963 the structure was frankly shabby. Supporting timbers so solidly laid by Innes were now showing strong evidence of decay, every succeeding blast of Culebra's raging winds shaking and rattling the window frames. Concerted effort by the pastor and his flock enlisted the efforts of most of the city's population, regardless of denomination, with the result that the church was restored to prime condition. Next year saw a rededication of the historic church.

But the next few years forced the painful realization that Trinidad was, in some respects, approaching the status of a ghost town. In 1966 its population had been sorely eroded, half the city's families being on relief rolls. Zion's congregation faced the grim fact that it was no longer self-supporting, merely trying to keep up a pathetic show of life. At this state of affairs the pastor, Rev. Albert J. Shandrick, called his flock together to reorganize, expand and rehabilitate.

Today, with his church emerging from a state of near paralysis, Rev. Shandrick comments, "At Zion the stirring of the Holy Spirit is evident. Eager witnessing, sacrificial stewardship, faithful attendance are signs of it. Our historic church is lovely, we keep it so. We are gathering capital funds to increase our facilities. We expect to set up Zion 'branches' in nearby communities without Lutheran witness (there had been no Lutheran Church nearer than 80 miles away). We are in fruitful dialogue with our neighbors of other faiths, not the least the Roman Catholics."

Present pastor of Zion Lutheran Church says edifice is "vibrant with uninhibited freedom in reverent expression." Walls are of soft brick, roofs slant sharply to add grace and shed Colorado's tremendous snows. Lower nave windows are of narrow Gothic design in brilliant art glass. Upper circular ones are filled with similarly colored glass. Principal feature is tower, certainly "uninhibited." Climbing stoutly upward past large rose window it supports quintet of needle spires, one on each corner, a giant one in the center, the whole reminiscent of Russian Orthodox design. One architect terms edifice "a monument to the creative talent of early builders." Another, "It would have been so easy for this to have been a monstrosity, but is without doubt a jewel." (Photo courtesy Andy Stanphil, Albuquerque, N.M.)

Handsome edifice of Central Presbyterian Church, Denver, stands at corner of Eighteenth and Chapman Streets. Built in 1891 structure is third in series of expanding homes for congregation, first small one located on Fifteenth Street. Several other Denver churches have grown out of Central, the Twenty-Third Avenue Church built largely of stone from old building at Eighteenth and Chapman (photo courtesy Denver Public Library Western Collection).

The Preacher Met Guns

WHEN REV. A. T. RANKIN went to Colorado to start a church he found the gold camps full of edgy, gun-toting prospectors, and in Denver, an embattled new editor of the *Rocky Mountain News* who kept his own guns handy, his helpers ready to reach for a rifle.

About a third of the people who populated Colorado in 1858 lived in a tiny gold camp near the confluence of Cherry Creek and the South Platte River. It was never much of a success as a gold producer but did develop into the "Queen City of the Plains"—Denver.

Argonauts on their way to the California gold fields in 1849 tarried at every stream to sample the gravels. In one such party from Georgia were Green Russell and his brothers Oliver and Levi who "raised color" in Cherry Creek but were determined to reach California and went on, remembering the location as promising.

Russell was among the thousands who failed to make fortunes in the Sierra foothills and in 1858 returned to prospect the Cherry Creek area more thoroughly. The gold he found there was negligible but enough to start rumors drifting eastward, and by the time the news reached the big population centers it was blown up out of all proportion. By Christmas of 1858 several hundred impatient gold-seekers were camped at Cherry Creek near its junction with the South Platte.

By next spring thousands were on their way to the camp. Most in the vanguard found little or no gold and returned eastward in anger and disappointment. Many still on their way west were persuaded to return without ever having seen the mountains. Yet the neighboring camps of Denver City and Auraria persisted and even grew. Then when John Gregory made his great strike in Gregory Gulch, 40 miles west, Denver City and Auraria were caught up in the resulting boom as the nearest sources of supplies for Central City and encircling camps. In time, having survived floods, drought, epidemics of grasshoppers and assorted vicissitudes, Denver City forged ahead as a permanent metropolis.

Before Denver merged with Cherry Creek and Auraria camps, the *Rocky Mountain News* was founded. The canny editor, William Newton Byers, realizing full well the bitter rivalry between Denver City on one side and Cherry Creek and Auraria on the other, built his little plant on the dividing line so he could have the business of both. He was so outspokenly vituperative in attacks on political candidates his newspaper did not support, he kept a pair of six guns close at hand and each of his helpers stayed close to a rifle.

Into this atmosphere of armed readiness wandered Rev. A. T. Rankin in August of 1860. Rankin had arrived July 31, sent out by the Presbyterian Foreign Board of Missionaries to establish a church in Denver. He found eight persons willing to form a nucleus and set the next Sunday as the date for first services. He prepared his notices and walked to the offices of the *Rocky Mountain News* to arrange for publication.

The minister was in the habit of keeping a meticulously accurate diary. After he visited the *News* he wrote, "While I was there a man rushed in and caught the editor by the collar, at the same time pulling a gun and threatening to shoot him. Half a dozen guns were then drawn to protect the editor. The ruffian withdrew, later returning with others shooting through the windows. They were then pursued up the street by the newspaper men. Two of them were shot."

Rev. Rankin preached regularly for the next four years using idle saloons, empty halls and private homes for the services. Then the congregation produced some funds, which, together with moneys from the Presbyterian Board, were enough to build a $6,000 church on Fifteenth Street between Lawrence and Arapahoe Streets.

As the city of Denver grew so did the Presbyterian congregation, and in less than a dozen years the first little church on Fifteenth Street was inadequate. A new one costing $50,000 was erected at Eighteenth and Chapman Streets, but by 1891 this building too was outgrown and the cornerstone was laid for the present edifice at the same location, the cost, a quarter of a million dollars.

"Mother

Imposing edifice of Trinity Methodist Episcopal Church at East Eighteenth Avenue and Broadway was erected in 1888. Original building was dedicated in what was then Auraria, December, 1858, and frequently termed "Mother of Methodism in Colorado" (photo courtesy Denver Public Library Western History Collection).

ethodism"

RINITY METHODIST CHURCH," wrote Francis Wayne in the Denver *Post* of April 24, 1938, in a feature on the Church's Golden Jubilee Celebration, "has a right to ring bells, crescendo its singing of hymns and give thanks since, although it has many sisters, it is known as the 'Mother of Methodism in Colorado.'"

The article proceeded at length: "Trinity Methodist Episcopal Church is the name of the original organization established by authority of the Nebraska-Kansas conference on the arid plains of what is now Denver, then Auraria in December, 1858. It is the name of the gray stone edifice standing proudly at East Eighteenth avenue and Broadway which opened for services Dec. 23, 1888, and which will celebrate its golden jubilee in a series of ceremonies May 1 to May 8.

"The program of the celebration includes an opening service Sunday morning, May 1, at which Bishop Ralph S. Cushman will preside. In the evening there will be an educational program honoring the memory of the Rev. Henry A. Buchtel, first pastor, later chancellor of Denver university and Colorado governor, who labored valiantly to build the church. Monday evening there will be a banquet at which a former pastor, the Rev. Loren M. Edwards, will be the chief speaker. Wednesday will be historical episode evening. Friday Bishop and Mrs. Charles L. Mead, long identified with Trinity, will be honor guests at a reception arranged by the board of trustees. Sunday morning, May 8, Bishop Mead will speak at the morning service and in the evening civic leaders will be given places of honor in the pulpit and the auditorium.

"No true history of Colorado can be written without headline space being set apart for a report on the development of Methodism, its churches and schools.

"Pioneer denomination in Colorado, its leaders found waiting them wild animals, Indians, trappers, hunters, wild-eyed adventurers.

"The site of what is Denver was known first as Montana, then St. Charles on one side of Cherry creek and Auraria on the other.

"The Rev. George W. Fisher, a local elder, preached the first sermon at the corner of Twelfth and Wewatta streets. Later, in June, came the Rev. William H. Goode, superintendent of missions, accompanied by Jacob Adriance, 23, a revivalist. They built a cabin, opened their Bibles in the lobby of the Pollock hotel, and did not disdain to sanctify a gambling 'hell' by using it for God's service. On Aug. 2, 1859, they perfected an organization to which they gave the name of Trinity Episcopal church. Henry Reitz, a painter, was the first member enrolled and with H. J. Graham and Alexander Carter he assumed responsibility as steward.

"After its organization the society worshiped in numerous places, scarcely ever meeting in the same place twice. Dwellings, stores, hotels, cabins were used for meetings until June, 1862, when members rented the People's theater at 1423 Larimer street.

"On March 1, 1863, a one-story frame building, formerly used as a carpenter shop, became Trinity Methodist Episcopal church and was used until swept away by the flood of May 19, 1864. Then on Feb. 12, 1865, a building was rented on Lawrence street.

"This served as the church until July 31, 1887. when the Tabor opera house was used for services. It was at this time that plans were drawn for erection of the present edifice which bears the title of Trinity Methodist Episcopal church.

"On April 1, 1888, in 'Denver's gilded age,' Methodists and members of other faiths crowded into the basement of the new church for the first service and within an hour contributed $60,000 to help to complete the one-fourth-million-dollar building. The formal opening was on Dec. 23, 1888, with lilies imported from California beautifying the altar. Music poured from a $25,000 organ donated by Isaac C. Blake; infants were presented for baptism at a fount brought from Italy and donated by a smelter and Mrs. Edward Eddy at a cost of $825. Dr. Buchtel was pastor, opening the services in a pulpit donated by Dr. and Mrs. William Buchtel, she the daughter of the late P. T. Barnum, circus magnate. Colorado sunshine flowed thru stained glass windows donated by Peter Winne and his daughter, Ida, and communion was offered from a silver service and table donated by Mr. and Mrs. H. B. Chamberlin.

"Bishop Henry White Warren, known as the "White Knight of Methodism," delivered the dedication sermon and A. L. Doud, surviving now to enjoy Golden Jubilee week, was first superintendent of the Sunday school.

"In education, as in social service and patriotic movements, Trinity church has been in the van. The seminary which flanked Lawrence street church developed into Denver university.

"Social, recreational and club work necessitated the erection of Trinity building next to the church and to and from Trinity pulpit have come and gone men of such impressive talent that many were called to the bishop's robes. Included in this list were Earl Cranston, David Hastings Moore, William F. McDowell, Robert McIntyre, who thought it wise to pace the age by popularizing the pulpit, and, still living, Bishop Mead.

"From the cabin and tent and gambling 'hell' the church has moved thru Indian, Civil and World wars, thru floods when Cherry creek rampaged. It has entered missionary fields, at home and abroad, has fought many a well-timed fight for civic righteousness.

"Now, after fifty years, wearing proudly the old name 'Trinity Methodist,' it prepares to produce a Golden Jubilee celebration and go marching on with Bishop Cushman and Dr. Houser leading the way to bigger and better and more effective activities and service.

"In charge of arrangements are F. R. Lilyard, chairman; A. L. Doud, Frank McDonough, Miss Alice M. Wilson, Miss Grace E. Wilson and the pastor."

Emanuel Temple, oldest church in Denver, was built in 1876 on site of first Sunday School in Rocky Mountain region, serving final religious usefulness as synagogue of Congregation Sherith Israel. As of 1969 classically handsome structure is in use as studio for artist Wolfgang Pogzeba (photo courtesy Denver Public Library Western Collection).

Children Met in Log House

THE OLDEST CHURCH in Denver in point of age and continuous service, is the small stone edifice at 10th and Lawrence sts. Emanuel Chapel has another distinction, in that it marks the site of the very first Sunday school in the Rocky Mountain region."

So wrote Joseph Emerson Smith in a Denver newspaper. The article continued:

"The late Bishop John Franklin Spalding of the Episcopal Church was told the story by none other than Col. Lewis N. Tappan, one of the organizers, and the bishop bore it in mind when, years later, he bought the ground for the first Episcopal Church to serve West Denver, building the chapel in the block that saw Denver's first hotel, the El Dorado, and where Denver's first white child was born, in the old log cabin hotel.

"In October, 1859, Colonel Tappan, recently arrived from Boston, to become one of Denver's most prominent merchants, was walking down San Luis St., now 10th St., when, near Larimer, he came upon a group of noisy children at play. They told him it was their recess and they were the pupils of Denver's first school teacher, Prof. Oscar J. Goldrick. Colonel Tappan entered the log cabin and accosted the school teacher with the question, 'Why not a Sunday school on the Sabbath?' Goldrick assented. In the Nov. 3, 1859, issue of The Rocky Mountain News appeared this notice:

" 'Union Sunday School—A union Sunday school for the children of Auraria and Denver will be held every Sunday at 3 o'clock p.m. at the house of Preachers Fisher and Adriance, near Cherry Creek. It is particularly requested that parents and guardians will endeavor to have their children attend the school regularly and punctually. Books and children's papers will soon be furnished to the scholars. The school will not only be a union school for both towns, but a union of all denominations.

(Signed.

" 'George W. Fisher, Lewis N. Tappan, Jacob Adriance, D. C. Collier, O. J. Goldrick.'

"This committee selected a one story log house, with a mud roof, on Cherry St., now 13th, near Larimer. The first Sunday saw 12 pupils occupying the rough board benches. D. C. Collier was elected superintendent, and the children were taught by the ministers from the Bible. The second Sunday saw 15, and the third Sunday 20. Colonel Tappan wrote the Baptist Sunday school at Lawrence, Kan., for books and lessons. The package was freighted across the plains free by James & Cartwright, and, much to the surprise of the colonel, when he opened the box he found they were the identical books sent, at his solicitation to the Kansas Sunday school by his old Bible class in Rev. Baron Stow's church in Boston.

"The Union Sunday School prospered until the next year, when denominational organizations were formed in Denver. The Sunday school books were then boxed and sent to the first anti-Mormon Sunday school in Salt Lake City, then presided over by Rev. Norman McLeod. The first churches were built in Denver. The Southern Methodist Church erected a small brick building at Arapahoe and 14th sts. in 1860.

"At the outbreak of the war, Rev. Mr. Bradford left for the South, and the trustees of the property sold it to the Episcopalians, the church being named St. John's. On 15th st., between Arapahoe and Lawrence, the brick First Presbyterian Church had been finished by 1865; and, in 1878, built a larger edifice at Champa and 18th sts. The Southern Methodist Episcopal, on Arapahoe st., spired the skyline of the little city. The Catholic Cathedral was at 15th and Stout, and, after much effort, the Seventeenth Street Presbyterian Church had been completed and opened for worship March, 1872. This handsome brick and stone Gothic building, with stained glass windows, stood on the present site of the Equitable Bldg. As the business section grew, all the early churches were razed, one after the other. None of the pioneers remain, except Emanuel, in its historic block in West Denver.

"Completed in 1876, it was the first place of

public worship erected in that quarter of old Denver. For years it retained the distinction of being the only church in a ward containing a population of more than 2,000. In the '80's, it was connected with All Saints' Mission of North Denver."

Emanuel Temple's usefulness dwindled steadily in a neighborhood of once aristocratic homes. Commerce leveled the old brick mansions and factories, warehouses, garages replaced them. Emanuel narrowly escaped the fate of its elegant contemporaries by being purchased by Jewish Congregation Sherith Israel as a house of worship. Instead of the King James precisely beautiful English, there rolled the sonorous Hebrew, while on the altar candles illuminated the gold letters of the name the church had always borne —Emanuel. Yet that too ceased to exist when after a few years the Jews moved to a better location, leaving the old church empty of life and color.

Church of the Annunciation in Leadville was undoubtedly one of finest edifices in Colorado, ecclesiastical or otherwise, when completed in 1881. Its famed steeple, extending 150 feet above the street, 10,200 feet above sea level, is said to be the highest in the northern hemisphere. Structure is prominent in center of this photo made from near Matchless Mine owned by Horace Tabor, then his widow, Baby Doe Tabor. Baby Doe looked out from this same knoll, seeing almost exactly same view during her lonely poverty stricken final years. Often termed "Cloud City," Leadville is topped by range of peaks towering above 14,000 feet, one of them Mount Massive, shown in background (for more about Leadville, see *Western Ghost Towns*).

When "J. C." Came to Leadville

WRITING IN *The Colorado Quarterly,* Prof. Muriel Sibell Wolle of the University of Colorado and prolific historian of the state says,

"The first raw Sundays in the brash, raw carbonate camp of Leadville were no different from any other day, except that the crowd elbowing its way along the muddy streets was bigger and

louder than usual and the saloons and shops got more trade. The new silver camp which sprawled the length of California Gulch, high in the Rocky Mountains, was only a year old but already steady streams of men converged there to seek fortunes in the heavy black sands of its creek bed or in the rich lodes hidden in the adjacent hills. Few of these men had time to worship on Sunday when there were so many riches to be had around them; so when on a Sunday morning in the summer of 1878 a new sound rang out over the raucous camp—the peal of a church bell—one of the miners, digging in his prospect hole, leaned over his pick to listen and then said to his partner, 'I'll be damned if Jesus Christ hasn't come to Leadville too.'"

"J. C." had been in and about Leadville since 1860. Along with hordes of miners came Fr. Joseph P. Machebeuf reminding them that gold was not the only objective in this life. The priest held Mass there in the gulch, the first religious service in that part of the Rockies.

Since Leadville is on the eastern slope of the Great Divide it was first considered to belong in the vicarate of Rt. Rev. John B. Miege of Leavenworth, Kansas, but later it was found more practical to administer the Pikes Peak area from Santa Fe, New Mexico, the responsibility then transferred to Bishop John Baptist Lamy. Very soon the bishop placed his friend Fr. Machebeuf in charge of the Leadville area. With newly ordained Fr. Joseph Raverdy, Machebeuf left Santa Fe in September of 1860, arriving in Leadville in October or early November.

In addition to California Gulch, Fr. Machebeuf cared for South and Middle Parks, traveling on horseback, wagon or on foot. Many times he was forced to cross over Mosquito Pass where he slept among patches of snow with stars for a canopy. Where practicable he traveled in a carriage equipped with some of the comforts of home—bedding, food, cooking utensils and feed for his horses. The rear of the coach contained vestments and communion service, and could be converted into an altar. From it many Masses were read in the mining camps.

Some time in the middle 1870s the Sacred

Heart Church was erected, becoming over-crowded in a few years. Fr. Machebeuf wrote, ". . . the madness of the crowds coming from all parts of the United States—every nationality and every shade of religious faith or no belief at all, except in money—all bound for Leadville, the new silver camp which outrivals, at least on paper, the richest mines of California and Nevada. The camp is only a few months old, but already there are 15,000 people here and there will be 30,000 before next winter. Some of the mines are reported to be producing as high as $4,000 a day.

"We have a church in Leadville but it is much too small. The Catholics come, but the crowd is such that one-half of the people strive to hear Mass kneeling in the cold and snow outside the church in the street."

By 1877 Fr. Henry Robinson had been named resident pastor of Leadville while Fr. Machebeuf continued to travel. From the start Fr. Robinson saw the need for a new and larger church for Leadville. But construction of the Church of the Annunciation was not begun until 1879, not actually completed until 1881, the first Mass offered on New Year's Day of 1880.

Fr. Robinson told a reporter for the *Herald-Democrat* that the new church cost $30,000. In addition to this amount, $12,000 had to be raised for St. Mary's School and $20,000 for a hospital. He was quoted as saying, "I am proud to say that all the money was collected in this city. I persevered until every cent of indebtedness was cleared. Many a time I had gone to the mines at midnight when the men were changing shifts to receive contributions even from my non-Catholic brethren. I received a great deal of assistance and on all occasions was treated with courtesy and respect; and among them I have many warm friends. I never appealed to them for charity in vain."

Annunciation's huge bell, christened "St. Mary's" was installed in 1885. When its clangor reverberating from 363 pounds of metal first shattered the air over the city, all citizens were startled. Not all were pleased. One group petitioned the city council to abolish the ringing of all church bells in Leadville but later backed down under a storm of protest from the majority.

In 1859 the site of Leadville was a favored summer camping and hunting ground of the Indians. That fall prospectors worked the upper reaches of the Arkansas River after leaving the gold fields of Clear Creek and Gilpin Counties. They found traces of gold but before any thorough search was possible, they were driven out by the severe blizzards of early winter.

In April, 1860, after the late spring at 10,000 feet, Abe Lee, one of the first returning prospectors, saw a glitter in the sand. "Gold! Gold!" he shouted. "I've got all the gold of Californy right here in this pan!" And so the gulch was named California and turned out to be one of the most famous mining camps in the world.

The city of Leadville passed through many up and down periods during its history. In the middle 1870s it almost became a ghost town when the rich deposits of placer gold became exhausted. Then it was found the heavy material clogging the placer beds was the richest kind of silver carbonates. Mills to refine it were built and soon a second and far greater boom expanded the population.

The silver panic of 1893 that turned other camps into ghost towns would have destroyed Leadville too except for the secondary metals it mined. Vast stores of molybdenum were found a few miles to the north, the rare material a most efficient hardener of steel, and the town of Climax was activated.

Strikes depressed the economy at times, the worst in 1896 prolonging idleness that cost 2¼ million dollars. One of the latest of the strikes took place at Climax but directly affected the lifeblood of Leadville. During the 12-week strike in 1958 Fr. Hamblin of Annunciation inaugurated a daily Rosary in petition for its settlement. The international publicity resulting brought praise from both sides of the dispute, and was credited with helping to expedite conclusion of the quarrel.

WASHINGTON
Big timber country

Little Methodist Church on Claquato Hill, three miles west of Chehalis, last of early territorial churches to remain standing in Washington. Only 20x30 feet with sanctuary 20x23 feet, church is surmounted by tower consisting of square, louvered structure upon which is superimposed octagonal louvered belfry, this in turn topped by conventionalized crown of thorns. Bell, still in place, was purchased by popular subscription, cast in Boston by Henry Cooper & Co. in 1857, shipped around Horn via Olympia. Because of donations of land, labor and material church edifice was free of debt from time of dedication. First services were held by circuit rider John F. Devore, member of Methodist National Board of Missions.

Over 100 and Still Going

IN 1857 Lewis Hawkins Davis built a small sawmill on his land claim at the foot of the hill where tiny Mill Creek flowed into the Chehalis River and turned out rough lumber from the abundant supply of logs cut nearby. A dedicated Methodist Davis used his first planks to build a church on the summit of the knoll.

Fortunately for the community that sprang up, it had an expert craftsman, John Duff Clinger, brother-in-law of Davis. Clinger was quite capable of doubling as architect, and so assumed full responsibility of constructing the church. He personally made door and window casings and built the unusual tower, framing it with mortise and tenon work of the finest quality. Even the lookouts supporting the roof projections on the gables were mortised and wedged into the ends of the rafters. As the oldest building still standing in the state of Washington the unique church is a monument to John Clinger.

Lewis Hawkins Davis, born in Windsor County, Vermont, became infected with the Oregon Fever in 1852. He and his family joined with a wagon train heading for the Willamette Valley, but in Portland he concluded the country thereabouts was already too crowded. Settlers' cabins there were within a few miles of each other and Davis was intent on carving out his own piece of

wilderness. He found just such a country in the tall timber north of the Columbia River and on the banks of the much smaller Chehalis, and took out his donation land claim.

Other settlers soon followed the lead of the pioneer, erecting their cabins on his land and forming a tiny village called after the Indian "Claquato," the term referring to the "high place" or knoll centering the spot.

The town of Claquato flourished largely because of its position on the old Military Road, then the main traveled road between the Columbia River and Olympia. When road and rail arteries shifted to the east to serve the towns of Chehalis and Centralia, the town on the "high place" withered.

The little white church fell idle except for Sunday School services, even these ceasing in the mid 1930s. After vandals did some damage to it, doors were padlocked and windows boarded up. Restoration was begun in the early '50s by Chehalis Post No. 22 American Legion and county officials. No structural changes were necessary, so well had Clinger done his job; almost all original material could be left in place. The interior was newly wall-papered with a pattern that matched the style of the period. Rededication of the restored edifice was celebrated August 16, 1953.

Pews (and pulpit, pastor's chair) were shaped by hand from planks cut on jig-saw mill. Even nails were hand forged by A. F. Gordon, local blacksmith. Furniture is in place exactly as in years preceding Civil War.

Lewis Davis, founder of Claquato, donated land and material for Methodist Church. Suffering severe fall in his mill, Davis lingered, then died. After services in his church he was borne up hill to grave, almost first in tiny cemetery.

The Church Outlived Them All

Baptist Church of Oysterville in photo taken some years before renovation was started. In old days when church was new belfry had much more ornamented openings, each course of fancy shingles on tower and belfry was made distinct by alternating white and dark paint.

WILLAPA BAY in Washington fulfills all requirements for growth and reproduction of oysters which need an almost exactly formulated mixture of salt and fresh water, the salinity varying at regular periods. When the white man came to the harbor, then called Shoalwater Bay, the inner beaches were one vast carpet of oysters, the supply hardly affected by their use as the main food of the native Indians.

In the summer of 1851 young Canadian-born Charles Russell saw an opportunity to make his fortune and started it by shipping a canoe full of oysters to San Francisco. Had he been able to obtain exclusive rights to the supply he would have enjoyed a successful business operation, but others marketed the oysters too. Using more modern equipment his competitors took over and swamped Russell's one-canoe enterprise.

Among the first settlers on the arm almost enclosing Willapa Bay were R. H. Espy and L. A. Clark who started ambitious harvesting, smoking and canning operations. One of the buildings Espy erected was the little Baptist Church.

Oysterville is virtually a ghost town now, the old courthouse, hotels, several saloons and most residences having long since succumbed to the ravages of rot and storm-driven tides. Only the Baptist church building persists and lately was given a new lease on life with renovation undertaken by C. J. Espy, son of the founder.

Espy carries on the Oysterville tradition. After a busy life spent in the East and other sections of the country, he is retired, spending his leisure in the old family home. His bedroom is the one in which he was born more than eighty years ago.

Interior of Baptist Church shows simplicity of nave and sanctuary. Partition down center of pews is in style of old New England churches which often segregated men and women. Church never had electricity, though recent wedding was illuminated by current brought in heavy cables. Nave was originally illuminated by pair of chandeliers supporting kerosene lamps, suspended on ropes running over pulleys to lower them for cleaning, lighting and extinguishing. One Sunday morning startled congregation found one crashed down on pews. For safety they were removed, side lamps substituted as shown here. When founder H. H. Espy died his casket was placed in tiny sanctuary for funeral, leaving little room for passage.

Unusual emblem topping old First Congregational Church at Kalama was erected in honor of newly born state of Washington, admitted to Union coincidentally with organization of church. Some jubilant members termed their new edifice the "Statehood Church," name not surviving. Almost adjoining far corner of building is site of still older, now razed Episcopal Church. Next is home of Hite Imus built in 1901, son Hite and wife still living here. Bell is seen still in belfry in this photo made by author in August, 1968, but in November Pastor Watteraud had bell removed to historic shrine near present church in lower part of city.

The Organ Came from London

HEN REV. R. D. NICHOLLS became pastor of the Kalama Congregational Church in 1903, the first disappointment he felt was its lack of a pipe organ. In London, England, he had been an apprentice in a pipe organ factory and now wrote his brother back home about the problem. The brother responded that he knew of an old used organ moldering away in a church basement. So it was purchased and, upon arrival in Kalama, was cleaned and reassembled. But—could anybody play it?

Kalama was Chinook for "pretty maiden" and that was the name they gave to the river flowing beside a rocky headland to empty its clear waters into the broad Columbia. Until 1853 the natives along the river saw only such itinerant whites as those on the *Chatham* and the smaller boats of Lewis and Clark. Then came Ezra Meeker with his wife and son. He built a rude but comfortable cabin to shelter the family while he and his brother went on north to the Puyallup River country where he took a donation land claim. Ezra Meeker had a talent for publicity which made him the Northwest's best known pioneer. Although his family did not stay long at the Kalama River, several other pioneers were glad to see a cabin in the wilderness and settled there too, giving the river's name to the settlement.

St. Joseph's Catholic Church of Kalama is spectacularly situated on steep hill facing Columbia River, looking across town and to much of Oregon. Franciscans, responsible for many early Washington missions, built St. Joseph's during Kalama boom. Remodeled and restored in recent years, St. Joseph's now has no resident priest, Fr. Patrick Godley, regular pastor of St. Phillip's at Woodland, Wash. making weekly journey to say Mass for about 50 families at St. Joseph's, 100 families at Ridgefield, Wash. and his own 50 at home in Woodland. "I'm a busy man," he says with obvious truth.

Due to abundant salmon and other fish in the rivers and plentiful timber in the nearby hills, Kalama grew steadily, and in the summer of 1869 it was learned the Northern Pacific Railway would build a line connecting Kalama to the new city of Tacoma on Puget Sound. A tremendous boom got under way in Kalama, actual work on the line beginning Feb. 15, 1870. A large ferry was put into service to take trains across the Columbia to Portland, from there continuing south.

During the height of Kalama's expansion the population swelled to an all-time high of 3,500, many being Episcopalians who felt the growth would continue. They banded together to build a handsome house of worship on the steep hillside rising above the business district. Their church was well attended until 1873 when the railroad and ferry docks were completed. Construction and office workers moved away, businesses failed, and the town realized the sharp pangs of depression. Kalama was now only a whistle stop where trains rolled on to ferries, hardly pausing. For lack of a sustaining congregation the Episcopal Church closed its doors.

While most businesses failed, saloons were doing fine. What better solace for the blues than the fiery liquids popular with loggers and fishermen on the lower Columbia? John Wicks, one bistro owner, felt he could double his trade with another outlet so bought the church for a "honky-tonk tune." Wrecking the structure, he hauled the boards down the steep hill to build another sin-spot beside the river. The saloon survived Kalama's most disastrous fire that destroyed twenty-five other buildings, only to float away in an unusually high freshet in 1894.

In 1888 Kalama gained several new citizens, the Hiram Imus family who had come out from Kansas. The group included Hiram, wife Mary Ann, son Hite (nickname for Hiram), daughter-in-law Fannie, sisters Emma and Laura Imus.

Next year, in 1889, this contingent of the Imus family, along with Cora B. Darnell and Mrs. W. S. Crandall, organized a Congregational Church, meeting in the Imus' kitchen. Thomas Moran donated a building site adjoining the upper edge of the lot where the Episcopal Church once stood.

During construction, some work being done by carpenter Hiram, members held services in the Kalama School. The first resident pastor was Rev. George Baker. The membership grew steadily from the original sixteen to more than a hundred in 1902. Rev. Samuel Greene, Congregational Superintendent of Sunday Schools for Washington Territory, organized a Sunday School in the spring of 1889. In 1903 a parsonage was built several doors down the hill and across the street from the church.

Then came Rev. Nicholls and the pipe organ, played regularly by Mrs. Hite Imus, daughter-in-law of Hiram. Her husband sang in the choir; son Raymond, now of Seattle, was general custodian. He carried wood, kept the fire going in the pot-bellied stove at the rear of the nave, rang the bell for services, took up the collection, tolled the bell for funerals and closed the building after all activity. For these services he received $4 a month.

In 1901 Hiram's son built the family home just below the site of the old Episcopal Church, adjacent to the current Congregational Church. The head carpenter on the job was John Stratton who worked a twelve-hour day for $2. During this period the senior Hite was Kalama postmaster and founded two newspapers, Kalama *Bulletin* and Rainier *Review*—Rainier being across the Columbia River in Oregon and, incidentally, the birthplace of this author. Both papers were printed on the handpress brought from Kansas.

In more recent years the scattering of the Imus family, always mainstays of the church, so reduced the congregation that the church closed its doors. It was eventually sold to the Assembly of God group who held services there for several years. Improving circumstances for them made it possible to build a new edifice which they did economically with material salvaged from Kalama's old movie theater. It was a smartly styled church of frame construction near the south end of the city. Four of the theater's stout beams were erected separately from the church to house the bell from the old structure on the hill. Assembly of God pastor, Rev. LaVern Watterud, says the bell will not serve except as a historical relic.

Church Stands Firm against Floods

Puget Island's Lutheran Church is set almost at the edge of one of the many sloughs pene-
trating the interior. Their levels and that of Columbia River, beset by floods in early summer,
are now controlled by encircling dikes. Original church, built in 1894 appears here as transept,
never having steeple. Parsonage was built in 1909, present and larger structure completed in
1929. "We had many fine pastors over the years," says Mrs. Svenson. "One we liked very
much was Ted Nystuen. He served from 1951 to 1957. But we are also very fond of our
present minister, Rev. L. Kleps."

John Slocum Go

Shakers term altar simply "table" but observe several Catholic-like rules concerning it. Sign of cross is made on passing, few ceremonial objects such as bells, crosses and candles being only items allowed. These are placed on white cloth, when not in use covered with another white cloth. Little crosses around "sanctuary" are actually sconces. Candle light was regarded as only "pure" light, kerosene and later gasoline lanterns frowned upon as inventions of devil, prohibited in church. Bell, once ringing for services here was given to Indian church at Queets.

Modern Indians at La Push are largely commercial fishermen, most owning elaborate boats and equipment. Shown here are vessels belonging to both Indian and white operators. In background is James Island, several acres of rock and trees standing guard at entrance of harbor, left. Bar in right background shuts out open ocean. Often violent winter storms send waves completely over barricade, but main force is broken. "The Needles" line of many smaller, jagged rocks extends several miles out into open sea, out of view at left.

the Message

Shaker Doctrine is noted for lack of uniformity among branches and ceremonies yet churches have some similarities such as being placed east-west, with door opening to west. Table stood in east, thus displaying one of many possible origins in Catholic doctrine. (Parade dancing, however, seems strictly aboriginal). Church on Quillayute Indian Reservation at La Push differs from conventional rule in that belfry is placed over door instead of table. Photo is made from window of one of many rotting Indian houses.

WASHINGTON'S Olympic Peninsula is its northwest corner, almost detached from the rest of the state by sounds, inlets and sinuously winding channels. Sometimes termed "The Last Wilderness," it retains a number of good-sized areas remaining inviolate from the white man's invasion.

Born of inner-mountain glaciers, two debris-laden streams, the Bogachiel and Soleduck, tumble their separate courses toward the sea, but on nearing it join forces in a pool some 200 feet in diameter. Out of it runs the Quillayute River, a mere six miles to the sea, its mouth forming a safe harbor, the only one in the long reach between Grays Harbor and Cape Flattery. Here is located the old Indian village of La Push, centered by the fading relic that was once the thriving Indian Shaker Church.

In several eastern sections of the United States are branches of the United Society of Believers in Christ's Second Appearing. Founded by "Mother" Ann Lee in England around 1747, the sect is often termed "The Shakers" because of gyrations and trembling of jerking muscles during trance-like rituals. Though there are marked similarities, the northwestern Indian Shaker religion seems to have little connection in origin or ceremonies with the older cult.

The Indians have versions as to the beginning of their church, none agreeing in exact detail because of a complete lack of written records, no minutes or notes of any kind being kept even today. Through all versions runs a similar thread concerning John Slocum, an Indian who would never be remembered except for the remarkable manner of his death. He had all the weaknesses of his brothers, including a passion for gambling, horse racing, drinking and profanity. He and his wife lived at Mud Bay, about four miles from Olympia. Sometime between 1870 and 1880 John died and was laid out by his grieving wife, Mary.

After some time, possibly days, mourners were startled to see John raise his hands in an attempt to undo the bandages wrapped around his chin to keep his mouth closed. Most of the mourners fled, but Mary aided him in removing all encumbering wraps, whereupon John called for the return of his friends. He had a message for them, he said.

He had awakened to see angels standing about. The leader beckoned John to follow him on a tour of what might await him and all Indians when death came. First, he was given a view of Hell, where many Indians were suffering the penalty for having indulged too freely in all the vices termed wicked. Then John was carried aloft for a vision as seen through heavenly portals, a clear picture of white clad Indian angels enjoying the rewards of clean living. Attempting to enter this beautiful domain John was restrained by his guide who said, "Your time has not yet come. You are to return to earth to preach to your fellows, to inform them of what you have seen." Then he awoke to find himself bound up in the death bandages. In another version he woke up in a canoe, high in a tree, having been interred in ancient Chinook fashion.

John recovered, and for a time lived an exemplary life. After a while he began a steady program of backsliding and soon was in the old rut. Then he fell very ill, and again was given up to die. His wife, Mary, held vigil over him for days while his life flickered. At last, unable to stay in the house any longer, she went outside to the beach to gather oysters. It was very cold and, as she returned to where her husband lay dying, she trembled and shook uncontrollably. As she stood over Slocum he raised up, perfectly well. All the tribe concluded that it was the shaking that had worked the miracle being, indeed, God's Medicine.

This time John Slocum really got the message loud and clear. He had the tribe build a little church where he thereafter preached the new gospel, combined with healing sessions by self-appointed "workers" who shook over stricken tribesmen, who reputedly recovered without delay. The movement spread rapidly, first coming to official notice about 1883. Law officers made many attempts at suppression, but official persecution later eased off, so long as churches were confined to the reservations.

The typical Shaker Church is painfully simple in its appointments. There are no pews. Two sets of benches around the walls are provided, the center being left open and free for the ceremonies. One set of benches forms a "U" at the entrance with an opening left for the door. These are reserved for non-participants. Another "U" almost joins the first, this set at the other end, broken only by the altar arrangements. These benches are at first occupied by those who will parade and shake. All entering members make the sign of the cross, then shake hands with all who are already seated, the women placing themselves to the right as one faces the altar, the men at the left.

During most of the period of activity in the La Push Church, regular devotional services were set at nine o'clock on Sunday mornings. When all members had settled themselves, the leader, or minister (this a loosely and temporarily appointed role) called out, "Pray!" Silent prayer continued for a few minutes, when the leader would begin his sermon. This was usually very informal, nearer a discussion, at the end of which the real ceremonies began. One man took up a hand bell in each hand and began ringing them in a uniform, regular beat. All members seated on the front benches rose and formed in lines around the floor, sexes separated. Most had brought their own bells with them and soon all were ringing as the lines moved around, in anti-clockwise circles. Those at the head of the line carried no bell, but held a lighted candle in each hand.

At first parading worshipers merely stamped out the rhythm of the bells, heels hitting the floor in hard, stomping fashion. Hands which had been held near the waist, palms upturned, were extended at shoulder height as excitement mounted. Faces, calm at first, grew ecstatic as if seeing a vision, then becoming contorted as spasms began. Starting at the neck, muscles twitched and jerked until all the upper torso became involved, the lower part being occupied with continuing violent dancing activity. "Shaking," voluntarily initiated soon took over as an uncontrollable, ecstatic frenzy. If the dance lasted for some time, as it often did, some members collapsed from exhaustion.

Collapse could also come from near heatstroke or suffocation, especially in summer. Windows were left closed, and with tremendous collective physical activity the atmosphere soon grew thick. Later, laws forced the opening of windows or doors.

At the conclusion of services, participants gathered at the "cookhouse" for a meal prepared beforehand by women members. Usually the dining place was a building erected especially for the purpose, the location next to or at least near the church. Where there was no special structure, the meal was taken at a member's home.

The Indian Shaker Church is a still viable denomination. The Federal Bureau of Indian Affairs in Portland states that there are many active churches, with Mr. Horton Capomen of Tahola, Washington, as Bishop. Old-time Quillayute Indian woman, Mrs. Roy Black of La Push, told the author why the church there is neglected. "We all used to go all the time. Most of the older members I used to know are dead now, and the younger ones either don't care about it, or sometimes go to the Assembly of God. Their church is lots nicer."

First Pastor Came by Boat

THE FIRST Congregational Church and Sunday School meetings in Cathlamet were made possible by the monthly calls of patriarchal State Sunday School Superintendent, Rev. Samuel F. Green. All travel in those roadless river towns was by boat. Arriving regularly on appointed Saturdays on the afternoon boat, Rev. Green would set to work arranging the schedule of services. After church on Sunday he would stay as long as possible, then hurry down to the dock at the sound of the small ship's bell.

In 1895 the Cathlamet Congregational Church was organized. Quoting from the minutes of the first gathering, "A meeting was held in Birnie's Hall, Cathlamet, Wahkiakum County, Washington, October 13, 1895, for the purpose of organizing a Congregational Church . . ." Officers were elected and resolutions made, the finished document signed by the new clerk, Mrs. C. H. Warren.

The first pastor of the church was Rev. Charles W. Wells, who began his ministry November 1, 1895, and it was during his tenure that the church edifice was erected. Assisting in financing was a loan of $500 from the Building Society, a worthwhile sum in those times. Most construction labor was contributed by members.

After a succession of pastors, all well liked, came Rev. William Head, on July 1, 1910. Serving a total of nearly 25 years in two periods Rev. Head made the strongest impression of any minister before or since. He gave all he had in mental effort and physical labor. Besides being an excellent preacher he undertook many projects to improve his church. A major project was the excavating of the basement and installation of a kitchen and dining hall there.

Rev. Head was possessed of a fiery temper, and had no patience with juvenile delinquents. His daughter-in-law, Mrs. John Head, related to the author, "He was on the roof one day, repairing the brick chimney. Some boys came by and, unaware that he was up there listening, said something about breaking a window for fun. Mr. Head shouted, 'Make a move toward that window and I'll kill you with these bricks.' The boys skedaddled, knowing full well the preacher's temper and marksmanship."

Several other pastors are remembered for their good deeds, among them Rev. Robert J. Allen, who was instrumental in greatly increasing the congregation and consequent financial condition.

Cathlamet Congregational Church, organized in 1895, briefly serving Baptists in recent years, now stands forlorn, slowly decaying. From lofty perch on rocky hillside old church watched historic period in development of lower Columbia region, glory days when river was only highway from ocean to large cities in interior. Local historian Howard P. Murphy, in tracing history of old bell now placed in memorial arch near new church, finds murky gaps in early story. Very probably it came from Troy, N.Y. foundries and shipped around Horn as other west coast bells were. Nephew of Mrs. Warren remembers helping unload bell from ship at Cathlamet dock.

During later years in service, swinging bell set up alarming vibrations in aging tower. For this and sentimental reasons congregation decided on its removal to new building. Removal from shaky perch presented problem until several loggers experienced in high-climbing successfully accomplished risky job. Historic church bell, first and last to ring in Cathlamet was then taken to hang silently beside new church some distance away.

Cathlamet's old cemetery, last resting place of Birnie family, Indian Chief Wahkiakum, many others prominently figuring in history of locality. Burial ground has been "cleaned up" since this photo appeared in author's book *Tales the Western Tombstones Tell*.

Sometime in the late 1950s the congregation decided to sell the old building in order to expand into a new one at another location. They found a buyer in the First Baptist Church and soon moved out, taking along only the bell.

For a time the Baptists held regular services. Likely the congregation could have held its own but for internal strife. A split reduced the group into factions too small to support a church. The old, historic building fell into disuse and now shows signs of decay.

Cathlamet was a very large Indian village on the lower Columbia River, just opposite Puget Island, complete with many of those classic examples of native Chinook architecture, wooden houses of immense size for communal living, some measuring 35 by 20 feet. Submerged piling-like foundations of some still remain.

The tragic story of the tribes and their decimation is the same as that for Puget and Sauvie Islands, Skamokawa and many other sites along the lower Columbia River and along the beaches near the river's mouth. James Birnie of the Hudson's Bay Co. was the first white man to live at Cathlamet and, while Birnie has many accomplishments to his own credit, what people noticed most about him was his Indian wife. It was the common, accepted custom in those times for a man to take an Indian wife in the absence of white women. At Cathlamet the Indians were Chinooks, the women shy, retiring. When one was selected by a white man as his wife or companion, she usually set up her own quarters somewhere behind his home. She cleaned his house and cooked his meals, but would not presume to sit beside him at the table, particularly when his friends were present. Birnie's wife however had been acquired while he was yet "back east" and she was of sterner stuff. Mrs. Birnie presided at all meals, taking her place beside her husband even in the presence of the august Dr. John McLoughlin.

Among many other benefits Mr. Birnie bestowed on the community was an all-purpose hall. It was located on the upper dock, safely out of reach of any but its most extreme freshets, south of Warren Packing Co.'s docks. Some remnants of the building still stood in 1953, perhaps later. Mrs. Maude K. Butler wrote in the *Longview Daily News* January 15, 1941, "It was truly a community hall because Birnie generously gave it rent free for all functions—dances, Sunday School, church, social entertainments—even funerals were held in Birnie's Hall."

Mrs. Lettie Smith Warren became the first superintendent of the First Congregational Sunday School in Cathlamet April 16, 1893, the group meeting in Birnie's Hall. Mrs. Warren soon discovered the place littered with "debris" on Sunday mornings, evidence of unrestrained dances held by fishermen and loggers the night before. Setting out early, Mrs. Warren and her mother, Mrs. Asenath Ryder Smith, carried to the hall brooms, mops and some kindling wood. After starting a warming fire in the old pot-bellied stove, the two cleared the premises for Sunday School. Most Sundays there was a fair attendance but one day only one little girl showed up. Discouraged, Mrs. Warren told her mother she would never again open up the hall for Sunday School. Her mother lectured her, "Lettie, as long as there is a single pupil you will get the hall ready for her." It is reported that attendance never again fell so low.

Cathlamet is not an expanding industrial town. Commercial riverboat service has long since ceased. Gone are the *Undine,* the *Georgiana,* the *Lurline, T. J. Potter* and others, famous old stern and sidewheelers. Logging disappeared after unrestrained cutting of once plentiful timber that once grew right down to the river's edge. Gill net salmon fishing, then wastefully practiced, is almost a thing of the past except during very short seasons. Not yet a ghost, the town waits for industry which is reaching to outlying sections of the Columbia.

The Pulpit Was Hers

Methodist Church of Menlo faces main highway, town itself being on short side road. Although some 75 years old, edifice is in perfect condition, kept sparkling white with frequent coats of paint. Fancy shingling was in high style at turn of century. Expert artisans bound regular cut shingles in tight bundles, then trimmed them to shape on bandsaw. Hand work netted man munificent $2.50 per ten hour day.

ENLO IS A COMMUNITY of farming, dairying and fishing people. Located near Willapa Bay the area is more than bountifully endowed with the rainfall that guarantees green pastures and heavy forests. The big timber is no more, but green pastures are still there with some of the finest cattle in the country.

Among early settlers were the Lillys and the Sowers, industrious folk who had to cut the trees before they could raise cows for milk. Nina Sowers was a little girl around 1895, and now Mrs. Wolfenberger, she still lives near Menlo and distinctly remembers the building of the graceful, white church that stands at the edge of the road.

"We lived five miles from the site, a long way in those days before automobiles. When my father would hitch up the horse and buggy to go to town for staples he often would take me with him. We always stopped where the church was going up to watch awhile. Father said it would be a good thing for everybody to have a church there.

"I didn't know it then, but I learned later that one family, the Lillys, were almost entirely responsible for the founding of the church. There was much doubt about which denomination it would serve. You see, Mr. Lilly was a devout Methodist and his wife was equally serious about the Baptists. The whole community speculated as to which one would win out. No one was too surprised when it was announced that it would be a Baptist Church, Mrs. Lilly being quite strong willed and determined, too. Mr. Lilly wasn't too happy about the outcome and he left a few details unfinished. Nobody could be positive, but some said he wouldn't have anything to do with the pulpit for example. Anyway, Mrs. Lilly built that with her own hands. More than likely it was just because she wanted to have a part in the finishing touches.

"Although everybody had thought there would be preaching every Sunday, it turned out that the town couldn't afford to keep and pay a steady minister. Mostly one would come from Raymond (like Rev. Roberts), or even Chehalis across the mountains. Of course with travel so slow in those days he couldn't come, preach and leave all in the same day. He would arrive maybe on Saturday, hold services Sunday morning and then stay with some family most of the rest of the week, resting and maybe getting in a little fishing or something, enjoying himself, you know. There was one preacher who could almost always be counted on to preach for special things like funerals or weddings. His name was R. V. McCash.

"When Mrs. Lilly passed away the church turned Methodist, nothing too sudden. It was really perfectly natural, since most of the remaining family leaned that way. And when the daughter, Miss May, decided to be a missionary to the Malays, everybody was shocked, but not surprised that she would go as a Methodist."

Old bunkhouses, just south of church, only remaining buildings of once large cannery complex that grew from oldest salmon packing plant in state.

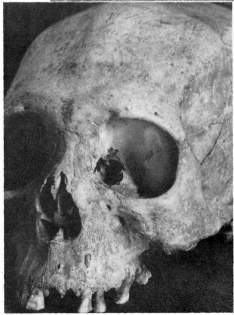

Skull of Chief Concomly. Explorer Clark wrote of Chinookville "The principal Chief of the Chinooks came to see us this evening." This would be famous Concomly, one-eyed head of entire tribe. Skull shows old injury to left eye.

Stella Maris . . . Star of the Sea

A RICH VEIN of history runs through the Stella Maris area near the old Indian village of Chinookville. It was from here that Lewis and Clark first saw the breaking surf of the Pacific Ocean and knew they had successfully completed their mission. And it was on these shores the bark *Isabella* was wrecked, her second mate and boatswain, Essexman James Scarborough, stranded. Less well documented is the story that Scarborough subsequently accumulated a rich treasure of gold and hid it somewhere on the hill named for him. When Patrick McGowan built a large cannery here, the rumor sprang up that he had discovered the Scarborough cache which made him rich.

Actually McGowan earned his money by hard work and canny judgments of how long to wait and when to go ahead. He established the first salmon packing industry in Washington on the site he claimed at Chinookville, not willing to attempt salmon canning. Early canning methods involved soldering the cans shut by hand, many of which later spoiled and exploded, resulting in damage suits. McGowan salted his fish and, as soon as the canning processes were refined, he stepped into that field well ahead of competition.

McGowan arrived at the mouth of the Columbia by a circuitous route from New York where he had been a clothing merchant. Attracted to the California gold rush in 1849, he soon discovered that chronic ill health prevented his actively mining the claim he located. Selling out he went to Portland where he married, the couple moving to the lower Columbia where they established a family of seven children. A number of his descendants still live in the area, Grandson Henry's widow, for one, now 96 years old. The church and site of the old cannery and several gaunt bunkhouses still remain.

Although there were hardly enough Irish or Catholic parishioners to fill it, one of McGowan's sons, in 1904, built a commodious church on his property, naming it Stella Maris—Star of the Sea. Later, he donated the building and ground to the Diocese, then at Nisqually. Catholic authorities dedicated the church more formally as St. Mary's.

For a long time the church was attended by a priest traveling once monthly from Portland's Church of the Holy Rosary. Through part of the 1920s and most of the 30s services were held at intervals by various priests, then closing in 1943. After that the structure rapidly deteriorated.

By 1961 old Stella Maris was in bad shape. Full exposure to marine gales and blasts of wind-driven sand had scoured off all traces of paint and removed many shingles.

Reported Fr. Lawrence Low of Seaview's St. Mary's Church in 1969, "In 1961 we took steps to make repairs on the church at McGowan. We replaced shingles and the round front window that had blown out in a storm. There was no use in painting it. I hold services there every August for the large numbers of salmon fishermen who camp on the grounds at that time. The rest of the year the old church stands closed. There is only one door that can be opened at any time, and that one is so swelled in winter no one could get in, anyhow."

A final word comes from Mrs. Daniel Whaldon of Chinookville who says with nostalgia, "My brother, Stewart Coyle, was the first child to be baptized at Stella Maris, and it was there that Daniel Whealdon and I were married in 1925."

St. Mary's Catholic Church at McGowan faces Pacific Ocean. Lashing marine storms have bestowed patina of color and texture.

Church Bell Cam

Little Episcopal Church, reflecting pioneer nostalgia for New England, was originally built at edge of bluff some blocks from present location. Hand-hewn beams, put together with pegs, were severely strained during transportation on rolling logs. Once securely placed on new foundations church was braced with steel bars running across nave, well above heads of congregation. Church is still in constant use.

PORT TOWNSEND

with the Fog

PORT TOWNSEND's picturesque St. Paul's Church was built in the days when the town was learning to live with belligerent Indians, who later became somewhat "domesticated" and then fawned on the whites, the most notable one being Chetzemoka, more familiarly known as the Duke of York (see *Boot Hill*). St. Paul's congregation was organized in 1860, the building erected in 1865.

Originally the church stood at the very edge of the bluff, fully exposed to ocean storms and soaking, impenetrable fogs. On one Sunday morning in the 1870s, when such a fog blanketed the port, the Sunday School teacher waggled her little hand bell, since the church lacked a tower bell. Out in the bay the revenue cutter *Wyanda* was moving rapidly shoreward, Capt. J. W. Sneldon allowing for more water than he had. When he heard the bell tinkle, he got his engines reversed in time to avert a crashing disaster against the docks.

After securing the *Wyanda* Capt. Sneldon sought out St. Paul's pastor and told him of the incident, adding, "There is much fog here, an excessive danger to ships. I will donate my ship's bell for your church if you will see to it the bell is rung at intervals on every foggy day as a warning signal." The pastor considered the offer heaven-sent and the belfry had a bell.

At least two ships were known to have been saved from being wrecked when pilots heard the bell's timely warning. On one was passenger Ira Sankey, noted Evangelist, who was so impressed by the account he was inspired to write the hymn, "The Harbor Bell." First sung on Seattle's skid road, the song became popular and reached over the world. Cockneys on the London docks, sensitive to ballads about bells, since by tradition their breed was always "born within the sound of Bow bells" (or Mary-le Bow Church bells), caught up the hymn as their own. Sankey once said of it, "The Harbor Bell has saved many thousands of souls."

Port Townsend is a city that "couldn't quite." From the air, water or promontory backing it, the town displays a large collection of substantial brick and stone buildings, seeming enough to form a city of 30,000. A closer look reveals every one of the imposing structures to be of Victorian vintage, most of them empty, some unfinished, although many of the ground floor windows carry displays to attract the tourist's eye, showing everything from tawdry plastic baubles to artistic and expensive statuary and paintings. In spite of the empty upper floor, Port Townsend is not a ghost town. The revivifying influence of the big Port Townsend Division of Crown Zellerbach Corporation saves it from such melancholy. Actually the city is a museum piece, a monument to a fantastic decade, during which it dreamed of becoming the "New York City of the West."

Founded a few months after the birth of Olympia and Seattle, the city at the entrance of Washington's inner waterway soon became the port of entry to Puget Sound. On November 3, 1899, the Albany, N. Y., *Argus* admitted, "Port Townsend ranks only second to New York City in the number of marine craft reported and cleared in the whole United States."

The bubble expanded with incorporating the "Port Townsend and Southern Railroad" and convinced citizens their city was indeed the Key City of the Sound. It was during this period that all of the two dozen buildings, now largely empty, were constructed. Then came the crushing news that the builders of the barely begun railroad still held $5,000,000 worth of unsold bonds.

The bubble of hope burst with loud reports. More than half of the city's population moved out. Banks went bankrupt, closed or merged. Businesses failed, new fortunes disappeared. The thirty miles of railroad track were abandoned to rust. Port Townsend stood in a state of suspended animation until the advent of the Crown Zellerbach industry.

First United Presbyterian Church was built in 1890, near end of Port Townsend boom, just before disastrous collapse of city's financial structure. Organ alone cost $2,500. Pipes are made of spotted pipe metal, wooden parts of California sugar pine and Michigan pine.

Belfry shows ship's bell presented by captain whose cutter was saved from destruction in dense fog.

One of many mansions built during boom. Adjacent to St. Paul's Church, this one was constructed by George Starrett, listed in 1897 city directory as "millman and capitalist." Still remaining in spiral staircase are frescoes titled "The Four Seasons," depicting four maidens suitably "attired." Voluptuous female representing "Winter" was nude except for fortuitiously placed wisp of drapery attached so some women friends of Starrett's would enter house. Victorian residence is now open to public as museum piece.

The Church Nobody Can Use

AT THE SECOND COMING of Christ, the world would be destroyed by divine intervention, the wicked would perish, the righteous saved. This was in essence the belief of the religious order founded by William Miller. He was a New Yorker, born in 1782, a veteran of the War of 1812, diligent student of divinity without formal training. Although a Baptist, he had advanced ideas and his followers were at first called Millerites, then Advent Christians. Before he died in 1849, new groups were formed using his basic philosophies, the largest being the Seventh Day Adventists, who lean heavily on their observance of the seventh day of the week as the Sabbath.

This is the nutshell background of the Advent Christian Church in Maryhill, an account of which is given by Archie Sanders, now of Vancouver, Washington. He was born at Columbus (later renamed Maryhill), and his family was intricately bound up in the history of the graceful white church still standing in Maryhill, now virtually a ghost town.

"A fellow named Miller came through town," Sanders related, "and he preached the gospel of the Advent Christian Church. He may have been a son of the founder, William, but I can't say for sure. At the time, maybe the 1870s, Columbus was a community of perhaps twenty, thirty homes and a school house. An even smaller community called Fruit Flat was on a bench directly above. The people were mostly Baptists and Methodists but had no church. Miller converted everybody to his faith and for a time preached in the little school house. Then I guess he moved on, but the people remained with his teachings."

Archie brought out some sheets with facts and figures, perhaps the only data preserved. In 1886 a move to build a church resulted in a donation of land from the claim of early settler Amos Stark. Builders were Amos, his brother Benjamin, William Chapman, doctor and minister, and Joseph Henderson, Archie's grandfather. Timbers and lumber were transported by wagon and team from Goldendale, each trip requiring a full two days. Included in one load were 2" x 24" planks

Panoramic view of Maryhill area looks southwest, includes section of Columbia River with Oregon shore in background. Arid landscape differs strongly from heavily forested mountains not far downriver. Advent Church is seen in left middle ground. Samuel Hill, son-in-law of rail magnate James Hill, built tracks along Washington shore, attempted "take over" of Columbus, use of name Maryhill for wife Mary. After his death community of Columbus did accept name of Maryhill. Hill was buried here near brow of upper bench, his tomb shown in foreground (more photos, story see *Boot Hill*).

Little church in classic New England style was built to serve Advent Christian congregation in Maryhill. Later it was used briefly by Baptists, still later, more briefly by Episcopalians. 1958 photo shows structure in fairly good condition but driving winds, deep snows, dessicating summer sun in upper Columbia Gorge have since taken toll. Vandals have broken out many windows, desecrated interior. Bell is still in place here, has since been removed with pews.

for the pews, steamed and shaped inside the building as it went up. During construction the weather was hot and Archie's mother Ida, then a girl of twelve, carried cold water to the perspiring workmen. The church was finished in late September, 1888, and dedicated the next month.

The first pastor was Rev. William Chapman who doubled as physician for the community. At first he lived at Fruit Flat(later moving to Goldendale, communting from there.

For a time the interior of the church was left unfinished. Then providentially, an itinerant plasterer named E. J. Carmen came along. He mixed up a batch of plaster, liberally mixed with horsehair and "did a wonderful job of plastering the walls," adds Sanders.

A bell had been ordered from the East but when it at last arrived at Grant, Oregon, the railroad station across the river, it proved to be too small. It was shipped back and the congregation had a long wait for a larger one.

After a number of years some of the Advent Christians began to waver in the faith, the former Baptists and Methodists willing to return to their earlier beliefs. The Methodists built a small church nearer the river and across the tracks, the Northern Pacific line having gone through by then. The Baptists retained the old church and renamed it.

Sam Hill, connected with the Northern Pacific Railway and who later built his castle and replica of Stonehenge in Maryhill, erected a small Quaker Church high on the slope, using for pews those taken from the Methodist Church which had fallen into disuse. The Quaker Church served only a year or two when it was torn down. Then the Methodist Church was also demolished and the same fate seemed to await the Baptist Church as population dwindled almost to the vanishing point.

In recent years the Episcopalians of Wishram, a small downriver community, laid plans to purchase the Maryhill Church and move it to their town. Under direction of Ralph Jacobson of Wishram the congregation purchased two lots there and took out an option on the Maryhill relic. But the Washington State Highway Department refused permission to move the church over the only connecting highway. With all plans frustrated, the Episcopal people removed the bell and heavy curved pews, stored them at Wishram to be used if and when their own structure would be erected. Then they allowed the option to lapse back to the Advent Christian Conference.

When members of the latter discovered their losses, they threatened to sue the Episcopalians, but as yet have not brought the matter to a head. Mr. Jacobson explains, "Yes, I did receive a threatening letter from the Advent Conference, but I suggested they read the fine print which gave us removal rights. After all, the entire church has been rapidly eroding through vandalism and natural forces. Certainly the bell would have been stolen long before this, or some hobo would have set the building afire."

The Klickitat County Historical Museum at Goldendale has made several starts toward saving the Maryhill Church, but all have been aborted through lack of funds. At this point the historic little church seems doomed to complete dissolution.

Russians Clung to Old Traditions

THE TOWN OF WILKESON came into being because of its location, almost directly on a vein of coal. The fuel was found as early as 1833 when Dr. William Frazer Tolmie of the Hudson's Bay Co. was thrilled to discover an outcropping near the juncture of Cowlitz and Toutle Rivers, then was deflated when he rushed samples to Dr. John McLoughlin at Fort Vancouver and heard the factor comment, "Your coal is of no value here. Why should we travel so far to mine it, then haul it to the fort when our surrounding woods provide plenty of fuel?"

Yet coal did eventually come into general use. When railroads came to the state it proved to be a far more convenient fuel for the boilers than the more bulky cord wood. Prospectors found a rich field on the northwestern fringes of Mount Rainier, the deposit conveniently near the surface and within easy hauling distance of Tacoma, an early established railhead.

Samuel Wilkeson was secretary of the board of the Northern Pacific Railway which built a line to the location, the town that grew up there being subsequently named for him. The rails reached Wilkeson in 1876, and by '79 coal was moving out to Tacoma. In 1883 the Oregon Improvement Company, a subsidiary of the Union Pacific, acquired control of the mines but worked them at slow speed for only two years until the '90s when The Wilkeson Coal and Coke Company took over. The glory days for Wilkeson were mainly finished, though some small mines continued in operation, and discoveries of sandstone deposits infused some blood in the economy. Today the place is near ghost, most buildings standing vacant and the once shiny tracks are now rusted and idle. During the period of largest coal production the railroads imported large numbers of Russian laborers. Since these men and their families adhered to the Russian Orthodox faith a church was constructed especially for them near the north end of town. It is believed the company aided financially, although Wilkeson was never the conventional company town. The church was solidly built and remains in excellent condition today.

A small group of these adherents are to be found in Wilkeson and vicinity still clinging to the Orthodox denomination, most of them descen-

Holy Trinity Church is small but conspicuous because of distinctive "onion" dome surmounting tower and traditional Russian Orthodox Cross at apex. Though tiny, congregation keeps church immaculate, according to Fr. Nicholas Sanin who holds monthly services here. Interior is filled with items pertaining to worship of Eastern Churches, with censers suspended from brass chains, icons representing Jesus, Mary and various saints which were always painted or in relief, never sculptured.

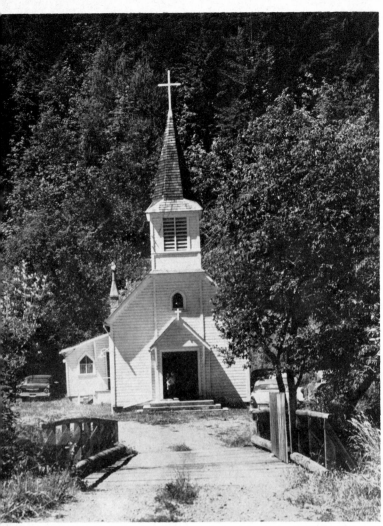

Our Lady of Lourdes Catholic Church in Wilkeson is still in occasional service, attended by Fr. Charles Crosse of nearby Buckley. Setting is picturesque, the snowy white edifice brilliant against background of dark green firs, maples and other vegetation of Washington's well-watered Cascade Mountains. Little bridge affords crossing over small Wilkeson Creek.

church on Thanksgiving Day of the same year. Once every month he travels to the old Wilkeson church to hold Sunday services.

About the old cross, still intact, Fr. Sanin says "Our people explain the presence of the two 'extra' bars this way. Although those Christians belonging to Western faiths venerate the cross in its simplest form, we understand that there was an additional horizontal bar. The upper was a sign identifying the victim, "This is Jesus, The King Of The Jews.' The lower arm was meant to support his feet, however inadequately. During the final death struggles of Jesus, he kicked this support awry, one end pointing down to Hell, the other Heavenward."

The other picturesque old church in Wilkeson is the Catholic Our Lady of Lourdes. Since June of 1968 it has been attended by Fr. Charles Crosse, regular pastor of St. Aloysius Church in nearby Buckley. Fr. Crosse is intensely interested in the history of Our Lady of Lourdes. "I know it was built in 1894, but beyond that I have found little. The sexton for more than fifty years, Andrew Krupa, has helped some, but the main mystery remains so far unsolved. Why was the church named for Our Lady of Lourdes? I have gone over baptismal records a long way back, finding few that were not of Slovakian origin. None with any French history!"

dants of those active in earlier mining operations. They have the comfort of monthly services in their church through the ministrations of Fr. Nicholas Sanin.

His main work is in Chemawa, Oregon, a suburb of Salem, where the Federal Bureau of Indian Affairs established a school for Eskimo and Indian children from Alaska.

Many have come from such places as Sitka, Wrangell and other coastal towns established by Russians who indoctrinated the aboriginal population with their Orthodox faith.

For several years Fr. Sanin held services for the Alaskan youths in one of the schoolrooms. In 1968 he secured two mobile homes, spliced them together, remodeling the resulting structure as a chapel and held the first services in the novel

86

NEVADA

Salvation in The Desert

Virginia City's Presbyterian Church in photo made around 1950 shows slight improvement over "vandal-wrecked shell" described by Muriel Sibell Wolle few years earlier. (photo courtesy David Mason, M.D.)

He Brought God to

Presbyterian Church in 1967 is much spruced up, now allowing for regular services. Church faces out over vast open valley, others facing wall of Mount Davidson.

Saint Paul's Episcopal Church nowadays is sadly dilapidated, still imposing. Worst damage now is in tower where rain and melted snow stream through steeple laid bare by frequent "Washoe Zephyrs." Earlier, more flimsy structures were leveled or entirely washed away by some destructive forces (For more on Virginia City see *Boot Hill* and *Western Ghost Towns*).

he Desert Wastes

F ALL THE OLD mining camps of the West, many of which fit the popular conception of ghost towns, Nevada alone claiming more than 1,300, Virginia City in that state is easily the best known. It may be only a remnant of the once roistering boom city but it is still a showy place of history with many of the original buildings, many of them little altered. While most visitors gravitate to the plentiful bars and gambling places, many are impressed with Virginia City's substantial church buildings, some of them in good repair.

The city is located on the eastern slope of Mount Davidson, placed so high that from any point the view is a tremendously impressive sweep of valley and mountain. Some early arrivals from more verdant parts were not enamored by the view. One man described it as, ". . . the fag end of Creation. There is neither water nor grass and every animal that goes out upon it dies. The Almighty had some great thought in mind when he planned Washoe, but halfway through he forgot. It was never finished. His creative power was exhausted."

Others may have shared these feelings but not those hardy religionists who came out to the raw, harsh country—men of several creeds but with one purpose, to save men's souls. One of them worked as a miner at Shaw's Flat near Grass Valley, California, but went to Paris where he studied at the Seminary of St. Sulpice. After graduating he returned to California but was soon involved in the "rush to Washoe." So as Rev. Patrick Manogue he went to Virginia City and was destined to play a leading role in the religious development of the raw camp. His first place of worship was a stone shelter thrown up on the mountainside. Steps of rough rocks led up to a simple altar centered by a small white robed Madonna Monogue had brought over the Sierra. The year was about 1860.

In old histories and journals are many stories about Fr. Manogue. One especially points up the fact that the priest was, "a stalwart, strong limbed and courageous crusader." Called to administer the last rites of a dying woman he was met at the door by a powerful and angry man.

"No damn priest enters my door" he raged, but a faint voice came from within, "Father please come in, I have sinned and am dying." Manogue threw the man to the floor, disarmed him and entered the room. Ordering the man to "stay there until I have finished" the priest placed his clean linen handkerchief on the bedside table and placed a candle on it. He annointed the woman, administered the last Sacrament and prayed until the eyelids closed. After all was finished he softly tiptoed out.

Later in 1860 Fr. Monogue built a small frame church. Almost immediately the structure was blown down in one of those mountain gales sarcastically termed "Washoe Zephyrs." The wrecked church was replaced by another and larger one. This one withstood winds well but soon proved too small. The next church was larger and built of brick at a cost of $65,000. All producing mines of the city contributed silver for a bell, Fr. Monogue shipping the metal to Spain for casting into a sweet-toned bell. The entire town got drunk on the day the new bell was hoisted into the belfry. In 1875 a fire that destroyed much of Virginia City reduced the proud structure with the silver bell to ashes.

Built two years later on the same site was still another church, a new St. Mary's in the Mountains. This magnificent structure termed the most beautiful in Nevada stands today dominating the already lofty skyline of the city. This church, also built through the efforts of Fr. Manogue cost $60,000, mostly raised by public subscription. During its heyday St. Mary's had a membership of 2,500 regular attendants. Communicants averaged 100 a month and at Easter time averaged 1,200 to 1,500.

Arriving in the Washoe district along with Fr. Manogue was Episcopalian Rev. Franklin S. Rising. As frail as his Catholic cohort was robust, Rising was nevertheless as active in promoting the religious welfare of his flock. Poor health failed to dampen Rev. Rising's keen sense of humor as is proved by his reporting an incident that amused him. He lived in quarters above a saloon. Answering a knock one evening he found a man with a request. His pal, he said, was a gambler who had just been shot and it would seem the wound would be quickly fatal. Would Rev. Rising "say something" over the dying man? Rising asked this visitor, "Do you think your friend would like the Eucharist administered before he passes?" The friend was more than a little baffled but tried to be agreeable. "Well," he said more familiar with faro than theology, "it seems pretty strange to me at a time like this, but I guess it would be all right for you to bring along your deck if you want to."

Rev. Rising had come out as a missionary of this church and was subsequently called rector of the parish. He was instrumental in the building of St. Paul's Episcopal Church in the early 1860s. The edifice came near being destroyed by a fire in the summer of 1868 starting in the church tower, a mystery never solved. Fortunately the damage of $2,700 was regained in insurance.

In September, 1872 the church building was enlarged and the interior rearranged, the seating capacity being enlarged by six pews. Two years later the edifice was again enlarged, so fast was the congregation increasing in these boom years. This time the cost was $9,000, the outlay gaining an extension of 20 feet at the east end and a gallery constructed across the west end. At the same time a large pipe-organ costing $3,000 was erected in the gallery. The congregation enjoyed all these improvements for just one year when the church was razed in the same fire that destroyed the Catholic Church. Also destroyed was the rectory and the homes of two-thirds of the congregation members.

The rectory was almost immediately rebuilt and a foundation laid the next July for a new church building. By December of the year following the fire Virginia City had a new St. Paul's Episcopal Church. Total cost, including furniture, new organ, etc. reached a total of $25,000. Toward meeting this, the sum of $12,000 was realized from insurance and $13,000 by popular subscription. On December 10, 1876 the new church building was opened for divine services. At that time there was a deficit of $2,000, this sum still not gained in 1881 when this history was compiled. It is worth a comment on the ups and downs of a large mining camp that a single pew in St. Paul's was in the possession of five families consecutively. Church membership in 1881 was about 80 persons, never having exceeded 100.

Founder Franklin Rising had long since been forced by ill health to resign his post and in 1866 he returned to his old home in New York State. Two years later he was killed in a steamboat col-

lision on the Ohio River.

The third largest church in Virginia City was that of the Presbyterians, as always embracing many Scottish immigrants. In all probability the most colorful Presbyterian minister ever preaching in the Washoe and elsewhere in Nevada was the Rev. J. H. Byers, fresh out of Glasgow University. Starting his American career in Elko, Nevada, he immediately ran into a series of experiences not dreamed of in the old country.

On June 3, 1876 Rev. Byers was called upon to preach the funeral services of Hon. H. H. Peyton, formerly a member of the legislature. This date, coincidentally, was also set for the passage through Elko of the famous "Lightning Train" from New York to San Francisco. In expectation of this earth-shaking event set for 4 o'clock, the funeral was scheduled two hours earlier.

At 2 o'clock the bell had been tolled, the church was half full and more people arriving. The corpse rested on chairs before the pulpit. Pall bearers were all in place and Rev. Byers was ready to being the service. He was just rising in the pulpit when someone near the door yelled "The train is coming!" The call started a mass exodus, every mourner, the pall bearers, even the sexton rushing out to see the train. Left behind, Rev. Byers glanced at his only companion, the dead body of Mr. Peyton, and later related, "I am sure I detected a slight straining movement as if he too, would like to have joined the crowd." Later, after the train had left, the bell was again tolled and the funeral resumed. The Hon. Peyton had missed seeing the Lightning Train go by.

On the 21st of September, 1862 a Presbyterian Church Society was organized and a meeting held in the Methodist Episcopal Church in Virginia City. Sixteen members were present, the Rev. W. W. Brier of the Home Missionary Society constituted these into a church and in December the Rev. D. H. Palmer arrived from New York to assume the duties of regular pastor.

For some time the congregation met in various homes but in 1867 efforts were begun towards having their own church. The operation that followed is best described in *The History Of Nevada* (1881.) "On July 7th, 1867 the church was dedicated. It had cost $4,700. The funds which enabled the society to rise to the dignity of having their own meeting house were secured through successful mining speculation. The Trustees had secured from some friends on the inside what is known as a point on the stock market. With the little money in the treasury they purchased a few shares of stock, these rising in a few weeks sever-

St. Mary's in the Mountains dominates city. One novelty incorporated in present structure was meant to save it from destruction from fires that destroyed several preceding ones. Water system was extended to vertical pipe terminating at apex of steeple. If fire threatened, huge fountain could be activated, drenching church. It was never called into service, and now would likely be useless. Water supply being carried from Sierra snows in old wooden pipes that have badly deteriorated, severely reducing pressure originally powerful.

al hundred dollars in value. They sold out before the crash and with the money thus secured purchased four lots on C St., the principal thoroughfare. On either side of the meeting house they erected buildings rented out for stores, and from which they derived an annual rental nearly sufficient to pay the salary of the minister, and meet the running expenses of the society. The organization reported last May, (1881) 105 members and the Sabbath School of 200 pupils. The location of the building proved providential, escaping entirely the holocaust of 1875."

Interior view of St. Marys is taken by available light to give natural effect. Real glory of nave is in columns of redwood, natural color and surface never having been marred by varnish or paint.

Little Catholic church stands lonely in field at Dayton's edge, removed from fairly solid business section of old buildings. Church was brought from lofty perch in Pine Grove Mountains in two sections (More photos, story see *Western Ghost Towns*).

Small school doubled as non-denominational church on Sundays. Exact location is between Pine Grove and Yerington, thought to be at or near tiny hamlet of "Pizen Switch". In earliest days of mining, cattle raising along Walker River, enterprising man set up board across barrel, sold vile concoction he called "whiskey." Short term customers took to advertising small cross roads village as "Pizen Switch." Those men engaged in moving Pine Grove church to Dayton had to pass by here, no doubt paused to refresh.

"Get Rich While Serving the Lord"

IN AN AGGRESSIVE EFFORT to build a Methodist church in Austin, Rev. Trefrel collected contributions in the form of mine shares. Then in order to realize money from them he returned to his native Vermont and approached his Methodist brothers with all the verve of a medicine man in glittering phrases like, "Grasp this marvelous opportunity to get rich while at the same time serving The Lord." The buyers all did, too, the Methodist Mining Co. proving to be a going concern.

Huddled in the hollow of the steep Toiyabe Canyon, Austin was the central point in a widely scattered cluster of rich mining camps. From here radiated trails and crude roads to Hamilton, Tuscarora, Eureka and several now faded towns. One nearby camp, Jacobsville (originally Jacob's Well) seemed at first to have a headstart. With its Pony Express Station and maintenance point on the later transcontinental telegraph line, two hotels and post office the hamlet was prominent for several years. Beginning about 1863 it suffered attrition, then desertion as people moved to the better situated Austin.

Yet growth there lagged for a time. Potential mineral wealth in the mining district was ample enough but the attraction of Virginia City's Comstock Lode dulled and with it Austin's lesser glamor. When continued discoveries in the neighborhood of Austin grew into bonanzas the district came into its own. On Sept. 2, 1863 Austin was made seat of Lander County, then comprising about a third of Nevada. A little later that same year it had a hotel, the International, and a newspaper, the *Reese River Reveille,* both institutions destined to flourish long beyond evanescent boom days.

In 1864 lots were selling for as much as $8,000 in gold. In a few more months 366 houses had been built, far too few to house the 10,000 swarming the nearby hills. By the next year there were a number of stamp mills, a Y.M.C.A. had been organized and Austin mining stocks were being sold on every street corner in San Francisco.

Before the year 1867 was out there were 11

Methodist Church in early days, shown in author's copy of old postcard from collection of Bert Acree. Famous Masonic-laid cornerstone is at corner opposite one nearest camera.

mills for 6,000 claims, several public schools and at least one private one. The latter advertised in the *Reveille* its specialty, the teaching of "The French language as it is spoken in Paris." Truly, Austin had come a long way in a short time.

The tremendous expansion of mining claims was accompanied by corresponding legal disputes, litigation proceedings supporting thirty-three lawyers. In proportion there were twelve physicians, five clergymen, many saloons, gambling houses and girlie dives. Yet spiritual needs were not overlooked, three houses of worship being erected—Methodist, Episcopal and Catholic. The latter two have histories conforming to those in most early mining camps but that of the Methodist is surely unique in its physical structure.

Methodism began in Austin when it was created a charge by the Conference in 1864, Rev. C. A. E. Hertel being assigned as first pastor. He held services in halls, abandoned saloons or wherever he could find shelter. But this was not rewarding enough for Hertel who left discouraged, to be replaced by Rev. J. F. Trefrel. This astute minister saw the acute need for a church, the richness Austin's claims and the paucity of actual cash in pocket of his parishioners. On his initial tour of solicitation he was often met with something like "Parson, I certainly would like to contribute to the building of a church, but all I have is a few shares in the claim we just staked." After some thought the Rev. Trefrel again made the rounds, this time accepting a share here, several there until he had accumulated an ownership in most of Austin's potentially wealthy mines. Still, the money was all on paper and not negotiable in the building of a church.

Rev. Trefrel's next step was to pool the claims and organize the Methodist Mining Co. Then he left Nevada's stony soil for the equally rocky hills of his native Vermont. In turn he approached all his Methodist brothers, exhorting them to buy stock in his company. Ever fluent, the Rev. Trefrel would build up to his effectual punch line, "Grasp this marvelous opportunity to get rich while at the same time serving the Lord." Although most sensational news of great riches in the Silver State had actually pertained to Virginia City and the Comstock Lode, still claims of the Methodist Mining Co. were in Nevada too, and therefor must have an equally great potential. Rev. Trefrel found another ready market among his friends in New Hampshire and as a result, set up a new company.

According to the *Daily Reese River Reveille* of July 3, 1866, in reviewing events leading up to the laying of the cornerstone of the First Methodist Church stated that the organization behind the church activities was the New England and Nevada Silver Mining Co. of Boston, Mass." . . . with a paid up capital of $250,000.00. Of this sum $75,000 was set aside for working the mines of the company, building a mill, etc; $50,000 for the building of a church, and the remainder for the purchase of mines and payment of expenses."

Mr. Trefren returned to Austin early in May, 1866, and immediately commenced preparations for the building of the church, parsonage and mill and the opening of the mines belonging to the company . . .

"The building will be brick, with stone foundations and basement, will be forty feet front, sixty two feet in depth, and the main story will be sixteen feet in height. On the southeast corner fronting Court Street is a tower ten feet square which will reach with brick to the greatest height of the main building and extend to a lofty spire constructed of wood. The lower story of the tower will constitute a study for the pastor and a bell will be placed in the belfry."

On July 6, 1866 the *Reveille* printed a near-full page detailing the laying of the cornerstone, headlined, "AN IMPOSING CEREMONY." The story continued, "The corner-stone of the First Methodist Church in the City of Austin was laid at half-past six o'clock last evening . . . The ceremony was performed by the Masonic Fraternity of Lander Lodge No. 8 and Austin Lodge No. 10. W. W. Wixom had been deputed by the Grand Master to perform the ceremony . . . The members of the Order were disposed in the form of a square, and the ceremony commenced. A melodeon had been brought to the ground, around which the choir ringed and performed an ode. Prior to lowering the stone a tin box had been filled with the usual appropriate memorabilia including a Holy Bible and a list of the officers of the two Masonic Lodges in the city. The box being placed, the stone was lowered and the architect advanced and delivered the plumb, square and level to the Grand Master . . . the elements of consecration, corn, wine and oil, were poured upon the stone with appropriate ceremonies. The Grand Master then struck the stone three times with the gavel. He then delivered the instruments of architecture to the principal architect, and after a song from the choir the Masonic portion of the ceremony was concluded."

Next came a lengthy program by the church, highlighted by an address given by Rev. A. N. Fisher, who listed in detail the history and accomplishments of the Methodist Church from founding to the present date. Singing of the Doxology and saying of Benediction concluded the ceremony, surely one of the longest and most detailed in Nevada in that day of little formality.

The church was finished in due time, a "splended" pipe organ installed and a fine parsonage built, all cost amounting to $35,000. The actual cash accumulated by Rev. Trefrel fell short of paying the final installment, leaving an indebtedness of $6,000. Before this amount could be collected the New England and Nevada Mining Co. silver stocks were declared to be largely of the wildcat variety. It appeared the original contributors were more free with dubious stocks and shares than with promising ones. The company was then declared bankrupt and the church property sold to the county for use as a courthouse.

The History of the State of Nevada, 1881, notes:

"Subsequently the property was redeemed by the Church Extension Society of the Methodist Episcopal Church which has advanced money to pay the indebtedness, most of which has been repaid and the society is almost out of debt. The Rev. Trefrel is now in Santa Cruz. In 1868 he was transferred at his own request from the Nevada to the California Conference."

On May 4, 1951 the historic Methodist Church became the property of Lander County Civic and Historical Society. The structure and those parts adjacent were transferred from California-Nevada Annual Conference of the Methodist Church.

A modern note is included in a letter from Mr. Bert Acree of Austin. He writes in 1969 "I was baptized in the Methodist Church on Easter Sunday, 1886, but never became an actual member of the church. I was the janitor for many years and remember the church as a lovely edifice and certainly a Historical Building. I hope it will be here for many years to come."

First cornerstone laid in Nevada was that of M.E. Church, Austin, historic ceremonies conducted by Free and Accepted Masons. Third such rites were conducted at laying of cornerstone in fraternal order's own home shown here, Nov. 2, 1867. Officiating again was W. W. Wixom, "deputed" by Grand Master. Included in Wixom's family was Emma Wixom, who as Emma Nevada, became state's most famous soprano (for more on Austin, see *Western Ghost Towns*).

St. George's Episcopal Church (right) looked like this in August, 1968, when photographed by Reese River Reveille cameraman. Occasion was ordination as Deacon for Herman Buck of Austin. Ceremony attracted, besides newsmen, clergy, laymen "from every corner of Nevada." Earliest Episcopalian services were held in Austin courthouse by Rev. D. M. Goodwin. St. George's Church, built in 1878 still serves congregation.

Methodist Church in modern photo (below left) taken by R. Allen Kennedy of Tonopah.

Venerable St. Augustine's Catholic Church (below right) still stands in good condition. Built in 1866, edifice is still used for regular services.

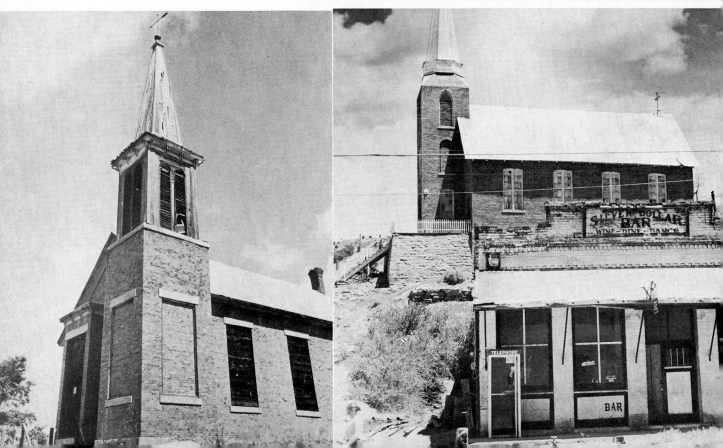

IDAHO

Among Good Indians and bad men

St. Joseph's Catholic Church still stands on brow of East Hill in Idaho City. Although no longer serving on regular basis, church has been kept in good repair. Most extensive renovations were undertaken by Fr. W. A. Henrichs who came to the basin in 1889. Residing at Granite he served St. Joseph's as a mission. Dismayed by finding foundations "all rotten" Fr. Henrichs began a campaign to raise funds for repairs. Although there were only 25 families in Idaho City at the time, their contributions were so largely augmented by Protestants that the desired sum came near to being realized. A benefit concert on Thanksgiving Day raised the rest. In 1937 Bishop Kelly ordered a new coat of paint and replacement of decayed sills and uprights.

They Came to Save the Wayward

IDAHO CITY DID NOT BECOME noteworthy for any peaceful history. The old cemetery on the hill above, many of the picket enclosures now centered by large trees, contained in 1863 some two hundred marked graves. Of these, one old timer said, only twenty-eight died natural deaths.

Idaho City's jail was the first in the Territory and was needed until 1870. It contained two rows of stout cells and stood in the center of an acre of ground encircled by a stockade. The hapless horse thief or murderer, once incarcerated, seldom saw the outside again, even if he was hanged or shot. All such concluding ceremonies were conducted within the palings, the prison yard being complete with gallows and cemetery.

The city was the center of a collection of camps including Granite City, Placerville, Pioneerville and Boise City. All but one have stagnated or disappeared except Boise which is the capital of the state. Granite City has nearly vanished, only a few ruins in the brush being now visible. Pioneerville is a huddled mass of rotting frame buildings, Placerville a peaceful group of occupied homes. Others in the once glittering area have long been forgotten.

Idaho City is a museum piece containing many relics, some preserved, others falling or already fallen into ruin. It was here in the early 1860s that Sherlock Bristol was prospecting when snow began to fall. He and several other men who joined him later, built some cabins and dug in to prepare for winter. They began mining the first likely spot, bringing water to wash the removed dirt, from the creek. Bristol directed one of his party to dig a well closer to the claim and after reaching a depth of eighteen feet the man let out a whoop. He had turned up gleaming nuggets of gold. This was the incident that built a city which reached 6,000 people the first year. It was first called Moorestown after J. Marion Moore, then Bannock City and finally Idaho City. The creek is still called after Moore.

To release the lively emotions of a polyglot population, enterprising gamblers, saloon keepers and madames quickly set up establishments as did those starting grocery stores, supply houses, theaters and blacksmith shops. And then came men of God to preach and pray for the lost souls. The first of these was a Roman Catholic priest.

Catholic missionaries had been in the Northwest permanently since November 1838 when Fr. Francis Norbert Blanchet went to Fort Vancouver as the new Vicar General of Oregon Territory. Although initial efforts were centered in the Willamette Valley where French Canadians had settled, attention soon spread to the roistering mining camps of Idaho where Irish Catholic miners were arriving in force. Credit for establishing the faith in the Boise Basin is given Frs. Touissant Mespie and Andre Poutin.

Finding a total of more than 10,000 people in the area, Fr. Mespie immediately set to work soliciting funds for a church in Idaho City, then still called Bannock City. Subscriptions soon warranted the purchase of a block of property on East Hill. An item in the Boise *News* described the edifice Fr. Poulin was building. The church would be twenty by seventy-five feet and surmounted by a twelve-foot cross. "A vestry will be attached and it is Father's intention to add a residence of larger dimensions as his means increase. The grounds will be decorated with shrubbery in the spring." The final sentence may well arouse some curiosity for the garden-minded. Obviously no nursery would be found in that early day and place. Perhaps the church grounds would be landscaped with the amply available white flowered native shrub that would one day be the state flower of Idaho, Philadelphus, often miscalled Syringa.

By early November the church was sufficiently complete so that on the 15th Fr. Mespie performed "the solemn and impressive ceremonies of dedication." The year was 1863 and the church was named for St. Joseph. It was the first of any kind in the Boise Basin but others soon appeared in other camps in the district.

Those responsible for finishing St. Joseph's and paying off the debt were not quibbling about methods. Lotteries were the most popular and profitable, one of them offering an organ as grand prize. Benefit concerts and dances were also arranged, one of the latter netting $380. "This amount," the *News* said, "will materially assist in fitting up the interior of the church and

Early Episcopal Church at Placerville near Idaho City occupies prominent situation on hill beside road leading to Granite. Long time resident of Placerville, Mrs. Edna Carpenter, says "I would rely on any information given by Bishop Rhea who was well known and beloved by all of us. If he said the bell in our church came originally from the Episcopal Church in Silver City that is very likely to be the case. Besides, this has long been my own understanding. The church now still serves as a nondenominational house of worship. In fact we had church there this morning (Sunday, January 19, 1969). As to a Catholic church here, I don't believe there ever was any. Up at Granite, a mile or two above here there is a large white cross on what they say is the site of the only such church in this part of the Basin." Since there actually was a Catholic Church at Granite, Mrs. Carpenter's information has been accurate (More photos, story see *Western Ghost Towns* and *Boot Hill*).

adjoining grounds." This continuing concern for the appearance of the surroundings seem to be unique in that rough-and-ready time, according to printed accounts.

The next few years brought changes. Fr. Poulin, always frail, further declined and was forced to retire to Portland. The next year a disastrous fire, on May 17, 1867, destroyed most of the city, not sparing St. Joseph's Church and the residence. Fr. Poulin, though almost given up the year before, had made a good recovery, returning to Idaho City only to find his church in ashes. It was characteristic of the ailing man that he immediately set about ambitious plans for a new and better church building.

So zealous were his efforts that a new edifice was soon under way, services temporarily continuing in "Brown's brick building." By the end of

the same year the fine, new St. Joseph's was ready for occupancy. Before final completion, Fr. Poulin had been called away, leaving the entire burden for Fr. Mespie.

The next several years showed a strange intermingling of strata in Idaho City, evidenced in a letter one observer wrote to an Oregon aquaintance. "The priest and saloon-keeper jostle each other on the sidewalks, and the gentleman's wife must walk a trail around that of the courtesan who lives next door and does her shopping at the same counter. These contrasts are so common that they attract no attention whatever." Another comment was that it was a "a disorderly town of . . . 2,500 white inhabitants . . . with many families, many clever men, many children, but no schools of any kind."

In an attempt to remedy this condition to some

extent the sisters of the Holy Name in Portland came to Idaho City, after investigating other Basin towns, and established St. Mary's Academy, later renamed St. Joseph's. Protestants, always a minority group in Idaho City, amazed the soliciting nuns by contributing heavily to the school fund. An Episcopal observer commented that nearly all of the $2,700 accumulated was collected from them. More, they sent their children to the finished parochial school and continued to provide funds for its support.

During the height of the mining boom various groups of Protestants had met in private homes, and at least two, the Methodists for one, had actually built churches. Apparently none of these assemblies proved long-lasting. In the fall of 1865 the *Idaho World* said, "The church-going community, if there be any, is badly off at present in this place. With the exception of the Catholic churches at several points in this country, there is no church of any denomination now open for religious services. The building originally erected in Idaho City for that purpose still stands, being occupied as a Court room, but no minister of the Gospel has proclaimed 'glad' or any other kind of tidings from its pulpit for several months. There is no Protestant church in the Boise Basin."

Although several Protestant churches were later built elsewhere in the Basin, it seems none ever took permanent roots in Idaho City itself. The peak period here was too short to allow any late comers time to get established. By 1869 many of the most important mines were already showing signs of exhaustion. Hundreds of Irish miners departed for greener pastures, their place taken by Chinese content with the leavings. The situation was not one to contribute to the church and as for school, the Sisters operating it took their customary summer vacation and failed to return. The new young priest Fr. Archambault undertook to run the school along with his duties in the church but when several more Catholic families moved away in 1870 the school registration dropped to a low of twenty-five. In spite of an obviously bleak situation Fr. Archambault stuck to the job, regularly saying Mass in the church and teaching the children still attending school. In January 1876 his once robust body became so weakened by overwork and poor diet that he fell an easy victim to diphtheria. Surviving after a hard struggle he found his voice gone, being forced to close the school and leave his church to occasional ministrations of Fr. Poulin who by now was helping at several other struggling churches in the Basin. Although later able to return temporarily to St. Joseph's, Fr. Archambault was transferred to Boise in 1877, leaving his church in Idaho city to the inevitable decline.

Old Silver City Cemetery contains remains of saints and sinners who now rest together in anonymity. Beyond graves is center of town, bare spot being part of Jordan Street. Large building with balconies facing street is famous old Idaho Hotel. *Avalanche* of July 7, 1868 reports, "First Catholic Church was built on Jordan St. opposite the Idaho Hotel and near the Chinese laundry."

A Church for $25?

IDAHO, A STATE WITH MOUNTAINS full of precious metals and minerals, is filled with old mining towns. Among these are many ghost towns, the queen of them all without question being Silver City. Today it is still most picturesque, sitting high in the Owyhee Mountains in southwest Idaho not far from the Oregon border.

The discovery of gold and silver on War Eagle Mountain was more than ordinarily spectacular, ore from the Poorman Mine assaying between $3,000 and $4,000 per ton. One mass of ruby-silver crystals weighing a quarter of a ton was found at a depth of a hundred feet.

The prosperity of any mining camp is subject to the vagaries of depressions and varying prices of metals. Silver City of necessity followed the general pattern, suffering its hardest blow in the financial panic following the collapse of silver values in 1893. As late as 1898 when its chief glories had faded there still stood six general stores, two hardware stores, a tin shop, two meat markets, four restaurants, a brewery and many other businesses.

Church records for Silver City are far from complete, many having been lost in fires of frequent occurrence. In the spring of 1865 school master J. A. Chittenden opened a "Sabbath School" which met in the school house for several months. Then it moved next door, north of V. Blackmer's on Washington Street.

A Union Church and School Society was organized in October of that same year, apparently meeting in members' homes until a year later when Silver City's newspaper, *The Avalanche,* announced the completion of the new "Community Church." By 1867 the project must have come to an end because in that year Episcopalian Bishop Tuttle complained, "No minister of any kind is here, not even a Roman Catholic. The Sunday School is the only thing witnessing to Sunday . . . although it is a 'Union School' and all kinds of children, even Roman Catholics are in it, we feel that it has a church leaning . . . We met for services this morning and will meet tonight in the Orofino Saloon, an old deserted drinking place."

Many large more imposing buildings still stand in Silver City but old church is given prominence because of isolated location on summit of knoll. Built as an Episcopal house of worship was later sold to the Catholics. No vestige of conventional trail or walk now leads up hill, worshippers possibly picking own way, one as good as another (for more on Silver City see *Western Ghost Towns* and *Boot Hill*).

Bishop Tuttle made frequent visits to Silver City during the years 1867 to 1877 and was always well received. On one such occasion the *Avalanche* reported, "Services were held morning and evening on Sundays at Jones Hall. On both occasions the Bishop discoursed eloquently and his sermons elicited rapt attention at the hands of a large audience. The Bishop's visits are always a source of pleasure to our people and there is general regret that such long times elapse between them."

There has been little information about the yet beautiful church that still stands today. Its position on an eminence commands the attention of all visitors and it is the target of many cameras. Was it Episcopal or Catholic? It had been alternately credited to both. Recent information appears to explain the confusion, though some exact dates are missing.

Betty Derig of Weiser, writing in *Idaho's Yesterdays,* organ of Idaho Historical Society, states that in 1940 she had a letter from Fred Richards, historian of Payette. Mr. Richards wrote that beloved Bishop Rhea had informed him of the disposal of Silver City's Episcopal Church. It seems that Bishop Barnwell (Episcopal) sold the church "some years ago" to Bishop Kelley (Catholic) for the sum of $25.

The Episcopal people must have felt that the price hardly allowed all equipment to go with the edifice. At any rate, when the Catholics took possession they found the belfry empty and the "seats" (the record doesn't read "pews") missing. The bell went to the Episcopal Church at Placerville, the seats to St. Michael's Chapel in Boise.

Interior of Cataldo Mission exhibits many examples of primitive, unschooled art. At upper left is conception of Heaven. Companion piece at right presents alternative, these old world works carried by blackrobes to wilds of Idaho. After well over century of exposure, colors remain unfaded. On bracketed pedestals right and left of sanctuary are figures of Blessed Virgin and St. John the Evangelist carved from blocks of wood by Fr. Ravalli. Same skilled artisan priest also constructed altar, painted several other pictures in church (photo courtesy Frances Cope, Coeur d'Alene *Press*).

Mission in the Forest

THE CHURCH BUILDING and evangelizing efforts of famed Father DeSmet among the northern Indian tribes were ordinarily confined to the country of the Pend d'Oreille but at times he traveled to Kootenai and Nez Perce villages in need of religious attention. During one of these excursions he paid a visit to the mission of St. Paul in the Willamette Valley of Oregon. On returning to Montana he stopped for a time with the Coeur d'Alenes and concluded there was opportunity for church goodness with these Indians. That same autumn, in 1842, he sent out Father Nicholas Point and Brother

Charles Huet to establish a permanent mission among the Coeur d'Alenes.

The site selected was on the north bank of the St. Joe River about one mile south of Lake Coeur d'Alene. The spot seemed an ideal one but next spring the several small buildings erected were inundated by the flooding river. In the hope that the phenomenon was an unusual one, the priest and his layman brother remained. By 1846 it was apparent that the site was hopeless and a new one located on higher ground on the Coeur d'Alene River, about forty miles northeast. After numerous adventures and tribulations in

Cataldo Mission on the Coeur d'Alene Reservation is termed by Catholic authorities "A triumph in Renaissance architecture, perfect in planned execution, striking in beauty of line and perfection of detail, erected in a virgin forest in utter wilderness." That a man could ride in on horseback, and with a few primitive tools construct it seems "near to miraculous." During Idaho's earliest pioneer period the Mission's lights shone forth in welcome to engineer, soldier, packer, hunter, scientist and prospector. The party in search of what turned out to be Idaho's most spectacular early gold camp, Leesburg, sought shelter here from heavy winter snows (see *Ghost Town Album*).

Montana, at St. Mary's and other points in the Inland Empire, Father Ravalli found himself here, charged with the task of building a mission. The job would have to be done with no other tools than a broad ax, an augur, some ropes, pulleys and a penknife. For a construction gang he had lay brother Huybrechts and a band of unskilled Indians.

Father Ravalli drew up his plans for the church, then in 1846 started the work of erection. Seven years later the mission stood finished, about forty by ninety feet and forty feet in height. The square timbers along the side walls, cut by broad axe, were twenty feet long, twenty-two inches on a side. Horizontal timbers, placed about halfway between floor and ceiling, were mortised into the uprights, the entire frame held together by wooden pegs.

With the framework in place, construction of the walls began. Holes were drilled at rather close intervals in the sides of uprights. Supple poles then were inserted into the holes and laced together with ropes made of braided grass. The Indians formed a sort of brigade, filing from river to church, each man bearing as much mud as he could carry. Another crew at the church smeared the mud on the skeleton walls, layer upon layer as it dried. To this day there are visible several handprints left by workers.

This method of construction, though termed "adobe," differs markedly from that employed in mission churches and residences in the great Southwest where the mud is first cast into large bricks, then sun-dried and later erected into walls. In this type of adobe construction the bricks are their own support, requiring no timbers except for lintels, roof beams, etc. At Cataldo the walls, by accretion became about twelve inches thick, approximately the same as the more conventional adobe brick ones.

While the natives were working hard at actual construction, Brother Huybrechts, who was no mean artist, carved panels to cover the ceiling, designing each one individually. He placed them himself, possibly not trusting the native laborers with the fragile sheets of wood. During the second year of construction the first services were held under its roof, and in 1853 the adobe edifice was pronounced completed.

In that same year Isaac I. Stephens, great territorial governor of Washington, enjoyed the hospitality of the priests at Coeur d'Alene Mission, recording there a tribute to the architectural beauty of the church. In 1858 the "Blood and Iron" warrior Captain John Mullan, while build-

ing his famous road, was an honored guest at the mission, calling it "a Saint Bernard in the Coeur d'Alene Mountains." From November of 1858 until February of 1859 the mission was home to Father DeSmet.

In 1877 new boundaries for the Couer d'Alene country had made severe inroads into the mud walls of the mission, eroding them in several places so as to let in some daylight. During that summer the structure was lined, inside and out, with clapboards, a luxury item unobtainable at the outset. Now the already historic structure was comparatively safe from further weathering.

In 1877 new boundaries for the Couer d'Alene Reservation were created, leaving the old mission stranded outside. There was considerable pressure by authorities to maintain the building as an agricultural community for the Indians. However, a survey revealed very little good land in the immediate vicinity, so the old mission building was abandoned and a new one built at DeSmet, southwest near Farmington. Even though an occasional nostalgic Mass was held in the old mission, the structure inevitably began to decay.

Until sometime in 1920 there was little evidence of interest in the preservation of historic structures in Idaho. About that time some citizens became conscious of the value of some of Idaho's historical relics, and that unless something was done to save them, such relics as the old mission at Cataldo would soon crumble into ruins. During the next several years interest grew under impact of feature stories in the newspapers, and in 1926 an organized "automobile pilgrimage" to the mission further stirred public consciousness. All this culminated in 1928 when a crew under direction of the Bishop of the Idaho Diocese went to work at the site.

The foundation walls were strengthened or rebuilt, about a hundred concrete piers placed to firm up and level the floors and exterior walls covered with new siding. Skilled artist-workmen brightened the frescoes and retouched altar decorations, leaving all much as it was originally.

The *History of Idaho* by Cornelius Brosnan notes, "Upon the completion of the restoration work in 1929, the custom was inaugurated of conducting an annual pilgrimage to this religious shrine. It is a source of pride to Idaho citizens that living in this war-torn world of today, that this memorial to the peace-loving fathers of long ago would appear once again as a shining and arresting feature overlooking the Coeur d'Alene River."

ARIZONA

Missionaries in the land of mesas

"There is a rocky hill near del Bac," wrote historian Rev. Edwin McDermott. "Kino had worked there during the day, hauling tezontle stone for the walls of his new church. He climbed that hill after the delegates had left and he looked westward. He envisioned a chain of churches, visitas and ranchos, stretching to the Pacific." Author made this view from same side hill showing extent of church grounds. Campanario at far end surmounts detached mortuary. Well shown here is dome over intersection of transepts. Low dormitory, utility structures in center, are of later date than church. Pair of leonine figures in foreground is larger version of wooden ones at ends of altar rails. Originals in church honored reigning House of Castile, whose emblem was pair of lions, responsible for most mission funding.

Figure of Virgin Mary, clothed in actual gown and lace, stands at right of altar. Legend has it that in early days of San Xavier young Indian girl engaged to marry soon had completed elaborate wedding gown. When intended groom was accidentally killed she placed gown on statue.

No blade of grass softens desert ground in cemetery of San Xavier Del Bac.

Lavish reredos above altar is heavily ornamented with gilded gesso and carved wood.

106

Mexico Said, "Spanish—Go Home"

Mission San Xavier Del Bac, just south of Tucson, is often termed "White Dove of the Desert" and is seen from afar because of open desert surroundings and slight elevation, location chosen by founding Father Kino in 1693. Design of church exemplifies late Spanish renaissance of Churriguesque style as carried out by native craftsmen. Central third of facade is unplastered, natural terra cotta richly encrusted with native attempts at Spanish baroque ornamentation, shells and arabesque swirling volutes. Pilasters are here brought into sharp relief by glancing early morning light. Of two massive towers only one is crowned by dome. Why? Question remains unanswered historically, only legend explaining that architect, having completed one, climbed second to lay out dome, fell to his death, leaving job undone.

IN 1693 FATHER KINO came to the Indian village of Bac on the Santa Cruz River. He walked to a slight elevation giving an unobstructed view of the desert for miles around. "Here," he said, "we will build a mission to convert and educate the Indians under God. We will call it San Xavier Del Bac. It will be the most beautiful in all New Spain."

If not his exact words these were his thoughts as evidenced in his naming the mission after St. Francis Xavier, patron saint of all the missions and namesake of Kino. Fr. Eusebio Francisco Kino, born an Italian at Segno, his baptismal

papers dated August 10, 1645, he was sent out to the wide-flung provinces of Spain in 1678. Three years later he landed in the New World at Vera Cruz. Until his death at Magdalena, 62 miles south of the border towns of Nogales in 1711, he spent his time in continuous travel and in establishing missions.

Actual construction of the first mission at Bac began in 1700. A chapel and numerous service buildings were constructed and cultivation of the fertile surrounding fields begun when the Pima and Papago Indians of the area joined in a general uprising since called the "Pima Revolt."

Church edifice is laid out in cruciform as opposed to most others of period in simple rectangular floor plan. Ceiling over nave and transepts is series of flat domes between transverse brick ribs. Dome over transept crossing is supported on high octagonal drum, pierced by high medallion windows.

Jesuit builders were forced to flee San Xavier in 1751, later returning to work when the heat of battle cooled.

In 1767, an upheaval in Spain's colonial policies resulted in the driving of Jesuits from New Spain and their replacement by priests of the Franciscan order. These had hardly begun work on the mission at San Xavier when hostile Apaches in continuing raids sacked the establishment, again driving off the builders. When construction was resumed, a new design was worked out and this became the nucleus of the present day mission. After nearly two decades of construction the new church was dedicated in 1797. For the celebration the sanctuary was decorated with furnishings and ornaments originally brought to the site by Fr. Kino himself and subsequently hidden from Apache marauders. Now everything seemed to point to long and uninterrupted operation of the mission.

In 1822 the area won independence from Spain and in two years was established as part of the Republic of Mexico. The new government was not sympathetic toward the mission movement established by the "oppressor" in the old world. Mexican authorities took over the farm lands and refused support to the church. San Xavier therefore was again abandoned, remaining deserted until the country again changed its allegiance, this time to the United States, in 1859.

The Mission San Xavier, now part of the Diocese of Santa Fe, limped along in a state of disrepair and neglect until the year of 1906 when Bishop Granjon began restoration. He saw to it that original plans were followed, with no major changes except in the atrium and the nearly fallen dormitory buildings.

As San Xavier stands today it is surely the best example of architectural style and state of preservation of all the Spanish missions in the United States. Situated about eight miles south of Tucson, it is surrounded by vast open spaces which isolate the magnificent structure for photographers. It is open to visitors except during religious services.

Mission Had Sad Fate

Ruins of obscurely documented Saint Augustine Mission lay just west of Tucson, across Santa Cruz River on Mission Road, seemingly same one termed Saint Jose when founded. Although some voices were raised at intervals to restore or at least preserve historical structure, massive ruins of soft, unfired adobe continued to melt away. In 1940, when walls were still partially erect, Tucson visitor from New England exclaimed, "Your beautiful Mission is no more! What have you done? In the East we would have enshrined such a structure forever." Adding insult to injury, city located garbage dump on top of still remaining traces (photo courtesy Arizona Pioneers' Historical Society).

WHEN THE JESUITS were expelled from New Spain in 1767 there was no permanent building in Tucson. The Franciscans came, headed by Padre Francisco Tomas Garces. He began immediately to build Mission San Xavier but turned the job over to others and spent most of the next twelve years exploring the area. During this period he collaborated with De Anza in marking out a route from Tucson to the Pacific, incidentally founding the city of San Francisco.

At this time the region around Bac and the Indian village that would be Tucson was being harried by fierce Apaches who burned houses, murdered villagers and killed stock. At last, De Anza, in 1768, ordered his garrison to set up a presidio on the Santa Cruz River some nine miles above Bac. Under this protection, some authorities say, Fr. Garces established there a visita which he called San Jose Del Tucson.

No document has been found to give Garces credit, only the building itself, but when the first American arrived after consummation of the Gadsen Purchase in 1853, they found not only a chapel but a large two-story rectangular church. Presumably this was the same mission but by then it was called Saint Augustine Del Tucson.

The name change is rather easily explained in view of the fact that saints' names were less permanent than place names. Changes in personnel and the priest in charge sometimes resulted in renaming the church. Here again, cloudy or entirely missing records of the mission make the story mostly conjecture.

The Arizona Historical Society's organ *Arizoniana,* summer issue, 1962, takes the local public to task. An article states, "The failure of responsible citizens to investigate and take steps to preserve the mission complex at the Pueblo of Tucson is a tragedy of the first order. The Carrillo homestead just south of the industrial school incorporated bricks from the ruined chapel of San Augustine. In 1899 a University of Arizona publication said, 'The people of Arizona have every reason to thank the Antiquarian Association for their efforts to preserve the interesting ruins of prehistoric ruins and relics civilizations. . . There is one instance however that we wish to call attention to. Just across the Santa Cruz River, about a mile from Tucson, are the ruins of the San Augustine Mission, the first manual training school in the U. S. and remarkable for its interesting history and antiquity.' Nothing was done. The mission lies beneath Tucson's city dump."

Juan Remembered

Wishing Shrine is one of Tucson's most leegndary historic features with atmosphere of old Mexico. Backing a hard-packed earth patio, adobe shrine is pleasant place for contemplation.

or Almost Century

JUST OUTSIDE THE CITY of Tucson at the foot of Sentinel Peak is a large section of an old village. It was originally a collection of brush huts called by the Indians Stijukson or Schookson after a dark-colored spring. Many of the Mexicans and minority groups now living there are descendants of the south-of-the-border people who infiltrated the settlement and built it into an adobe pueblo beside the free-flowing Santa Cruz River.

Sometime in the late 1870s the village grew larger and more prosperous, the legend of the "Wishing Shrine" developing with it in the superstitious minds of the child-like people. It concerned young Juan Oliveras.

Although not long married the youth became infatuated with his wife's mother and was drawn into an affair with her. Detected in one clandestine act, the over-amorous Juan was ordered outside by his father-in-law and in the ensuing struggle was killed.

The church said he could not have proper burial rights so the body was put in the ground where he fell and the village was supposed to forget the matter. Several Mexican women did not. They had known Juan Oliveras and wanted to perpetuate his memory. In compassion they placed lighted candles on his grave, prayed for his soul and replaced the candles as they burned down.

In time a shrine was fashioned over the grave, a parapet built of native dried mud bricks surmounted by a gracefully designed cross. Facing a sun-drenched patio the structure resembles a churchly sanctuary exposed to the weather.

Many candles burn there or gutter out, some single tapers, some in elaborately branched wrought iron candelabras. The melted wax of a hundred years has soaked the wall and several feet of adjacent ground. It is said a wish uttered as a candle is lighted will be granted before dawn, but only if the candle burns completely down. Mothers of errant daughters trudge to the shrine, touch a match, kneel with head bowed. Wish or prayer, superstition or religious expression of hope, the Wishing Shrine is something more than a curiosity for tourists.

100 years of candle burning gives age and meaning to shrine. Paper flowers and fresh blooms in vases, saturation of candle wax in walls and adjacent earth offer strong resemblance to church sanctuary and altar, especially at night.

First Priest Came in 1690

ODAY THE RIVER called Santa Cruz is a weak thing, filling its banks only in rare periods of heavy rains. Not so in the seventeenth century. The stream then was more steadily robust, fed by more rainfall. In the heat and dryness of mid-summer it followed the southwest habit of retreating below the sandy bed for a time but remaining visible in several places the year around. Growing in these areas was abundant vegetation that supported an Indian population, mostly of the Pima tribes.

Late in 1690 some of the people of the village known as Tumacacori gathered to see if they could induce Father Kino to establish a mission among them. For some time they had heard of the black-robed priest who brought strange animals and plants good to eat, and of the paraphernalia he used. Accordingly they built a ramada, a simple shelter of brush, placed a cross un-der it, prepared a place near it where Father Kino could sleep if he should come to Tumacacori.

A delegation was sent southwestward to the village of Tucabavia with hopes of intercepting Fr. Kino. The priest later wrote, "It was our intention to turn back from El Tucabavia to Cocospera but some messengers from San Cayentano del Tumacacori came to meet us, carrying some small crosses which they gave us, and kneeling with great veneration and asking us on behalf of their people to visit their village also."

Father Kino and another priest did accompany the petitioners to their village, consisting of some 40 houses rather closely packed, said Mass and baptized several babies. This was the first bringing of Christianity into what is now Arizona. Then the priests resumed their journey southward. Later that summer Kino returned to Tumacacori

Tumacacori Mission as it stands today. Distinctive facade has features in common with Byzantine and Moorish styles with deeply recessed portal framed in traditional Spanish Renaissance manner. Dome at left arches over sanctuary, supportng lantern at summit. Steps made easy access for neophyte whose duty it was to tend beacon. Construction of church utilized combination of adobe (unfired clay) and hard-fired red clay brick. Walls are generally very thick, averaging five and one-half feet at bottom, some over nine feet, notably those in baptistry (more in *Boot Hill*).

to give the natives only a part of what they wished to hear. There were not sufficient funds, he said, to establish a permanent mission here, or even to send a resident priest. But he would see to it that the place was made a visita which meant that a priest would visit as opportunity offered.

During the next few years Kino was as good as his word, also sending the people a nucleus herd of sheep and goats, and instructing them in the cultivation of the seed wheat to augment the native corn. Before long the people at Tumacacori had cattle too.

Then followed a period filled with privations caused by the fact that Spain was at war with England and unwilling to bother with far away missions, let alone mere visitas. Kino died while dedicating the mission at Magdalena and Tumacacori was all but forgotten.

In 1741 conditions were somewhat better, Tumacacori again receiving visitas. A population listing for the village in 1765 shows 199 persons representing 87 families, probably as many as ever lived there. It is almost certain a chapel existed there at that time, no doubt a very simple structure. Vague records seem to indicate that there were two such rude structures there over the years, the first a wattle and plastered mud affair, little more than a shade-giving ramada, the second more elaborate and built of adobe bricks. At least one, more likely both, were severely damaged by fire in raids of the ever menacing Apaches.

The record becomes clear for 1773. It was then Tumacacori became a real mission, the head of the area, an old church register referring to the village as "este pueblo de Joseph de Tumacacori."

Sometime around 1800 the present church building was started and the village was not ready for such monumental construction. The climate had taken a drier turn, several periods of draught killing four successive wheat plantings. As fast as the population increased by births, it was decimated by murderous Apaches. But the chapel was "split into two separate halves" according to an early writer. The decision for a new and far more elaborate church was made with the thought that early, rough construction could be done free by Indian labor, the finishing by artisans who could be paid by that time, it was hoped. So the work went ahead.

There were constant difficulties until about 1822 when the structure was dedicated, being usable although far from finished. The most conspicuous evidence of work left undone is the truncated bell tower, appearing as if wrecked by earthquake (as were several mission towers in California in 1812). Fragmentary evidence indicates that early in 1822 Fr. Esteric sold some 4,000 head of cattle, evidently to raise funds to complete the building but there was difficulty in securing payment and work was stopped.

The new church functioned for only a few years. The last entry in the record of rites is, "August 26, 1847—At Tumacacori, for at least one baptism." This was noted by Fr. Rojas who must have been the traveling priest for the area, the entry so made indicating that Tumacacori no longer had a resident one and this was the end of the mission as a viable church. This assumption is born out by the entry for Oct. 25, 1848 in the diary of a noted traveling historian, Cave Couts. It reads in part, "At Tumacacori there is a very fine church standing in the midst of a few conical huts made of bushes thatched with grass, huts of the most primitive kind . . . No priest has been in attendance for many years although all its images, pictures, figures etc., remain unmolested and in good keeping."

The following winter was as wet as others preceeding had been dry. The raging Santa Cruz washed out much of the village, including the primitive brush huts described by Couts. This must have been the time when the natives abandoned the village and church completely. Thinned in numbers by Apache raids, disheartened by loss of their priests and now without shelter, the unhappy Pimas gathered up their belongings and furnishings of their church and traveled to San Xavier del Bac to the north. After turning over their sacred relics to that church, they annexed themselves to its pueblo and there finished out their lives.

During succeeding years the Tumacacori mission church was left to decay and vandals. Before 1860 the roof timbers collapsed, allowing rains to penetrate at will. At least one family took up temporary residence in a room of the building. Over the entire period of abandonment the floor was repeatedly dug up by searchers for the glamorous but wholly mythical "treasure of Tumacacori." It was within a few months of the one hundredth anniversary of its dedication that the mission church began to receive repairs which were calculated not to restore it to its original form but stabilize it as it now stands.

Tumacacori as it looked on July 3, 1889. Old photo made by George W. Roskruge is shown here to point out lack of conspicuous change occurring during last 70 years. Actually great depreciation had taken place in decaying beam ends, allowing collapse of roof.

Detail of facade, raised ornamentation still showing faint traces red pigment used as contrast to general cream-white background.

At rear of chapel and adjoining cemetery is mortuary where bereaved ones could watch over body until it was buried few steps away.

Sanctuary and part of chancel in photo taken by available light to retain natural effect. Dome above sanctuary did not depend upon wooden vigas for support, remaining intact when roof over nave collapsed. Continuing protection of sanctuary accounts for partial preservation of nearly 150 year old paintings. Note remaining brick platform once supporting altar. At right is seen partially restored pulpit. Nave never supplied with benches or pews, Indians kneeling on floor made of hard-tamped bits of accidently broken bricks, troweled smooth with mortar and painted red. Original floor was completely dug over by treasure hunting vandals.

The Miner Took to Preaching

ORE THAN A THOUSAND years ago Indians scrambled up the steep sides of Mingus Mountain to obtain gaudy face paints in oxidized metaliferous deposits on the spot where one day a city of 15,000 would be built. Perhaps about this time the aborigines mined the almost pure copper found there, fashioning it into weapons and tools. Mining by whites began around 1884.

And this sparked the mushroom growth of a city so fantastic that even today as a ghost there seems to be a mirage of great activity shimmering on the mountainside. From the upper city limits to the lower side there is a difference of more than a quarter of a mile in altitude, the height reached by only one sinuously snaking road. Other streets are so steep and so consistently dead-ended as to quickly discourage the inexperienced driver. Many a house with top below the level of the street above bears the garage on the roof. To get to a basement from the front steps one must climb a steep hill. And the houses were built so close together, many residents, it is said, could scratch a match on the chimney next door. When Town Marshal Fred Hawkins discovered a prisoner missing from jail he would get out his field glasses and scour the country visible from his or any other home. If he spotted a camp fire anywhere between Jerome and the blood-red cliffs of Oak Creek Canyon thirty miles away he knew he had located his man.

Although not as large as the famous Tombstone, Jerome was even tougher, with a fringe of saloons and brothels along its lower border. Yet if man preferred the society of God he had ample opportunity to choose one of several faiths in the bad old town.

The Catholic Church was always well attended at Mass and the clergy was not averse to mingling with laymen of all creeds. The Independence Day celebrations held in 1895 featured a popularity contest between a well known saloon keeper and a Catholic priest. It attracted large crowds, including a sizable contingent of elaborately dressed women of the red light district. The prize was about three hundred dollars and an ebony cane with gold plated knob which, fortunately for the prestige of Jerome's churches, the priest won. He kept the cane as a souvenir and turned the money over to this church.

There was one Mexican mine worker, Sabino Gonzales, who wasn't a particularly devout Catholic. Although attending Mass more or less regularly he felt more real sympathy towards Methodism but unfortunately the Methodist Church of Jerome drew a racial line, making Latins feel unwelcome and excluding blacks entirely.

Sometime during Jerome's heyday Gonzales was seriously injured in the mine. He recovered all his mental faculties but was left with little physical strength so he concentrated on a project which had been simmering in his mind for several years. He would build a Methodist Church for any of his countrymen who might have religious feelings similar to his own. He secured a site just below the town jail, a spot nobody else wanted, and from one source or another salvaged boards and other building materials. Generous donors contributed timbers, cast-off furniture, stucco for the exterior.

His church finished, Sabino Gonzales became the preacher too, attracting sizable crowds of his fellow miners. And attendance stayed high until the fortunes of Jerome fell during the general recession of the 1930s, then rose when the mines again boomed with a huge demand for copper during World War II. With the end of the war Jerome died as did the Mexican Methodist Church and everything else.

About two hundred people still live there, capitalizing on Jerome as a ghost town. Rev. Gonzales, now in his eighties, is one of the survivors. His little church is no longer active but when the regular Methodist Church holds occasional services, the old Mexican pastor is welcomed more warmly than he was back there in the boom days.

Mexican Methodist Church is in fair condition, upper floor occupied by family, lower used as antique shop. Behind it is one of oldest cemeteries in Jerome. All traces of graves have vanished, picket enclosures and wooden headboards used for kindling by woman living nearby.

Portion of phantom city Jerome clinging precariously to side of Mingus Mountain. At top are terraced sides of United Verdes Big Pit, more than 1,000' deep. More than $80 million in copper was dug here. Big blast in mine once started massive slide that has continued at rate of 6 inches to 8 inches daily.

Initial slippage moved many buildings several feet downward from street shown at extreme upper left. Jail, once located there, is now 300' lower (small cubical building, left center). Others are seen as crumpled slabs of concrete. Across and on near side of deep gully is seen Rev. Gonzales' Mexican Methodist Church, safely out of slide's reach (More about Jerome in *Ghost Town Trails*).

117

And the Congregation Chewed Dust

ORSES IN THE MINING CAMP of Vulture City were a prime necessity and as such presented one big problem. They were used to operate all the machiney and they had to be fed. The surrounding area, so dry and desert-like, offered no solution and in 1867 mine operator Jack Swilling faced a dilemma. In desperation he went down to the Salt River Valley to prospect for fodder and saw a ray of hope brightening his prospect. This was in the form of prehistoric irrigation ditches paralleling the stream and he talked to the farmers about running water in them and growing hay. They agreed to try and the first crop was a lifesaver for everybody.

Among those preparing the old canals and building new ones was "Lord" Darrell Duppa, scholar, adventurer, bon vivant and inebriate from England. He saw clear evidence that a much earlier city had existed there and suggested that the present settlement of hay farmers be named Phoenix for the mythical bird consumed by fire every five hundred years and immediately rose triumphant from the ashes. At the first election the name was official.

Founded by missionaries like Father Kino, Arizona was strictly Catholic for years. This domination ended in the mid-1870s when there were enough Protestants in the area to merit sending their missionaries into the mining camps. About 1875 Sheldon Jackson, head of the Presbyterian Synodic Missions for Colorado, sent Rev. William Meyer out to the raw stage-stop of Phoenix. With marked understatement Meyer reported, "Phoenix is certainly one of the most fertile fields for missionary work in the frontier Territory of Arizona."

On June 1, 1879, three years after he arrived, the First Presbyterian Church of Phoenix was organized. The first "edifice" was definitely unique in church history. At each of four corners was erected a stout cottonwood tree trunk with a "Y"-shaped top or crotch. Spaced between were smaller boles with similar "bean shooter" form. Slender poles were laid across these supports to form roof "beams" and these were covered with leafy branches. Walls were made of vertical ocotilla canes closely laced. The structure stood on a dusty lot south of the old Courthouse Plaza, the congregation composed of eight members at regular services.

Although well ventilated and shaded from Arizona's hot summer sun, the arbor was a dust trap, clouds of it sifting in with every wind. And dried leaves constantly sifted down. The church members considered a building nearby that was successively a carpenter shop, saloon and dance hall. When vacant it was quickly rented as an improvement over the brush church. Subsequently the Presbyterians moved through a series of humble structures, one the storeroom of Hooper and Company.

An important date was March 29, 1887 when the church was incorporated, the first of any denomination to be so organized in Arizona. Since then the fortunes of the Presbyterian Church have consistently improved, culminating in the March 9, 1927 ground breaking of their present house of worship. Earlier a site was chosen at the northwest corner of 3rd and Van Buren but no construction was done during World War I. When it ended the space was considered too small so that property was sold and the present site selected near the main highway.

Historic Brush Church in Phoenix was home of First Presbyterian Church in 1879. Construction was of native materials, structure proving breezy, dusty and altogether a poor makeshift (photo courtesy Arizona Pioneers' Historical Society).

Ocotillo grows in southern deserts in abundance, was once only material available for fencing, ramada walls, etc. Here canes are used as fence in now deserted mining camp of Vulture, which was responsible for founding of Phoenix. Cactus-like, woody stems plentifully equipped with stout spines, were more closely woven in construction of brush church in Phoenix.

Methodist Church, one of oldest structures in village of Lonerock, was last to shelter any large gathering. Among first settlers in ranching area were young David Spaulding and bride Sophia who had come from Scotland in 1898 and 1903, respectively.

As town grew because of strategic location at crossing of main stock trails, Spauldings were pillars of village and Methodist Church. Sophia, widowed in 1935, continued to live in old home, regularly attending church services, even after town began to fade. After several accidents caused by falls, Sophia died in 1961. By this time Lonerock was almost complete ghost but beloved pioneer woman's funeral in her church attracted overflow crowd from entire state.

Methodist Church, Antelope, built in 1897, almost only relic standing in historic old cattle town in central Oregon where herds of antelope once roamed encircling hills. Few years ago there still remained the old time saloon and barber shop, former still bearing scars of bullets fired in day when six-shooters were law. Fire and time have obliterated these, need for lumber on neighborhing ranches sacrificed two-story hall where once sheepherders and cattlemen fought it out on dance floor (more about Antelope in *Western Ghost Towns*).

OREGON

Pioneers in the Pines

Old Fox Valley Baptist Church saw slow decline in valley population as one disaster after another discouraged residents, never very numerous. Regular church services had long ceased by 1953. In that year Rev. Glen Fry of Village Missions again preached in old church regularly, but rapidly deteriorating condition of structure forced removal to school house. Rev. Dale Sherman is present pastor. Church structure now is slipping into decay. Old bell, weighing over 1,900 pounds and hauled by four-horse freight team from Heppner, still hangs in belfry (photo courtesy David Mason, M.D.).

Veteran of the

AVING SERVED several religious faiths and now awaiting uncertain fate, Portland's most famous church is likewise its spectacular ancient, the finest standing example of "Carpenter's Gothic" in the West. This is the "Old Church" at the northeast corner of S.W. 11th Avenue and Clay Street.

It began its colorful life as a "silk stocking" institution in the days of carriages and porte cocheres, private pews and private feuds. This was in 1880 when Portland was deep in lumber booms and fortunes were a-making for a few, a-breaking for the many.

On June 23 of that year, at the instigation of Hon. William A. Ladd, members of the First Presbyterian Church met at the business firm he headed, the Ladd and Tilton Bank. Their purpose was to form two religious boards of trustees, the more important one to govern the Calvary Presbyterian Church. These were men for the new city, pioneer men of drive and stability. A fund of $6,000 was raised to initiate a church structure and bids were sent out. When these were submitted the project was immediately shelved, funds pledged being wholly inadequate for the building of the church.

During the next two years as the city forged rapidly ahead in population and prosperity, the Presbyterians organized several Sunday schools which became active and gave them encouragement to once more attempt the formation of a permanent church society and the realization of a church building. Several meetings netted $20,000 which signaled the start of the venture. Famed architect Warren Williams volunteered to draw the plans, his services considered a donation to the building fund.

The location selected drew severe criticism from some members who said it was much "too far out in the country." It was true the area chosen consisted of open fields and woods but it was argued this distance from the center of town made the property less expensive. With building costs estimated at $24,000, the church was put under construction, the final costs nearly $36,000.

The cornerstone for the new Calvary Presby-

terian Church was laid Sept. 11, 1882. The first services in the sanctuary were for the installation as pastor of Rev. E. Trumbull Lee who then preached the first sermon. Rev. Lee served the church for four years during which time the membership rose from 64 to 195.

Rev. John Morrison of the Centennial Presbyterian Church in Oakland, California, followed Lee. He faced some difficult years when the business crash came in 1893, membership then falling off alarmingly. Recovering from the financial disaster with the rest of the city and country, Calvary Presbyterians continued to hold regular services in their splendid church for fifty years into the new century.

Giving a graphic picture of the Presbyterian situation, George Murdane tells of joining the church in 1928. "It wasn't so easy to get into a church in those days," he explains, "at least not that one. I had to appear before six elders. It was like an inquisition. Then they told me to go into the next room and wait. At last they came in and told me, 'We've decided to let you in.'" Murdane recalls that by this time all the open spaces around the church had been filled, not with fine homes and businesses but predominantly with shacky, nondescript dwellings, most of them clustered in nearby "Goose Hollow." He noted the congregation and Sunday school participation had declined sharply, partly because of the poor surroundings. Being full of energy and enthusiasm Murdane undertook to canvas the area for new members.

"I took a friend along and we met some strange characters. We would knock on a door and talk to a couple, and when we came back next week the woman or man would be different. I was greeted at one door by a man with a gun aimed at my middle. 'You're gonna get it now,' he snarled, and when I hurried to explain, 'I am from the First Presbyterian Church,' he asked, 'Why in hell didn't you say so right away. I was expecting a man who has been seeing my wife.'"

Mr. Murdane did add a few members as a result of his efforts but the following year saw another financial crash that almost wrecked the ros-

Mauve Decade

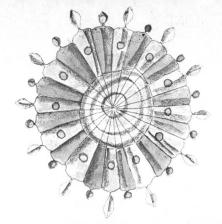

Having in turn served Calvary Presbyterian congregation, Calvary combined with Unity, Evangel Baptist, Southern Baptist, later known as Metropolitan Baptist, the famous Portland structure shown is now simply termed the "Old Church."

Photo was made on quiet Sunday afternoon, week day traffic and parking problem almost intolerable. Picturesque example of "Carpenters Gothic" is frequently subject of photographs and paintings. Near extreme right is seen overhang where elaborate shelter for carriages was once attached.

One of pair of chimneys that add yet another distinctive note to the Old Church. Building is heated by two furnaces once stoked with cordwood. One heats auditorium, other warms offices, children's rooms, etc. Corridor connecting to main entrance is lined by wooden, white-painted umbrella and galoshes racks, reminiscent of days when congregation walked through cow pastures.

Tower detail shows uniform architectural style, copied and modified in wood from French Revival Gothic. All details were done by artisans using hand tools. After cobwebby climb up spiral staircase author confirmed absence of bell. Pastor's wife, Mrs. H. C. Price, said that to her knowledge there never had been one. Also she indicated several cracks where severe storm wrenched tower structure.

ter. Recovering from this calamity the Calvary Presbyterian now combined with the Unity congregation and it grew until it was too big for the grand old church building. In May of 1948 the property was sold to the smaller Evangel Baptist Church, the Presbyterians having erected a new edifice in the northeast part of the city.

On Oct. 1 of the same year the old cornerstone was uncovered for removal to Calvary's new building, the occasion reported in the Oregon Journal by Walter Mattila. "Friday a stone mason pried open the stone in the presence of his five year old son and found the contents a soggy mess except for two silver dollars minted in 1882 and an 1856 Liberty quarter." Moisture had seeped into the supposedly tightly sealed copper box and the only document at all intact was a charter for the City of Portland for 1880. Copies of four daily newspapers were reduced to brown flakes, Mattila said. Referring to 1882 newspapers well preserved in the library files, he found full descriptions of the cornerstone ceremonies,

noted, "The congregation included the fashionable Corbetts and Ladds" and that the ceremonies began with prayer and hymns of praise. As the stonecutter finished the removal of the stone, one last vigorous whack sent a chip of granite into the eye of the little boy who was too closely observing the job.

The Evangel members made many changes in the interior of the old church, dividing large rooms into smaller, laying a floor in the dirt basement and otherwise attempting to make space for kindergarten, nursery, extra Sunday School classes, etc.

In 1951 the Evangel Baptist Church sold the building to the Southern Baptists who at once showed a growing discontent. Long before this the quality of the neighborhood had greatly improved. The decrepit hovels had given way to large apartment houses, a large stadium and more recently to the sprawling complex of Portland State College. Later a freeway was built to slice through the area, cutting off convenient ac-

Pews in auditorium were hand carved from fir planks, now showing mellow luster. Pipe organ was made in Boston by Brook and Hastings, classed as "wooden tracker." Old bellows requiring vigorous effort in operation still exist in basement, though fine instrument has long been electrically powered. Entire works were shipped around Horn on sailing vessel, landed at San Francisco, thence transported over old "Oregon Road" by oxen teams. Unexplained is why organ did not travel entire distance by water. Lamps once used acetylene gas, generated in basement where heavy joists are held by square, hand-forged spikes. Original controls are still in auditorium wall cabinet.

Exceptionally fine stained glass window was imported intact from Rome before Panama Canal was dug. Hand-blown stained glass panes bear many colored cut glass "gems" studding intersections of design. Window faces south on Clay Street. Original plans called for another facing west but lack of funds delayed, then eliminated project.

cess to south and west.

In 1965 the Southern Baptist Church underwent some progressive changes. It took on a new name, Metropolitan Baptist Church, and the firm resolve to build a new church in the West Hills area. Plans were drawn and the old building offered for sale. And "who will buy my violets?"

Many eager investors and property owners would like the land for commercial purposes, any of these requiring the building be placed under the wrecking ball. At the "For Sale" announcement a general hue and cry was raised by historically minded Portland citizens who quickly found emotion tinged with the hard facts of life, one being the land and building renovation would cost at least $125,000, the estimate rising by the month.

After much discussion and publicity in the press an "Old Church" organization was formed, and presently seems near a solution. Money is being raised to purchase the property, renovate the building and use it as a community center. Two main objectives have so far been accomplished, largely through unflagging efforts of Chairman Mrs. Peter Hurst. Two gains have been made—tax-free status and nullification of a stipulation by original Presbyterian owners that the church never be used for any other than religious purpose.

Fine examples of Victorian architecture adorn neighborhood, this one adjacent to Old Church bears sculptured "cameo," once often seen but now disappearing.

Case of the Missing Porch

Fortunately for record, historic, ornate porch caught eye of architecturally aware Dr. David Mason few months before its destruction. Church people now interested in complete restoration say this is by far best record, expect to use it as aid when rebuilding porch (Photo courtesy David Mason, M.D.).

William Sargent Ladd was one of early Portland's first citizens. Head of one of its largest banks he also served a term as mayor and chairmaned countless civic committees. Figuring prominently in the building of the Calvary Presbyterian Church, Ladd contributed heavily to its funding, making one stipulation.

Physically handicapped, confined to a great extent to a wheel chair, he asked the builders to design and construct a porch under which his carriage and horses could stand protected from rain while he was helped out and into his chair which would be wheeled to a special door leading directly and without steps to his private pew. The wooden canopy was built and in a style that complimented the charm of the whole building. It stood unchanged until 1964 when it quietly disappeared.

Persistent inquiry revealed not one explanation but three. A student of nearby Portland State College had illicitly parked in the driveway and

on hurriedly leaving knocked down one of the columns. A fugitive from the law, hotly pursued by a police car, sought to escape in a sudden turn through the porch but failed to either clear it or get away. The infamous "Columbus Day" storm blew down part of the canopy so all of it was torn down and had to be removed. No one seemed to know what actually had happened to it.

When recent newspaper accounts appeared concerning efforts to save and renovate the old church, two young men, Ben Milligan and Jerry Brusco, came forward to say they had the dismembered carriage porch and explained the circumstances. Driving past it one day they noticed workmen removing the familiar little appendage. Being jointly interested in saving Portland's Victorian memorabilia, they asked for and received the dismantled sections. So the porch was saved and will be available if and when the church is restored.

was Headquarters for Chinese Tong

Ornate Bishop's House, Portland, built in 1879, originally adjoined Catholic Cathedral which was built one year earlier on site shown here as vacant at right. "Victorian Gothic" structure was constructed primarily of brick with facade of iron, almost certainly mined, refined, cast at Oswego, now Lake Oswego, community few miles to south where limonite mines and foundry flourished from 1867 to 1894. Cast iron fronts were popular in this period—note ornamentations on old building in background here.

PROTESTANT AND CATHOLIC CHURCHES were established in the Willamette Valley during the mid-1840s but it was another decade before any were built in what would ultimately be the metropolis, Portland. These were Methodist and Congregational churches, first noted in 1851.

The exact date of the first Catholic mass said in Portland seems uncertain but it was held in the home on Front Street between Taylor and Salmon. In 1851 a collection of $600 was taken up toward the building of a new church on a good-sized piece of ground acquired near Fourth and

Couch. This was part of the land owned by Capt. Couch and probably donated by him to the church authorities. With the little building near completion a Christmas mass was said there in 1851, the edifice dedicated the next February 22. The location was soon found unsuitable and the church was moved to the corner of Third and Stark at a cost of $500 on four lots purchased in 1854 from Benjamin Stark, one of Portland's earliest settlers. He came as supercargo on the *Toulon,* remained to study law and was admitted to the bar in 1850.

Francis Norbert Blanchet, who was sent out

from Montreal as a Catholic missionary, establishing the church at St. Paul in the early 1840s, was later made Archbishop of the Diocese with headquarters at the largest town in the valley, Oregon City. With his transfer to the much faster growing Portland, a fine brick cathedral was built on the Third and Stark location in 1878. A year later the Bishop's House was completed next door to the west. This building still stands today.

Some of the first floor space was rented out, one tenant being an insurance agent, the remainder used by the Catholic library. The second floor was almost entirely occupied by the Young Men's Institute. On the third floor was the sumptuously furnished meeting room some twenty-four feet square with seventeen-foot ceiling. Large fireplaces graced east and west walls, both fitted with heavy mantels, the east wall also supporting a balcony or gallery for use by musicians.

With the building of a new cathedral at Fifteenth and Davis in the late 1890s the one at Third and Stark was razed. Since there was a buyer waiting for it, the Bishop's House was spared and some of the subsequent renters were "surely unsuspected by the archbishop," as related in one account. Most notorious of all occupants was a Chinese tong headquarters.

For some years Portland had the largest Chinatown on the Coast excepting San Francisco's, their associations termed "tongs" being ostensibly benevolent orders. Yet some came to be largely under the influence of "hatchetmen" of "highbinder" groups of which Portland had five—Hip Sing, Hup Sing, Suey Sing, Hoo Leong and Hung Sing. Since their operations were distinctly outside of law and order, meeting places were secret, one suspected to be the tong quarters in Bishop's House. One affray ending in the death of several Orientals took place only a block away. Much later, during "prohibition" days, a speakeasy occupied the building.

Original Catholic Church in Portland was built in 1851 at another location and soon moved to this site at Third and Stark Streets (facing on Third). In 1878 brick Cathedral was erected on this same corner. Later, Bishop's House was added on Stark Street at left, about where two story frame is seen here (photo Oregon Historical Society).

San Francisco architect P. Heurn designed Cathedral and probably Bishop's House. Elaborate cast iron traceried window on 3rd floor marks location of large room where Bishop Blanchet often presided over meetings. In 1965 William Roberts remodeled exterior and interior, retaining most of original flavor. Fire escape defacing front was removed, original tottering cross replaced and gabled hood repaired.

The Church Went Voyaging

HE REV. ST. MICHAEL FACKLER came to the Oregon Country by overland wagon train in 1847 and forthwith took out a donation land claim near Champoeg. He preached in various settlers' cabins in the vicinity and at least once ventured as far as Milwaukie to hold the first Episcopal services in the village on Dec. 19, 1851.

Those Milwaukie citizens of Episcopal leanings were so enthused by Rev. Fackler's sermon they became determined to have a church edifice where they could hold regular services. A committee including two wardens and eight vestrymen organized the church at first called St. John's Mission.

Milwaukie's founder is usually considered to have been Lot Whitcomb, although one Andrew Fellows had built a small cabin on the east bank of the Willamette River, stayed a while and moved on, Whitcomb's land claim then including the Fellows' cabin.

Whitcomb was a man of tremendous energy and he immediately put up a larger cabin, sawmill and very soon a shipyard where he built the steamer *Lot Whitcomb*. He also proved himself to be civicminded, donating two lots for church purposes to the infant Episcopal organization which were already improved with a skeleton of a barn facing the river that could be used as a church. Ten more feet were added to it, the whole covered with cedar boards. The congregation put in a stove, some benches and an improvised pulpit, the structure becoming the first Episcopal Church in the Oregon Country.

St. John's Episcopal Church, in Milwaukie, built as barn in 1851, consecrated as church in 1855, was first moved a few blocks in 1862. Ninety-nine years later it traveled several miles from Milwaukie to Sellwood, suburb of Portland, most of distance by water. Cost of moving was $4,000, sum raised after emergency transfer was made.

Dent Thomas, Sellwood, headed successful campaign for funds, some contributors being Nathan H. Whitcomb, grand-nephew of Milwaukie founder, Lot Whitcomb, who donated building in 1855; great-grandson George Tuley; great-granddaughter Marie Smith. Sons and Daughters of Oregon Pioneers contributed largest single sum, $500 (photo courtesy Al Monner, *Oregon Journal,* Portland). (More about Milwaukie in *Boot Hill*).

The "city" of Milwaukie at this time was much like other pioneer centers in the Pacific Northwest. Streets were nothing more than stump-studded wagon tracks plowing through deep mud in fall, winter and spring, dust in summer. Hogs wallowed in deeper puddles, cows and horses wandered at will. Citizens seldom ventured out at night, and when they did they carried kerosene lanterns in order to find their way through total darkness. It was during this period of bucolic simplicity that Spencer's School for Girls, first diocesan school was built. Erected in 1861 it was centrally located, some distance from the church out on the fringe. In bad weather the girls found difficulty in walking the long trail through the woods between church and school so on December 4 the next year the little church was moved "into town."

Bishop Scott, consecrated as the first Bishop of the Oregon Country, January 8, 1854 later wrote in the *Oregon Churchman* about the moving job, "The little church which was consecrated in 1855 (June 14) and stood a little out of the village has recently been moved to a central location nearer to the main street. The citizens generally turned out, putting their shoulders to the wheel and making the removal common work. When completed one of the oldest proposed three cheers for the church, which were heartily given, after which another proposed three cheers for the bishop which were heartily given accompanied by the ringing of the bell."

In 1928 with the permission of Bishop Walter Taylor Sumner and a gift of $100 from him, the church was moved across the street so that a basement could be put in. This included a small kitchen and a lavatory. The building was heated by a wood-burning pot-bellied stove until 1946 when a furnace was put in.

Now the little church stood on the corner it was to occupy until 1961. It was still little unchanged from the original "unfurnished building," although the profile had been slightly altered by the addition of a simple belfry accommodating the ship's bell donated by Whitcomb. By 1869 the congregation had scraped together enough money to make some improvements. The chancel was enlarged, new carpets put down and chairs placed. gan" placed near the altar.

In 1888 more drastic remodeling took place, giving the building the lines displayed today. The old square windows were changed to pointed, Gothic ones. A new roof was added, and siding placed on the outside walls. A tower and steeple were added to the front and the bell elevated to the new, higher position. Inside a new chancel with stained glass window was put in place and the walls covered by fir boards placed diagonally, much strengthening the frame. On Sunday March 31, 1889 the newly remodeled church was reopened with a sermon by Rev. John Sellwood, then 83 years of age.

As time went on the town of Milwaukie grew into city status, though never the area's metropolis as envisioned by Lot Whitcomb, that honor going to nearby Portland. The Episcopal congregation, once comfortably fitting into the tiny box-like pioneer church, now began to burst the seams. In 1948 a fine new church was erected next door, a corridor connecting the two where the sacristy had been. For a time the original building was occasionally used for special events, gradually falling into complete disuse. By 1960 the congregation concluded that the space occupied must be used for other purposes. The old church must be removed or razed.

On Saturday, May 11, 1961, Ormond Bean of the Portland City Council saw a news item in the *Oregonian* concerning the old Episcopal Church. If all local efforts to save it failed, the historic structure would go under the wrecker's hammer. Mr. and Mrs. Bean drove to the site where preparations for razing were already under way. Mr. Bean was told by the contractor in charge that a reprieve would be granted with expiration date the following Wednesday.

Mr. Bean then went into vigorous action. Parks Superintendent Harry Buckley was very much interested in the then infant Oaks Pioneer Park to be established near the end of the Sellwood Bridge and encompassing the old Oaks Amusement Park. Mr. Buckley agreed that the pioneer church certainly would grace the entrance to the park. Then things moved fast.

A barge was floated up the Willamette River to a point just below the church. Already placed on rollers, the building was eased down the hill and onto the barge. The way was through mid-Milwaukie, holding up all busy traffic, but there were no protests. The barge was floated downstream but as it was about to pass under the Sellwood Bridge, those in charge saw that the church would not pass underneath. So the barge was held in the current while the steeple was removed and laid flat on deck. At the site the church was hauled up the steep hill.

City park bureau personnel, anxious to provide authentic landscaping, went all out to make a

130

garden of old-time roses. Director Art Nussbaumer and head gardener William Robinson canvassed possible sources and in March the latter went to the Lafayette home of pioneer descendant Mrs. Sparks, securing from her home yard and Lafayette cemetery many old roses of early days. Included were Damask, York and Lancaster, Mission and several varieties of moss roses. These and a cutting of persian lilac were nurtured in park gardens, then planted in beds near the old church. A special feature was and still is a solid bed of the lovely and very old hybrid perpetual rose, Madame Caroline Testout, for many years the official Portland Rose and as yet not replaced. Cuttings for these were secured in old Sellwood gardens, a few blocks from the present site of the church.

St. John's now stands at entrance of Oaks Pioneer Park, Portland. Original barn-like structure had door at front end, remodeling in 1888 closing this when tower and steeple were added. At that time and for subsequent life of church entrance was made through side doors opening on porches reached by half-dozen steps. Now old front door is as before with side doors eliminated.

Original bell donated by Lot Whitcomb is still in tower. If it was ship's bell, it has long since been converted to be rung by conventional methods, old wooden wheel for this use still attached to bell.

While church was being readied for removal to new site Pastor L. F. Evenson noted old timbers were exposed so fastenings of wooden pegs were visible. He made 35mm slides and on learning that story would appear in this book he had reproduction made for author. Beams are likely oldest existing examples of cut timbers in Oregon Country, coming from primitive type of sawmill owned by Lot Whitcomb, and used by him in 1851 or '52 to build simple structure afterwards remodeled as St. John's Episcopal Church.

Willamett

Summer view shows oaks (left) in full foliage. Trees at right are madronas, part of group of four planted at corners of Purvis family plot in cemetery adjacent to church. Monument in center is fine example of type much used around turn of century, material being zinc, with advantages of permanency, comparatively light weight. "Fad" was of short duration. There were about 200 graves here in 1950, a few burials continuing to be made in lower section reached by unique aisle of evergreen trees.

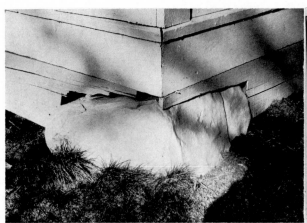

Large, native stones one at each corner, provide solid, termite-proof protection from wet ground, largely accounting for excellent condition of hundred and ten year old church edifice.

Bronze marker in front of Spring Valley Presbyterian Church.

ioneer

THE ZENA CHURCH and several fine old homes are the sole visual reminders today of what was once a thriving village near Lincoln. In the late 1850s, '60s, and early '70s Zena was a "suburb" of Lincoln and dependent on the port town for flour and supplies.

Originally termed "Spring Valley" for the nearby well watered glade, the place took on its odd name when Daniel Jackson Cooper arrived in 1863. He built a general store which attracted so many neighboring farmers a post office was needed. Cooper became the postmaster and was given the honor of naming it. Legend says his wife Arvazena suggested it would be nice to name the office for her, her sister Melzena, wife of Cooper's brother, asking the same. Daniel Cooper compromised with the common second syllable.

Zena post office was established March 22, 1869, when the community was the first station for change of horses on the stage route from Salem to Perrydale. Construction of the Zena church began in 1858 as a community project led by C. C. Walker, his brother W. W., B. F. McLeach and Nelson Walling. The lumber was produced at Oregon City, hauled around the rocky barrier forming the falls, loaded at Canemah on one of the river steamers, then hauled to Zena. Sills were hewn into shape with a broadaxe by brawny "Breeze" Gibson, general carpenter work overseen by experts Albert and William Patrick.

Before the edifice was finished the congregation sent to England for a bell. By the time it arrived by way of Cape Horn the church building was near completion, the belfry erected on the roof and ready to receive its precious burden. But the bell weighed over 400 pounds, creating a problem in elevation unforeseen by the builders. After several frustrating attempts at lifting it into place, the bell was placed on a platform in front, there to repose for several years. At last Captain P. F. Clark came along with enough engineering skill to direct the successful raising.

For many years the church bell called the congregation to weddings and births as well as services, warned of fires and other calamities, and was tolled for funeral processions. Although there are about three burials a year in the old cemetery, funerals are no longer held in the church, the last one being for Lloyd Philips in 1902.

Oregon was admitted into the Union on February 14, 1859, making it the 33rd state. When the long-delayed news reached Zena, there was a burst of enthusiasm about having a flag to fly over the church for the numerous community events that would be held there. Major Walter M. Walker (for whom a school in Salem is named) spearheaded the movement for the flag and arranged to get the considerable amount of wool cloth necessary for its construction.

Historic woolen flag, lost for many years, then discovered in phonograph horn. Unfurled, it was hung in honored place on church wall.

Mr. Ben Maxwell, historian and long-time writer for *Capital Journal* of Salem, now deceased, made this excellent photo during flag's short exposure to moths. Shortly afterwards, banner was folded, encased in tight, glass-fronted case like deep picture frame and rehung in same spot. In view now is little more than blue field with unique arrangement of stars, but damaging moths are denied access (photo courtesy Salem Public Library).

Mrs. Phoebe Walling McGrew and Mrs. Cynthia Chtwood organized something like an old time quilting bee among the women of the area. Red and white stripes were cut and sewn together and added to the blue field. Since the material was much too heavy to be transparent the stars had tob e cut in duplicate, a set sewn on each side. About the time this stage was reached news came that Kansas had also entered the Union, necessitating the addition of another star.

The finished banner, 11½ by 7½ in size was proudly flown over the church for several years. When, about 1864 after West Virginia and Nevada were admitted, the flag was adjudged outmoded. Mrs. Samuel Barker was the official recorder and keeper of records for the community, and she was entrusted with the flag for safe keeping. Concerned about what moths might do to the woolen fabric, Mrs. Barker sewed the flag in an oilcloth pouch and stored it in the attic. Years later, in an effort to make space, someone stuffed the bag into the open mouth of an old Victrola horn where it lay hidden for many years. The death of Mrs. Barker further clouded the memory of the flag's location.

With the celebration of Oregon's centennial a search was made for the historic flag and it was discovered in the old horn by Mrs. Barker's son Roy, who with his wife Ethel, continued to live in the old house. Found to be in fairly good condition the flag was displayed on the wall of the church for a time, later folded and placed in a glass case.

In the spring of 1969 vandals broke into Zena church, making off with the historic emblem.

Zena's post office was closed in 1902, the year before telephones came to town. The church itself, so stoutly built, was unable to withstand internal strife between various factions. Originally sponsored by Cumberland Presbyterians, the congregation was splintered by heretical interpretations of an early minister. Dissolution followed in 1866 after which the church remained idle except for occasional services held by various ministers of different faiths. In 1881 the church became a member of the Presbytery of Oregon. During the 1890s and early 1900s Rev. W. J. Crawford, a Baptist preacher conducted services with regularity in the prim, white structure. Then followed a long period of inactivity with a resumption of occasional services through the 40s and 50s. More than twenty ministers are known to have conducted services there.

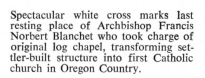

Spectacular white cross marks last resting place of Archbishop Francis Norbert Blanchet who took charge of original log chapel, transforming settler-built structure into first Catholic church in Oregon Country.

First Catholic Mission in Northwest

IN THE MID-1830s sovereignty of that part of the Oregon country lying south of the Columbia River was in doubt. It could belong to either Britain or the United States. In a move to use its influence to clear the issue, the Catholic hierarchy, through the Bishop of Quebec, agreed to send missionaries to establish the faith, "on the banks of the Cowlitz River or at Cowlitz Portage, falling into the Columbia River from the northward while giving assurance that the missionaries would not locate themselves on the south side of the Columbia River."

The missionaries included newly ordained Fr. Demers and Father F. N. Blanchet, who on their way from Montreal, celebrated the first mass in the area, on the Big Bend of the Columbia.

On "French Prairie," including Champoeg and nearby points along the Willamette River, almost all the Canadian settlers had been waiting for the traveling emissaries of the Church, but when notified they would be delayed, all but three returned home—Joseph Gervais, Etienne Lucier and Pierre Beleque.

Although traveling for six months and in need of rest, Blanchet and Demers listened to the French Canadian settlers and were told that on

assurances from the new vicar they might be provided with a priest. Accordingly French Prairie residents had erected a log church so that the priest could begin his work at once. But this was "disputed territory" the missionaries reminded them, yet it may be assumed Fr. Blanchet privately assured them their wishes would not go unheeded for long.

Toward the end of 1838 the missionaries left by canoe with four Indians for the Cowlitz site and celebrated mass in the house of a Canadian settler there, one Simon Plamondon. Fr. Blanchet selected 640 acres for the site of the projected mission and leaving instructions for the building and maintenance of it, returned to Fort Vancouver for Christmas.

On January 5, 1838, Fr. Blanchet arrived on the Willamette where the church had been built four miles from Champoeg and was soon to be called St. Paul. He moved into a small room at the rear of the crude log chapel and on the next day, Sunday, Feast of the Epiphany, the little church was blessed under patronage of the Apostle St. Paul, mass said for the first time in the present state of Oregon in the first Catholic church in the Pacific Northwest.

St. Paul's Catholic Church as it stands today. South transept was built in simple form in 1846, walls erected with bricks fired in kiln set up on spot, clay dug from pit at rear of building. Church was greatly enlarged along Victorian Gothic lines from 1889 to 1903 with added tower and belfry which are conspicuous for miles.

"Replica" of 1836 Catholic mission church at St. Paul raises questions. Style is very similar and belfry almost identical to that of St. Mary's Church, designed and built by Fr. Ravalli, individualistic architect and artist, at Stevensville, Mont. in 1866. How could this near duplicate at St. Paul have been constructed by unskilled trapper-farmers 30 years earlier? Fr. Maxwell at present St. Paul's said model had been made by retired carpenter Adam Wetch who still lives in village.

When found Mr. Wetch said he had never seen any drawing of the church in question but was familiar with the St. Mary's Church, having been its custodian for some years. It is from this memory picture his miniature church was built, original structure no doubt simple log cabin without tower, belfry or vestibule.

Dollhouse-like interior of model church looking past tiny font. Chapel of first log church may have looked much like this. To give scale benches are actually about 3″ high. In belfry above is miniature antique bell, actually used many years at mass and other services in present church.

Blanchet spent the following four weeks at St. Paul, instructing, baptizing the settlers' Indian wives and offspring, many of whom had already been baptized by Jason Lee, Methodist missionary. Relations between Protestant and Catholic missionaries, already poor in this early period, were further strained by such practices.

Before leaving, Blanchet took possession of a section of land around the church with the view of eventually establishing a permanent mission there. He obviously had every confidence Dr. John McLoughlin would secure the necessary permission from higher Catholic authorities. This did soon come about, and Fr. Blanchet served as pastor until he became archbishop of the diocese with headquarters in Oregon City, moving to Portland in 1862.

Historian Edwin O'Hara, in his Pioneer Catholic History of Oregon, quotes "an old pioneer" who wrote of what he termed "Oregon's idyllic period," the middle 1840s: "There was a time when St. Paul was the home spot of the Pacific Northwest . . . a time when Americans had not yet taught their prairie schooners the long way across the plains. In those ante-pioneer days the Canadian French made their homes on the beautiful prairies and, in the absence of their country women, espoused the dusky maidens of the Calapooyas who raised for them a bright-eyed group of half-breed boys and girls. The Catholic Fathers were there to bless the union and guide the lives of these youths and the condition was one of peace and plenty."

"United We Stand in the Worship of God"

THEREAS in the Providence of God, a few names of us, the professed followers of Christ; who hold one faith, one Lord, and one Baptism, have thrown together in the Wilds of the West, and being Members of Churches in the United States, desirous of keeping the worship of God in our neighborhood, and in our Families—Agree: that we hereby Constitute and come into Union—first giving ourselves to the Lord, and then each other and Covenant, that we will meet together to Worship God, and keep the Commandments and Ordinances of God's house, and hereby Constitute into a Church."

Thus, without benefit of minister, deacon or recognition council, did five pioneer Baptists found the first church of their faith west of the Rocky Mountains. Indeed, the little group had also established the first church of any Protestant faith of the Pacific side of the continent. The historic meeting had convened in the rude log cabin of David T. Lenox, located on Tualatin Plains, the north end of French Prairie in the Willamette Valley of Oregon. The date was May 25, 1844. On July 13 the tiny church received two more who were to be "considered in the Constitution."

Lenox was a native of New York who had moved successively to Kentucky, Illinois and Missouri, where he had bought a farm in Platte County. He had been active in the Baptist communities of each location, and had served as an officer in one of the associations. Influenced by the persuasive oratory of Peter H. Burnett, who was seeking recruits for an emigrant train soon to leave for Oregon, Lenox agreed to go with him.

When finally organized, the Burnett train was of such magnitude that it was broken down into

West Union Baptist Church, Tualatin Plains, is definitely oldest in Oregon and west of Rocky Mountains. This severely simple edifice, however, was not first Baptist church built, having been preceded by tiny building erected in Oregon City. Since the latter was soon washed away in one of Willamette River's periodic rampaging floods. West Union Church remains as the oldest *standing* Baptist church in Oregon. Commemorative services are still held in old church every August (more photos, stories in *Boot Hill*).

four parts, one captained by David Lenox. His section, which included his wife, Louisa, and seven children, left Westport, Missouri, in May of 1843 and was the first of any wagon train to reach the Oregon Country. Many months of weary travel had seen the travelers to Walla Walla, then the Columbia River, which they chose to take rather than the mountain route so late in the season. In November the party arrived in Oregon City.

Anxious to get settled, Lenox soon traded some of his stock for a donation land claim on the Tualatin Plains where he erected a simple, one-room log cabin, eighteen by twenty feet. There were no windows, the floor paved with rough-cut puncheons, in one corner a mud-and-stick fireplace. For some time all meals consisted of boiled turnips, wheat, flour and deer meat. "Coffee" was made from dried peas and the sweetening was crude molasses. Already crowded with the owner's family, the room often served as overnight shelter for newly arrived immigrants, often sheltering as many as eighteen people. Here, until a church could be built, were held at least some sort of services every Sunday.

For nearly nine months the West Union Baptist Church had no preaching by a minister of its own denomination. Sometimes young Henry Sewell would read a chapter from the Bible and do his best to exhort the little congregation. At least two Methodist ministers preached in the cabin on occasion. One, Alvin F. Waller, obliged several times. Once he brought along a Methodist woman from Oregon City, the lady carrying an infant in her arms. At the end of the service, almost before anyone knew what he was about, the Reverend Waller sprinkled the baby, administering the ordinance of baptism. "Hard Shell" Lenox jumped to his feet, outraged, shouting that the church would disown the ceremony, declaring that "there is not a 'thus saith the Lord' for it between the lids of the Bible." Rev. Waller then attempted to persuade the congregation that all would be better off to convert to Methodism, with the result that he was almost forcibly ejected by Lenox. After this incident the congregation struggled along with no minister at all until the advent of Vincent Snelling, first Baptist minister in the Pacific Northwest. On February 8, 1845, Snelling delivered his first sermon to the West Union Church, and he and his wife were received into membership.

The discovery of gold in California caused such a drain of manpower from the Willamette Valley that all plans for the building of a church structure had to be pushed aside. By the middle of 1853, enough Oregonians had returned so that construction could start on a plot of land donated by Lenox.

One of the noblest trees in dense forests of evergreens along coastal and near-coastal areas of the Pacific Coast is the one locally called cedar, elsewhere Giant Arborvitae, actually *Thuja plicta*. Lewis and Clark found the natives building houses of cedar logs, the material that split so easily and proved very durable. Taking this cue from the natives, the men of the West Union congregation cut cedars on the banks of the nearby Willamette River, towed them down to the nearest point, then hauled them overland by ox team. Once on the site the logs were broadaxed into huge squared beams and laid on the bare earth in a quadrangle measuring 30 by 40 feet. On these foundations was erected a frame structure built largely of the same durable cedar, split into light poles or rails. Joists were hewn from fir logs. Cost of the finished building was $1500.

West Union Baptist Church was dedicated on Christmas Day, 1853. Members of the congregation came on foot, horseback and by ox-team. They came from as far away as twenty-five miles, as they had done for some time, to attend regular services. And they continued to come to the little church that so strongly resembled those of their faith in the mid-West and New England. For over a quarter of a century the church continued to be the spiritual center for the community. Then, in 1878, for reasons not now known, the congregation was dissolved. The building then stood vacant and neglected for a long time.

In recent years the Oregon State Baptist Convention has annually held a Memorial Service in the church, on the third Sunday in August. In advance of this program the structure received a few repairs. A new concrete foundation was substituted as a safety precaution, but builders maintained the original logs would have continued to serve for a long time.

Present day annual services are basically religious but with a strong historical slant. Speaking in turn, one year, were four retired Baptist pastors over 90 years of age. Another such celebration had, as honored speaker, Dr. Brougher, then 96 years of age. And present at the 1964 gathering were "twins": Pastor Thomas Dulin of West Linn, Oregon, and Layman Leonard Will of Dayton, Oregon. Both hailed from Shelby County, Missouri. Both had been born on the same day, one hundred and one years before!

THE CHAMPOEG BELL

The rude little Episcopal Church was built in 1860 but there were no funds for a bell. Even if one could have been purchased it would have to be shipped from the East Coast around the Horn, up the Columbia and Willamette Rivers. But the church members could pray, said the minister. "God will provide in His own time." And there came a flood which brought wreckage and debris down from Champoeg, and in it, when the waters subsided, was found a church bell . . . Heaven sent, the people said.

Butteville was just downriver from the larger Champoeg in French Prairie, considered Oregon's most historic spot, where the celebrated "Wolf Meetings" were held and where in 1843 the vote of the settlers decided the area would become part of the United States instead of England, represented by the Hudson's Bay Company.

Champoeg grew into a bustling village but in 1861 the Willamette raged and swirled over it, carrying away the entire town, including the Protestant Church. Butteville, on a higher elevation, was spared, except for damage to docks and warehouses, and instead gained a church bell.

The hamlet's Episcopal congregation, while feeling that God had indeed answered their prayers, hung the bell in their own church belfry with the reservation that some day it might have to be returned. They need not have worried. Although Champoeg was resurveyed and streets laid out, it was never rebuilt.

The Butteville Episcopal Church was later destroyed by fire and since the settlement had shriveled, the replacement church was too small to accommodate the bell. It was hung on an elevated platform in front and from this position still rings every Sunday morning as it did in Champoeg more than a century ago.

"These Twelve Good

"Old Scotch Church" of simple Gothic structure, in Hillsboro, one of most handsome in Oregon Country. Built by group of Scottish immigrants who remained neighbors all their lives, church was dedicated in 1878. It has tall, eight-sided steeple, steep roof contributing to graceful, soaring effect. Stained glass for windows came from Scotland.

Ien and True"

ALL TWELVE CHARTER MEMBERS of the Tualatin Plains Presbyterian Church came from the same area near Glasgow, Scotland. They all settled in the same Oregon area. All remained there . . . all attended the same church all their lives. Eight of them rest in the burial grounds surrounding their church.

At Columbia Academy, the four-room school about four miles from the present site of the church, these twelve Scots assembled on November 16, 1873, to organize a Presbyterian church in this land of their choosing. In part, these are the words of the first minutes, written in solemn fashion, the precise script now faded to a pale brown.

"After a sermon this day by the Rev. A. L. Linsley, D.D., Portland, Oregon, he along with two of his elders, Messrs. Holman and Wadhams organized the Tualatin Plains Presbyterian Church, consisting of twelve members." The record was put down by Rev. George Ross who became first pastor of the church, then serving for twenty-one years. He was still in service of the congregation until his death in 1894.

During the next few weeks, on horseback and in buggies, the men combed the countryside for a suitable site on which to build a church edifice, services being held meanwhile at the Academy. Then at another meeting the minutes read, "At a congregation meeting at the home of William Chambers, Rev. George Ross, acting as chairman, it was unanimously agreed to buy two acres of land from Jacob Hoover as a site for the church and burying ground. Mr. Hoover being present then very generously said, 'I will donate one acre to you and sell the other for $25.00.'" The offer was accepted and thanks given to Mr. Hoover for his liberality. The site thus settled upon was a densely wooded area situated on the banks of McKay Creek, some two miles north of Hillsboro.

Plans for actual construction were settled on March 11, 1898, request made for a simple plan that could be realized for around $2,000. Soon a Mr. Ballantyne had submitted his drawings and plan for a gothic-style structure, estimated cost $2,120.

Construction began immediately, keeping cost under control by use of much labor and materials donated by members of the community. Trees cut from the site were processed in nearby sawmills, so that hauling charges were small. Materials and equipment for the interior were donated by members and friends of the congregation; pulpit and large Bible, still in use today, were gifts to the first pastor by Mr. and Mrs. Benton Killen. The sterling communion service was purchased for the church by Mrs. William Chalmers, wife of one of the first elders.

The land intended as a burial ground was readied as construction proceeded. Almost before it was smoothed off, the ground received little six-year-old Margaret Smith Chalmers, who died May 28, 1876. Inscribed on the little gravestone were the child's last words, "The Lamb has come for me."

A later burial was that of famous mountain man Joseph Meek, generally credited with swinging the balance to Oregon in the historical "voice vote" at Champoeg, in 1843. Meek died in 1875 and was originally buried on his home place not far away, but when the property was later sold, his remains and those of his family were removed to the church yard (see *Boot Hill*).

Some changes and additions have improved the old church, none altering the general appearance or basic construction. In 1905 an annex was added at the rear to provide more space for Sunday School classes. Some years later this was enlarged, a half-basement dug and heating plant installed. Still later an organ was purchased, with speakers for the sanctuary, and a new well drilled, fitted with a pump so cemetery lawns could be watered.

In 1959 additional remodeling made more space upstairs behind the sanctuary, and by further excavation of the basement a kitchen and dining room were provided. At one time a fire threatened to destroy the old landmark but was extinguished, leaving only some blackened scars on the original steeple timbers.

The Diary Tells the Story

THE LOCUST GROVE Liberal United Brethren Church served many years of usefulness, perhaps glory, but it would be well not to look for any spiritual function in the building today. In the extremities of old age it sinks slowly into decay as a hay barn.

Its builder was Milon Alonzo Van Gilder of Wasco, who came out from New York in 1889 with his wife, daughter and four sons. A man of systematic habits, he began a diary in 1874 which was recently brought to light by daughter Inez Sargent, still a resident of Wasco. From the old document comes the story of the building of the church.

Worshipful Master of his Masonic lodge in New York, Van Gilder found several of his new Wasco neighbors interested in Masonry, and organized the first lodge in the area, becoming Worshipful Master of it. One of his lodge brothers, a Mr. Woodward, living on a homestead claim about four miles west of Wasco, increased his acreage by planting ten of them in trees as allowed in the land laws. The area being cold in winter with long, hot summers, Woodward selected the very hardy locust tree, and his acres came to be called Locust Grove.

The small school Woodward built for his own and neighbors' children often served for Sunday prayer meetings, but there was a definite need for a church building. The community placed the problem in Van Gilder's hands, and by May 6, 1895, plans had progressed to the point of ordering building lumber. The nearest sawmill was in Goldendale across the Columbia River in Washington, and the lumber was hauled in heavy wagons to the north shore and ferried across the river.

Previous to 1885, a good-sized town named Grant stood on the Oregon or south shore of the Columbia at this point, serving as a shipping center for wheat farmers, having begun as a gathering place for overland immigrants intending to float down the Columbia to the Willamette country. All slips and most of the town were washed away by the spring floods of 1894, the lumber ferries being forced to land on rocky or muddy

Gothic windows provide incongruous background for stacks of baled hay.

Graceful, New England style Locust Grove Church at Wasco actually does stand in grove of locusts. In days when travel was difficult, often impossible because of mud or deep dust, farmers were glad to attend nearby church. As automobiles came into use, congregations gradually thinned, preferring more elaborate churches in town or taking trip instead of attending church at all. Rural edifice neglected, fell into disrepair. Locust Grove Church has reached low estate of barn for hay storage, stock feeding rack standing where buggies used to discharge worshippers.

beaches. Foreseeing this difficulty, Van Gilder met the ferry, with its heavy loads of church lumber, with two extra teams of horses, all wagons being landed successfully and hauled up the steep grade.

With the arrival of building material, all farmers joined hands in the erection of the church. The starting date was June 3, 1885, and by the 22nd, a Saturday, the building was finished. Inez Sargent remembers, "That very evening we had church in the new building. I was a very small child, but I can still see those happy faces, people were so happy to have a real church. The next day was Sunday and the church was formally dedicated with the morning services. Everybody was so starved for the spoken word that services were held every single day during all of the next week."

The first regular pastor at Locust Grove Church was the Rev. Mr. Adams, a very forceful speaker. He was followed by several short-term ministers, the Reverends Peel, Parker and George McDonald, the latter residing with the Van Gilder family. He was a graduate of the "Liberal" branch of the United Brethren College at Philom-

ath in the Willamette Valley, and Locust Grove, at first nonsectarian, was thereafter allied with the United Brethren denomination.

Inez Sargent recalls "quite a few of the farmers in the neighborhood had never been baptized, so Rev. McDonald saw to it that they were. Some preferred total immersion; they were taken in the spring to the creek not far away. Water is low or absent in the summer and too cold or frozen in winter time, but in late May we would make a picnic of Baptizing Day, taking our lunch along to eat after services. As for myself, I have always been a coward about water; just sprinkling was plenty for me."

With the later advent of the automobile, people began to attend services in the larger towns, or not at all. The old Locust Grove Church was never officially closed, but increasingly sparse attendance finally forced abandonment. Comments Mrs. Sargent, "The last time we went to church it was a very sad thing. There were only half a dozen people in the congregation. We couldn't get a minister any more, and we knew we would never gather there again."

Clatsop Plains Presbyterian Church, now officially Gray Memorial Chapel, stands isolated and conspicuous on inner of two dikes paralleling Pacific Ocean. Square structure is appended by extended wing to north. Church faces east conforming to earliest Christian custom but a contributing reason may be shelter offered congregation entering during bad westerly storms.

Directly behind church is narrow sheltered space between ridges fronting ocean occupied by cemetery started when shipwrecked bodies were found on beach. Other graves are exclusively for pioneers, among them the two surmounted by large boulder.

The Altar was a Cedar Log

THE "GRAY MEMORIAL CHAPEL" in the Oregon Country had its birth on Clatsop Plains, not far south of Astoria at the mouth of the Columbia River. In September, 1846, a group of "old School" Presbyterian pioneers met at the home of W. H. Gray, Oregon's missionary-author, and organized the church. Gray wrote one of the first histories of the state, much of it from first-hand experience, which was important in that it anticipated the histories of Hubert Howe Bancroft. Gray also was Port Inspector at Astoria for many years.

Other members of the church-founding group were Mrs. Gray, Mr. and Mrs. Alva Condit and Rev. Lewis Thompson, who lived on Clatsop Plains and was a cousin of Capt. William Warren who figured prominently in the history of the area. Rev. Thompson preached to the minute congregation until 1870, services held in one or the other of the rough cabins in the settlement until 1850, when a flimsy shack was put up for a church. This was built on a ten-acre plot donated by Robert Morrison.

Morrison and bride were out from the East in 1844, stopping for a year in the Willamette Valley, then taking out a donation land claim of 640 acres on Clatsop Plains. The couple lived with the Solomon Smiths until the birth of their first son William, Morrison by this time having laid out his new farm and area for the church.

Shortly after it was built, a ship was wrecked in the surf and, when several bodies were washed in on the beach below the church, Morrison donated two acres for a cemetery which now holds the bodies of most of Clatsop's pioneers.

The first church was built by Thomas Owens and his son-in-law, John Hobson, the project a near miracle. Tools and building materials were almost non-existent, the altar fashioned from a cedar log Owens dragged up from the beach. Small wonder that the structure was flattened in a violent winter storm three years later. Local conditions were so improved during that period that a new and stouter church was erected on the spot.

Another storm caught Rev. Mann, the second pastor, called in 1870, while he was crossing the turbulent Columbia. A giant wave overturned his boat and, while he survived to preach until 1877, all church records were lost. Catastrophies continued to 1931, when Rev. Thomas Kirkwood was drowned.

The replacement church withstood the buffeting of storms until 1927, when the weather-worn building was torn down to make way for a modern edifice. The movement for this church was started and largely funded by the daughter of founder W. H. Gray. The cornerstone was laid in 1929, the handsome brick structure prepared to withstand the elements for many years. The present pastor, Rev. Clarence Baerveildt, greatly interested in the background of the church, assisted in assembling this material.

Plaque mounted on stone reads, "Beneath this native stone lie Oregon's first schoolteachers, Solomon Smith of New Hampshire, Missionary, Millwright, Farmer, Merchant, State senator and his wife Helen, born Celiast, Princess-Daughter of Coboway, Chief of the Clatsops." (see *Tales the Western Tombstones Tell*).

"*I Am the Alpha*

Providence Baptist Church was erected in tiny clearing chopped out of dense forest of Douglas firs. Surrounding trees have several times been in peril of loggers, stopped at least once by courts. Adjacent and partially surrounding venerable church is graveyard, long neglected but recently placed under perpetual care. Grass is periodically cut, tottering stones propped, elaborate wrought-iron fences painted against rust.

PROVIDENCE

nd Omegay!"

GENERALLY SPEAKING, early day Baptist ministers had an extremely simple, uncomplicated approach to preaching, as compared to those of Episcopal or Presbyterian faiths. And this accounted for their greater initial success. To enter the Baptist ministry, little was required of a candidate beyond his effectiveness as a good Gospel preacher. Considering the low cultural level of most western congregations, a highly educated, high level minister could inspire discomfort and suspicion rather than a yearning for salvation. Moreover, an educated preacher would require a higher salary, and most primitive churches were ill-prepared to pay good wages. Indeed, many pioneer preachers received no pay at all, keeping body and soul together some by such extra-curricular activity as farming or carpentering.

Joab Powell was the classic example of the untrained but successful preacher. Barely literate, he nevertheless converted more souls to his church than did any other preacher in Oregon. Physically, Powell was formidable, a ponderous, square-cut figure, weighing in excess of 275 pounds. He wore homemade jean pants, a heavy black overcoat and high boots in all but the hottest weather. The boots were usually muddy, often carrying an overlay of dung from his barnyard. His black hair was seldom cut and never combed. He hated to shave and often appeared on the platform with a stubble of beard.

A lover of chewing tobacco, Powell invariably fortified himself for the delivery of a sermon with a mouthful of plug. Stepping before his congregation he would open with, "I am the Alpha and Omegay." Warming to his subject, the preacher would feel the need to empty his mouth of a copious load of dark brown juice. Hardly interrupting himself, he would turn his head slightly and let go. If the resulting deposit seemed a little thick, it was spread out by a heavy, booted toe.

Powell's sermons were delivered in sing-song fashion, but the intonation was forceful, earnest and well sprinkled with quotations from the Bible, of which he had a photographic familiarity. About halfway through his exhortation, if the weather was the least bit warm, Powell unfas-

tened the buttons of his ungainly coat and threw it to the floor. Then followed the vest. As sweat poured down his face, he drew out a huge red bandana, always kept in a hip pocket, and mopped his brow. Near the end Powell would exhort, sing, pray and entreat until he got the response he desired. If, as it rarely might, the congregation remained sitting on its hands, the pastor looked heavenward and intoned, "There is not much rejoicing in Heaven today."

Stories about the burly minister amount to legend in Oregon, but some reflect the popular conception of his character. Religious prejudice was rampant in that day, and most Protestants felt Catholics were an evil lot, that the Pope was working on a plan to take over the entire Oregon Country. Residents of French Prairie, predominantly Catholic, disliked and feared any advances made by Methodists and Baptists. It came to Powell's ears one day that a husky blacksmith of the St. Louis parish had sworn to exterminate him if he so much as set foot in the environs. Powell hoisted his weight on his horse and rode directly to the blacksmith shop, seized his detractor by the collar, and "soundly thrashed him," according to the story.

Invited to speak before the Oregon legislature, the preacher remarked as an opener, "I have been called upon to set forth the gospel to you as the chief sinners of Oregon." Nevertheless, there is today on the capitol grounds an equestrian statue of the famed circuit rider preacher.

Powell, though owning a farm from which he derived his living, was seldom at home. Leaving his several sons to care for the lands and stock, he got aboard his horse and roamed the farthest corners of the Willamette Valley, preaching in hundreds of communities with, or without a church. For these services he never asked payment above that of "board and keep."

Such tactics were bound to make him some enemies. On one occasion the minister came under attack because of alleged "lack of probity in a cattle selling deal." The Baptist Central Association, after investigating the accusations, reported them "false, *maliciously* raised" and "spread to sink the minister's reputation."

Powell's farm was near the Santiam River, his Baptist neighbors all Missourians and mostly from Jackson County. On April 9, 1853, Elder Joab Powell, Rev. Berkeley and Art Cheadle organized what was then called Missionary Baptist Church.

Land for the church and cemetery site was donated from two adjoining claims that met at the crest of one of the several rolling hills in the area. Phillip Carmichael and John Belcher were the donors of the land, then entirely covered with a dense growth of huge Douglas firs. Many of these magnificent trees still stand today.

The building committee made these recommendations, here reproduced verbatim from *Providence Baptist Church "Minute Book,"* February 5, 1865:

". . . your Committee would Suggest that a House 45 feet in Lendth and 35 feete in wedth 14 feet of 1 Story of a Substantiel fraim of heavey timbers well weather borded and Seald with 2 doors in frunt and a suitable number of windows a neet plain pulpit well Seated with 2 stoves and Chimneys well painted out and in Side, Such a building would in the opineon of your committee meet the wants of the church and bee of Lasting Eutility

your Committee believe It to bee theair duty to Suggest the Probable Cost of Such a building but it would be quite unpossable for them to arive at enything acurate but it will Require Sume were near $1200 you Comonitee believe however that a Considerable Porpotion might be Raised in Material and labor wich would lessem the burthen Materelly and fall Much Lighter upon the Church . . .

"your Committee beleave that the better plan to Rais funds for the Erection of Such a building would be by volentory Subscription beleaving that Such a course would not onley meet the approbation of the Church, but would afford ample opertunity to all those that might deseire to assist trusting that theare are meny who would feel it their privelige to do so from the fact that Respecable publick buildings of this Sort dose to Some Exstente Enhance the value of reals Estate and bespeakes the morals of the Community within its locality."

Earliest graves in old west were marked, at least temporarily by simple wooden markers. Some few of these remain in drier sections like Nevada, Arizona, Utah. In Pacific Northwest where rains are frequent, wooden headboards are vanishing relics. One pictured here is surely candidate for oldest if not only wooden grave marker in area. Placed lengthwise of grave, 7' board is constructed of yew wood. Ancient legends give yew many properties, one its power to frighten away witches, other evil forces. They were planted in temple grounds, later in church yards, especially in adjacent burial plots.

Distinctive marble headstone marks grave of eccentric but effective early day Baptist "hellfire" preacher Joab Powell. Similar stone at left (out of photo) stands on grave of wife.

JOHN DAY

The First Elders Came by Horse

THE TOWN of John Day in northeast Oregon, at the junction of Canyon Creek and the John Day River, has a history as wild and picturesque as the most turbulent of gold camps. The man for whom it was named is one of Oregon's most tragic figures. John Day hired out as a hunter with the Wilson Price Hunt expedition to Astoria in 1811. While the party was fighting its way through the Snake River country, Day fell ill and was forced to remain behind. Two of his friends chose to remain with him, one of whom died from the effects of starvation and a winter's exposure. Day and his other companion, Ramsey Crooks, struggled through the Blue Mountains and along canyons of the river later named for him, at last reaching the Columbia River after great suffering and, as a last straw, had their ragged clothing stolen by Indians. When sighted by the Robert Stuart party ascending the Columbia, the emaciated pair was barely recognized as human. As a result of his experience, John Day became violently demented, dying soon, some say, at Astoria.

When rich deposits of gold were found in Canyon Creek, the town of John Day was founded at a natural crossroads between The Dalles on the Columbia and gold camps south and east. During the years 1862-64 the mail was at first carried over the long stretch by horsemen riding over primitive Indian trails. Then a rough road was hacked out through the sagebrush and over rocks, enabling stagecoaches to rumble over the rough stretch, this termed the Military Road. Besides mail and supplies, these conveyances often carried thousands of dollars worth of gold from Canyon City through John Day to The Dalles. Hold-ups and murder by Indians were all too frequent.

During these first years there was little thought of religion in John Day and no churches at all. By the 1880s gold had become secondary to cattle, sheep and ranching. A more placid period made possible a more thoughtful atmosphere, and Charles Belshaw, who had been a devout Advent Christian member in his home town, now found himself the only such believer in all the country roundabout. As he talked to others in John Day, he found a number who saw much merit in his faith, and it was natural the group met for infor-

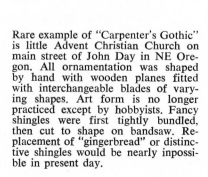

Rare example of "Carpenter's Gothic" is little Advent Christian Church on main street of John Day in NE Oregon. All ornamentation was shaped by hand with wooden planes fitted with interchangeable blades of varying shapes. Art form is no longer practiced except by hobbyists. Fancy shingles were first tightly bundled, then cut to shape on bandsaw. Replacement of "gingerbread" or distinctive shingles would be nearly inpossible in present day.

mal prayer and services. For some time "church" was held first in one home, then another.

By 1885 there were enough regularly attending members to think seriously of building a church, and that year the influential William Chapman officially organized one. Elder James Orchard held the first services, with ten members. He and succeeding ministers, Elders George Ketchum and Hope, had to travel the long 150 miles from The Dalles by horse.

For ten years the church prospered, but membership dwindled during the depression years until services necessarily ceased and the building fell vacant. In the late 1930s Elder Oliver Lucas of Oregon City and a friend traveled to John Day to see what could be done for the church. They found that, although members of the Advent Christian Church seemed non-existent, now there were many adherents of the related Seventh-Day Adventist Church. The elders from the Willamette Valley then successfully negotiated with these members to buy the old Advent Christian structure.

In time John Day saw the decrease of Seventh-Day Adventists, with an increase of Baptist adherents, and as a natural adjustment the church was used jointly by each congregation. This is the situation prevailing today, with ownership of the building officially in Seventh-Day Adventist hands.

Lonely little Methodist Church at Richmond, unused for many years, stands among sagebrush and juniper covered hills in central Oregon. Village grew slowly from collection of farm houses without nucleus until settlers organized to establish needed conveniences. With nearest source of supplies in Mitchell, 19 miles to south, first essential was store, built with lumber produced at nearest mill in settlement of Sixshooter. Next most necessary structure, all agreed was Methodist Church. This and several succeeding buildings seemed to call for town name. Passions of currently raging Civil War caused serious clash over christening. Final choice of Richmond, showed where preponderance of feeling lay.

One-time flourishing ranching community is now a ghost town, though summer usually finds at least one old farmhouse occupied by vacationers. Methodist Church is slowly deteriorating, dry climate of area retarding complete collapse. Woodpeckers find spaces between walls ideal shelter, as entrance holes indicate.

"An Edge with The Lord"

Pioneer Methodist Church in Jacksonville photographed by author with covered wagon during Oregon's Centennial Year celebration. Building still retains most original furnishings. Melodeon, small reed organ, was brought around Horn on sailing ship, unloaded at Crescent City, Calif., hauled here on backs of mules.

At that time church bore signs using large letters, "First Protestant Church West of the Rockies." Below in much smaller letters, "Built in Southern Oregon." Failing to gather import of fine print, author captioned photo appearing in *Western Ghost Towns* as "First Protestant Church West of the Rockies," has since been corrected many times. Actually Jacksonville's Methodist Church was dedicated in year following ceremony for West Union Baptist Church in Willamette Valley (see also *Western Ghost Towns*).

HE SOUTHWESTERN CORNER of Oregon was swarming with prospectors in the early 1850s. Many of them were unsuccessful in the California fields and, unwilling to return home empty handed, cruised farther north. The truth of the old saying, "Gold is where you find it," was proven in the winter of 1851-52 when a pair of erstwhile Californians, James Cluggage and J. R. Poole, made a strike on what was later called Jackson Creek (see *Western Ghost Towns*).

A lively mining camp, first named Jackson City, then Jacksonville, rapidly developed near the strike site. During the next year it suffered through bad fires, Indian wars and epidemics of disease. Shaking off one trouble after another, Jacksonville grew to be the major city of the area, but when the gold was gone, and without other industries to sustain it, the city became a near-ghost. Always retaining some population, Jacksonville has lately capitalized on its historic status, featuring a very fine museum in the handsome old Jackson County Court House. Among other historic structures is the Pioneer Methodist Church, "catty-corner" from the museum.

Among the first prospectors there was little thought of religion, but with the advent of a more settled population in the next several years, several houses of worship were established. Late 1853 brought the vigorous and enthusiastic Methodist worker, Rev. Joseph S. Smith, later Representative in Congress from Oregon.

Smith immediately set to work an effort to build a church in his faith. First step was to raise funds, so he delegated three women to the job—his wife, and the Misses Overbeck and Royal. These ladies, unused to the roughness so prominent in any mining camp, shrank at first, expecting great difficulty in wringing money from miners, gamblers and the various purveyors of sin who already made up much of the population. The timid solicitors gained confidence right away when the first saloon owner forked over a handsome contribution, at the same time remarking, "This is my take for last night. It might give me an edge with the Lord when I kick off."

History does not record if the girls were sensitive to the donor's motive but does state sufficient funds to build the church were collected. The building was immediately put under construction, but before it was finished workmen found gold on the site and the half-completed edifice was moved to its present location. Final construction was of hewn logs, roof covered with hand-hewn cedar shakes. When completed in 1854, Rev. T. F. Royal had replaced Rev. Smith, who had entered politics.

The population rapidly increased as the church was going up, and there was an immediate rush to use its facilities for the Sacrament of the Holy Communion, for weddings as well as regular Sunday services. An old account reads, "Vows were taken here that united many happy couples, and here came people bearing the remains of all that was mortal of their loved ones for final obsequies before taking that long, sad journey up the hill to where the beautiful God's Acre lies."

Lone jewel of faith—little Church of the Brethren in Mabel where most early activity was built around sawmills, logging camps, saloons, brothels. Longest surviving pastor was Brother Herman Ritter who preached there 50 years. He married Mary Elizabeth Nedrow in Illinois in 1894, first job teaching 61 in tiny country school while boarding from one family to another on $25 monthly salary. Searching for more meaningful life, young couple made way to California where Ritter managed to study for ministry. Ordained in Church of the Brethren, he was sent to preach godliness to ungodly loggers at Mabel, staying until he retired in September, 1953 (See also *Ghost Town*

NEW MEXICO

Mines and Missions

St. Anne's Church, browsing among ruins of now ghostly town of Madrid. When Christmas
lights were turned off in 1941 strings, bulbs and all were left in place as sentimental, nostalgic
gesture. Company offices, most other larger buildings also retain garlands of lights not turned
on in almost thirty years.

Town o

St. Francis Church stands as only solid building in Golden, one of several ghost towns neighboring Madrid. Gold, not coal was found here, the period of activity much earlier, original diggings by aborigines in 1600s. St. Francis was probably built around 1830. Walls of stone structure still stood in 1950s, but roof was gone and general collapse threatened. Full repairs were carried out by Fr. Angelico Chavez who wisely retained original off-square lines. Fr. Hukenbeck of St. Joseph's in Cerrillos still says occasional Mass here. Though only one or two faithful remain in Golden, church is filled with former residents who can't forget lively days.

"Christmas trees" in treeless region were manufactured of poles, pipes and wires. Each hill on both sides of town was crowned by illuminated, make-believe tree. Lower slope of each displayed creche or other Biblical scene. Seen here at extreme right are remains of "Bethlehem" centered by large cross. Last time display was lighted was on Christmas of 1941. Lower left is St. Anne's Church, lower right school.

Christmas Lights

URING MADRID'S earliest years the population remained small. At first mine operations expanded and brought an influx of workers and their families. Most of them were of Indian, Mexican or Spanish extraction from the immediate area, but increasing needs added Italians, Slovaks and Croations, all Catholics.

This period saw the erection and dedication of St. Anne's Church, a handsome structure of plastered adobe. At the height of the population Mass was said every Sunday, although there was seldom a resident pastor. In the years preceding 1918 a priest made the long trip from Santa Fe on horseback, just as the earlier missionaries did. Sometimes the bishop would come to Madrid to give confirmation, and on such special days thirty-five to forty supplicants would be grouped into two or three lines, ready to file into the church.

There were gold, silver and turquoise mines in the valley as early as the 1600s. Golden, San Pedro, Cerrillos flourished and died. Then vast deposits of coal were discovered near the center of what had been a series of near ghost towns, and Madrid came into being.

In its prosperity Madrid followed no accepted pattern. Even the name was pronounced awkwardly, with the accent on the first syllable in defiance of conventional Spanish speech. And, instead of fame by violence, this mining camp is noted for its spectacular display of lights at the Christmas season.

In the earliest days of big-time coal mining little thought was given to religious or aesthetic decoration, but when Madrid expanded into a major coal-producing center and electricity was introduced, produced by a small generator, the company allowed one light per house—one bare bulb dangling from the ceiling in the small frame shacks shipped in from another camp.

Then came new manager Oscar Huber and a huge power plant. Huber changed things, wiring homes for general lighting and for the new simple appliances.

With the free use of electricity some residents began putting a few lights around the front porch to help celebrate Christmas. From this simple beginning grew an official annual program unsurpassed by any other community. Every house and building was generously garlanded with strings of lights. Huge cut-out figures of Mary, Joseph and the infant Jesus were erected on the hillsides and studded with lights. Along the summits of the two ridges enclosing the town were erected numerous Christmas trees some fifty feet tall. This was desert country, so Madrid's trees were fabricated poles for trunks with crossed pipes for branches, all lavishly strung with light bulbs. Fr. Giles Hukenbeck, now of Cerrillos, says, "I first saw the Christmas lights in Madrid in 1932. I thought the trees on the hills were giant real ones, the whole effect was unbelievably beautiful."

The years from 1930 to 1940 brought a series of ups and downs to Madrid. With World War II came the last spurt—20,000 tons of coal going to Los Alamos to help build the first A-bombs. The Christmas lights were turned on for the last time in 1941. When the mines were closed and the switch thrown off, the choralers sang "Auld Lang Syne" while most of those watching wept openly.

155

Case of the Restless Padre

IT WAS CHRISTMAS EVE of 1889. In the mission church of Isleta the faithful were gathered to celebrate midnight Mass. There was a deep silence as the priest raised his hand. Then with a deep rumbling sound the altar swayed. After a short silence the trembling natives heard a loud knocking, as if someone were kicking on the floor. In superstitious panic the entire congregation rushed outside. Everyone knew what was happening. The coffin of a long dead priest, buried beside the altar, was again rising to the surface.

Almost three hundred and fifty years before this the original pueblo of Isleta, a few miles south of Albuquerque, was discovered by the Spanish, in 1540. No one knows how long it had been there. The Spanish built a mission church in the village, in 1613, which was nearly destroyed when they were driven out in the 1680 revolt. It was rebuilt by new Spanish forces in 1693, and this is substantially the same structure that stands today.

In conformity with the custom of the period, priests who died were buried inside the church, usually near the altar. A long standing story relates that at intervals the coffin of one of these padres rises to the surface of the paving and is exposed to the light of day. Identity of the occupant of the restless casket has never been positively identified, is sometimes mentioned as Friar Francisco Padilla, a member of the Coronado expedition, who was set upon by hostile natives and killed. However, this event occurred in 1540, long before the church existed.

Another possible is Francesco Latrado, an over-zealous padre who constantly berated his flock for drunkenness, lack of faith and other failings. At last short tempered Indians put a stop to the irritation by slaying father Latrado, scalping him, and paraded the grisly souvenir up and down the main street. While it is known the corpse was buried somewhere in Isleta, the grave is unlocated.

Then there is Father Juan J. Padilla who, in

Mission San Antonio de Isleta at Isleta pueblo south of Albuquerque is unique in combining wooden towers with adobe construction. Both towers and massive facade have been added during various restoration projects. Simple structure imbedded in "frosting" remains much the same as it was in 1693. (Photo courtesy New Mexico Department of Development).

Plank coffin of restless padre at floor level in church. Rev. Fred Stadtmueller examines contents of tin box found in casket. It contained copies of reports made during exhumations of 1895 and 1948 (photo courtesy Lou Wade and *Old West Magazine*).

1733, was assigned to the new mission of San Jose de Laguna, some miles from Isleta. About twenty-two years later he set out on what was supposed to be a routine trip to one of his *visitas*. Though subsequent events are not a matter of official church record, an interesting version has been offered by Julia Keller, historian of the University of New Mexico. Miss Keller's story relates that the padre was caught in a severe snowstorm and, losing his way, he let his horse wander. He came to a house where a devout lady was happy to shelter the priest and soon had a hot meal ready for him.

Hardly had he sat down to eat when the husband came staggering in, blind drunk. Infuriated at seeing a strange man in the house, he stabbed Father Padilla to death. When the man had sobered somewhat, he realized his mistake but was afraid to take the body to the mission. Instead he threw it over the priest's horse and tied it to the saddle. Then he whacked the beast on the rump.

Next morning an Isleta squaw saw the animal standing at the mission gate and called the resident priest. Isleta burial records do show that one "Juan J. Padilla, killed by stabbing thrusts," was buried inside the church beside the altar. Unfortunately for the story this record indicates the burial was in 1775, a date 20 years too late. Regardless of this discrepancy, Fray Angelico Chavez, in 1947, identified the body buried in location as that of Father Juan J. Padilla of Laguna.

Whatever the true identity of the priest, the natives long held the belief that at certain dates the coffin worked its way to the surface, that the cottonwood box was opened, the well-preserved

body washed and, after an all night wake, reburied at the former depth. So persistent were these reports the Catholic church, in the early 1800s, ordered an investigation. The coffin was exhumed, the body found to be strangely flexible so that the arms could be bent at will. Plain were wounds on the left side and at the lower part of the cranium just under the ear. There was a parchment with a date partially decipherable, 177... The coffin was reburied in the same grave.

After the strange events of Christmas Eve, 1889, the church again made plans for an investigation which was not accomplished until 1895. At that time Archbishop Chapelle named a commission of laity and church officials, including Father Docher, to examine the coffin once more. Again it was found close to the surface, the body in still good condition but mummified rather than "flexible." There was a purple stole around the neck, the record states, but nothing to account for the frequent antics of the casket was discovered.

The stories continuing, the casket was once more lifted in August, 1960, when such modern aids as pathological technicians, archaeologists and a photographer were present, as well as church officials. Nothing new was found. The body was less well-preserved, the purple stole somewhat disintegrated, but there was no clue to the mystery of the strange levitation.

More recently a cement paving has been laid over all of the graves inside the church. If the coffin of Father Padilla again rises, no one will ever know.

Phoebe Hearst - Angel

PINOS ALTOS was settled very early and has a long history of struggle between Indian tribes and whites (see *Ghost Town Album*). After 1860 prospectors found gold in the area and settled there to mine it.

In those days Mesilla was the center of the Catholic diocese, Pinos Altos only a mission or way station for itinerant priests. On their annual visits they blessed the marriages of couples who had elected to live together, christened babies born of such alliances and said prayers over new graves.

The story is told that one traveling father spoke to a man known as the Irish Catholic parent of a series of babies, all properly named Michael, Patrick, Brian, etc. "Well, Mike—I expect there is a new child this year." . . . "Yes, father —another boy." . . . "And what will his name be?" . . . "Well, father, I've racked me poor brains for good Irish names, so it's Martin Luther." It took whiskey and a good dinner to bring the priest around to good humor and willingness to bless the new child.

The first Catholic Church in Pinos Altos (Tall Pines) was built in 1868, the structure now only a pile of fast melting adobe. Until about 1870 there were few Protestants in the town, and they had no services in their faith. During the next two decades scattered and infrequent Methodist and other Protestant services were held in the school house or some private home, ministers supplied by the churches of nearby Silver City. About 1890 a regular Methodist minister, Rev. Ruoff, was assigned to steady service divided between Pinos Altos and Central, just east of Silver City. The reverend took a fancy to Pinos Altos and made his home there.

He soon began to agitate for a church building and the Methodist Extension Board agreed to authorize one. Mr. and Mrs. Frank Bell donated a part of their claim, the Good Enough, as a site, and the church ladies campaigned for funds by solicitation and proceeds from box lunches at social suppers and bazaars. Most miners in the district, even some Catholic ones, pledged funds; yet with all this the treasury failed to come up to the need. Then an "angel" fluttered down.

George Hearst, father of William Randolph Hearst, had cattle interests in the southwest and some desire to invest in a good gold mining claim. He sent Ben Thayer to investigate the possibilities in Pinos Altos but died before any developments could take place. Thayer did, however, view a display of Bell and Stephens, owners of the Pacific Group mine, showing one day's run out the Silver City mill—eight gold bricks a foot high and a hundred and nine and a half pounds troy, in value—$20,367. The Hearst man hurried back to the heirs who, on August 10, 1897, bought out the Bell and Stephens combine and moved into Palos Altos to start mining on a grand scale.

The widow, Mrs. Phoebe Hearst, also went to see what she had signed for and heard about the struggle to raise church funds. She was interested and agreed to make up the deficit, on one condition—there must be a library annex complete with books and periodicals.

The Methodist Church board eagerly accepted the offer and construction started at once. Apparently the original plans were used and the finished structure provided for no library annex. To rectify the error, a corner of the nave near the front door was marked off for the purpose. The furniture consisted of some hastily gathered tables and chairs, the reading matter—Silver City newspapers and a few magazines, including *Scribner's, Argosy, Puck, Life, Review of Reviews*. And the Gold Avenue Methodist Church was dedicated May 18, 1898, the year Rev. Ruoff retired to be replaced as pastor by Rev. Henry Van Valkenburgh.

Church librarian George Lincoln noted certain lack of patronage and took the problem to the board. Were the periodicals suitable for miners' reading? And would magazines for them be offensive to women and children? All agreed to one suggestion. "We must face the facts. Our population is naturally made up of Catholics and many of them would come to read if they were allowed to enter a Protestant church." Lincoln then had the Ladies Aid make some curtains and hang

Gold Mining town of Pinos Altos once supported heavy stand of "Tall Pines" but early mining activity soon depleted trees, using them in shoring and for fuel. By time Methodist Church shown here was erected, building material had reverted to New Mexico's always plentiful adobe mud.

In comparatively recent years old church was sold to Baptists who used it mostly for Summer Bible School. About this time wooden platform supporting seldom used bell was found to be so rotten as to be unsafe. Rather than repair structure, bell was given to rural church near Mountain Park, New Mexico (more photos, story in *Ghost Town Album*).

them to cut off the corner, separating library from church. "Results were amazing," reports Dorothy Watson, Los Pinos historian. "The library became a very popular place."

An Epworth League was organized about the same time, as well as a Sunday School, both flourishing for many years. A fine choir became famous in that part of the state, and the Gold Avenue Methodist Church was a continuing success.

It was, that is, until the rich veins played out. The Hearst interests were among the first to decamp, Phoebe Hearst withdrawing her support of the church library, which then died on the vine.

With the advent of the automobile local people lost interest in the church, driving to the larger, more impressive ones in Silver City.

The regular pastor resigned, and for a time visiting Presbyterian, Episcopal and other clergymen preached irregularly. When this plan was discontinued, the structure was turned into a community center, open to all. It was used for Forest Service movies of fire prevention, lecturers and entertainers. When these uses became infrequent, there was a movment to use the church as a museum, but this came to nothing. Now the old church in the "Tall Pines" stands abandoned, slowly melting away.

"Rebuild . .

Lower of "twin" towers has wider window. Both are supported by buttresses extending full width from base to belfry. Clearly shown in this close-up is network of minute cracks that would lead to large ones and dissolution but for periodic re-plasterings.

ebuild . . . Rebuild"

THE FORTRESS-LIKE Mission San Francisco de Assissi de Taos is famous for its exceptionally thick walls, five feet in most sections, ten at the bases of numerous buttresses. Explaining this is the fact that the entire building (except wood in lintels and ceiling) is constructed of mud just as it came from the ground. All walls are of sun-dried adobe brick, some containing an intermixture of straw, and over this is laid a heavy coat of "plaster," also made of mud somewhat thicker than slurry.

Parishioners are thoroughly imbued with the legend of St. Francis in the role of "repair man." Falling ill on his way to join Crusaders in the 13th century, he lay at death's door for a time. In a vision or dream he heard the recurring message, "Go forth, Francis, and repair my church, for it is nearly falling down." After recovering Francis went forth with holy zeal to rebuild old churches.

Although rains at Taos are not copious, they do erode the mission walls to some degree. Every year or so church members heed the traditional call to "Rebuild . . . Rebuild." They embark on a "crusade" to replace the surface before small cracks become big ones. Women mix mud and water as men erect spidery scaffolding around the building including the two towers. From this flimsy support they apply a generous coating to the surface. Nine days is the average period of work required and, with removal of the last bit of framework, all join in a huge fiesta without inhibitions or restraint.

Confusing to strangers in New Mexico are the

Imposing structure blends with landscape by virtue of natural earth color. Structure is variously given from 108 to 120 feet. Bell towers differ in height, window-piercings. Courtyard enclosed by six foot wall is almost solidly filled with graves, mostly of church personnel, Indian artists who painted some of pictures inside.

three villages with the name Taos. There is Don Fernando de Taos, best known and in modern times called simply Taos. Nothing really colorful has happened there since the massacre of a hundred and sixty people (see *Boot Hill*). In more recent times the place has become a famous rendezvous of artists and writers.

Two and a half miles north is San Geronimo de Taos, now known simply as Taos Pueblo. This is strictly an Indian village, with restrictions on tourists and cameras (these readily abrogated with silver). The original Mission of San Geronimo was built by Fr. Pedro Miranda in 1680. The second, with still visible walls four feet thick, was built in 1704. Nearby, and traditionally on the site of the first, is the third and present mission built in 1848.

Then there is Ranchos de Taos, a short distance south of Taos. All three locations are just west of the Rio Grande, here a tumbling stream of sparkling clear water fresh from the southern mountains of Colorado. Closely on the east rises the Sangre de Cristo range, the Taos trio lying at an elevation of about 7,000 feet, subject to cold, snowy winters.

Indian tradition has it that Ranchos de Taos was founded by agriculturally minded members of Taos Pueblo seeking more fertile fields nearer the Rio Grande. Another story is that those natives having sympathy for the Penitente Order left the hostile atmosphere at home, seeking religious freedom at the new location.

Also somewhat dependent upon tradition is the date of original construction of the Mission of San Francisco de Assissi, or more familiarly Saint Francis. Present personnel claims 1710 as the year it began, with a forty-year period required for completion, that the church later fell into disuse and was repaired in 1772. This latter date is indisputably registered at the Diocesan headquarters, Durango, Colorado. The period of disuse could easily have been during concentrated attacks on the village by Comanches.

Since rape and abduction of Taos women was a main objective, Comanche blood was plentifully present in local residents. Even now, every January sees the pageant of Los Comanches held in the plaza in front of the church. Enacted mostly on horseback, the play depicts the capture of two Taos children and their subsequent rescue. The happy ending concludes with a grand parade into the church. Sometimes even the horses try to get in.

Interior looks much as in early days except for addition of pews. Indian worshippers originally knelt on bare, hard-packed earthen floor. Vigas (roof beams) 25 feet from floor and spaced unusually close, are supported on corbels, pre-carved and painted with vegetable dyes. At left is painting of bare-footed Christ standing on shores of Galilee. No masterpiece, picture is nevertheless famous. When seen in darkness, background shows self-luminous clouds, heavy cross appears over shoulder and distinct halo floats over head. Phenomenon, consistently observed for 60 years, remains unexplained by any examination so far. At picture's lower corner stands small statue of St. Francis dating from 16th Century. Many church artifacts with same dating came from Spain.

Preacher Parade

Gaunt, decaying buildings along main street of Lake Valley have varying history. False-fronted structure at right was saloon, bawdyhouse in earliest days, then turned into community church. In center is lodging house for any wandering preacher who could be ensnared into holding Sunday services. On day Dr. Mason and author made picture there was not another soul in Lake Valley or for many empty miles around (see also *Ghost Town Album*).

ILVER DEPOSITS were fantastically rich in Lake Valley (see *Ghost Town Album*). One pocket of the shiny metal was so large it was hollowed out from the inside and termed the "Bridal Chamber," a railroad spur running directly into it. Intense while it lasted, the big boom in Lake Valley died out quickly. Many people moved to greener pastures, four-fifths by the mid-Nineties, the rest remaining to live out their lives in homes they had come to love.

The town never had a proper church, vice and sin holding the upper hand all through prosperity. But when the violence subsided the ladies thought it high time to invite God to Lake Valley.

In 1896 they formed a distinct type of Christian Endeavor Society, charter members being Mrs. D. S. Miller, Mrs. Margaret Williams, Mrs. Parvin, Mrs. Sarah Jones and Mrs. Elizabeth McLean. Founder and moving spirit was Mrs. Parvin, who brought the idea from Muscatine, Iowa. Dues were ten cents per month.

The ladies immediately set about establishing a community church. They persuaded Major Morgan, a veteran of the Union Army, to let them use a dilapidated saloon-rooming house he owned on the main street. The place had a reputation of the worst kind, having housed sin in its most rampant form, but it was cheap and available. The members put in a new floor, covered the inside walls with oil cloth and painted the false-front. They placed seven kerosene lamps where most needed and generally spruced up the old place to make the "house" a church.

Most of the time services were conducted by members reading from the Bible, a twelve-year-old child officiating several times. Then one Wednesday a Methodist minister stopped in town. He was invited to preach the next Sunday's sermon and, when he accepted, was "put up" in the little building adjoining the church. From then on any stranger was asked if he had ever been a minister and, if so, he was provided free lodging for as long as he would stay. A backsliding, ex-

Workmen cutting immense granite blocks destined to become part of Mormon Temple, 20 miles distant—shown in old photo, circa 1871. During earlier stages teams of oxen were required for hauling (photo courtesy Church of Jesus Christ of Latter Day Saints).

communicated bishop was once a welcomed guest who preached for his supper. Through the years following there was a continuing parade of Mormon, Episcopal, Presbyterian, Baptist, Quaker and Catholic travelers who were or had been men of the cloth.

The Lake Valley ladies also built a small public school, reset fallen tombstones in the cemetery, placed and repaired picket fences. Contributions were sent to the aid of flood victims in the eastern United States and sufferers from famine in China. Funds for all those projects were earned through cake socials, benefits, Fourth of July picnics. But all forty years of this beneficence ended when Lake Valley became a ghost town and the ladies disbanded.

UTAH
Land of Brigham Young

Famed Mormon Temple illuminated by floodlights. Now surrounded by large hotels, business buildings it once stood alone on plain near Great Salt Lake, conspicuous for miles. Foundations made of granite blocks measures 16 feet in width, height. Length of building is 186½ feet, width 118½ feet. Each tower soars 210 feet, is surmounted by statue of Angel Moroni, work of Cyrus E. Dalin, famous Utah born sculptor. Moroni was last of series of ancient American Prophets whose writings constitute Book of Mormon (photo courtesy Church of Jesus Christ of Latter Day Saints).

"This will be the Temple of our God"

THE MORMON PIONEERS arrived in Salt Lake Valley on July 24, 1847. They had come to this inhospitable country to escape persecutions which had troubled them continually up to that time. Four days after their arrival, Brigham Young, their leader, walked to a spot of ground between the forks of a small mountain stream and, putting his cane to the ground, declared, "Here will be the temple of our God." This was before a cabin or shelter of any sort existed in the valley. A stake was driven on the spot by Wilford Woodruff, one of Brigham Young's close associates. On that spot was later built the Mormons' most sacred structure, the Temple.

Construction was started in 1853. A granite quarry was opened some twenty miles to the southeast. The only means of transportation was by ox team, and in early days of construction a yoke of four oxen required three to four days to make the round trip required to transport a single block of foundation stone and return. Through the years of building, work progressed very slowly, but with great care. A railroad eventually replaced the ox teams, work then being greatly expedited. Even so, forty years were required to complete the great structure.

On April 6, 1893, construction was completed and a reverent dedication celebrated. Prior to sacred ordination a steady stream of visitors had been escorted through the unfinished building, as has been the practice since in the construction of all twelve Mormon Temples. Since dedication only members of the church in good standing have been permitted to enter portals of the Temple.

All work on temples is based on the conviction that life beyond the grave is as much of a certainty as mortality. The majestic building on Temple Square, and all other Temples built by the church at great cost and untold sacrifice, are tangible evidence of the assurance members have that in the resurrection they shall again take up their bodies and continue to live as individuals.

Temple Square, center of Mormon faith, in photo copies from advertising brochure "Among the Rockies," distributed in 1910 by Denver and Rio Grande Railroad. Square remains unchanged except for growth of trees, now obscuring main features of famed park. Structure at left is Assembly Hall, similar to other regular meeting house of Latter Day Saints, worship being open to general public. In center is Tabernacle, like inverted bowl, 250x150 feet, resting on 44 pillars of sandstone, each nine feet thick. Unique roof, actually immense sounding board, constructed long before availability of steel girders and rods is made entirely of wood. Roof is composed of two shells. Nine foot space between is filled with massive bridge work of timbers, latticed and pinned together with huge wooden pins. Enclosed pipe organ is marvel of pioneer ingenuity, built by Joseph Ridgers. Music of organ and Tabernacle choir has for years been heard over nationwide Sunday morning radio broadcasts. At right is Temple.

TEMPLE SQUARE
SALT LAKE

Almost A Church

IF THE FIFTEEN BUILDINGS that still stand in Grafton, the most prominent is the gaunt, two-story adobe structure slowly melting into ruin. Although having all the appearances of an early church, the building never was so distinguished, according to the author's source, Mrs. Jacob Truman of St. George, and her brother, Anthony Russell of Ogden, grandson of Alonzo Russell, first bishop of Grafton ward.

"I was born in Grafton on October 14th, 1896," writes Mr. Russell, "growing up there to the age of 24. So far as information goes in my memory of the 'old adobe building' in your photograph . . . was made of adobes from an old adobe hole located in the lower part of Grafton to the west. The lumber in the building was hauled from Trumbull Mountain on the Colorado River . . . was of excellent quality, almost entirely free from knots. A thousand feet was considered a very good load.

"There used to be a bell in the belfry, it had been donated by James Munroe Ballard, the town's second bishop. The building was a cultural center over and above its use for religious meetings. Every Christmas there would be a community Christmas tree bearing gifts for every child in town.

Regular district school sessions were held there, along with dances, dramas and all sorts of wholesome entertainments. So were funerals. I have heard many a sermon preached there by my grandfather when I was a small boy—but never once to my knowledge was there ever mention of any dedication service there. Strange, too, because several Apostles of the Church of Jesus Christ of Latter Day Saints have delivered sermons to the people in that building.

"The last district school held in that building was in the winter of 1917-18. I was the last school teacher in Grafton."

As for Grafton, the town was one of the settlements along the Virgin River, which formed a colonizing effort by Brigham Young to grow cotton on a commercial scale. The first settler was Nathan Tenney, whose child was born during a rampaging flood, the river coursing through the bedroom where the mother lay in labor (see *Ghost Town El Dorado*).

If the river was not washing away the farms, Indians were attacking the farmers. By 1866 harassment became intolerable, and the village was abandoned entirely. The Indian troubles cooling during the next two years, Grafton farmers resettled the town. By 1877 the Saints of Grafton had increased to the point of organization into a ward, with Alonzo H. Russell as first Bishop. He acted until 1887 when he was succeeded by James Munroe Ballard. After a three-year rest, relieved by William Ison, Ballard returned to officiate until 1907, when the ward was dissolved and the Saints transferred to Rockville.

Old meeting house, most prominent of few lonely buildings still standing on banks of Virgin River in ghost town of Grafton. Old structure served community as church, school, hall for socials, Christmas parties, dances, funerals. As town's only residents, cattle wander at will through gaping doorways. Immediately at rear flows old "Rio Virgen" on its way to Zion National Park. Prominently shown here is Mount Kinesava. Trees visible here are Mulberries, surviving from days when Grafton saw boom in growing of silkworms, the leaves serving as natural food for "worms." Altogether in the Mormons' Dixie region, much silk actually was produced, woven into fabric, fashioned into dresses. The new fabric was far more comfortable next to bare skin than earlier produced woolen homespun.

A Place Th

 MORMON HISTORIAN wrote in *Under Dixie Sun,* "The motive that prompted the members of the Church of Jesus Christ of Latter Day Saints to build temples must be understood. Without this knowledge it would be impossible to know why a people with limited resources and under such trying conditions, would devote their time and labour and sacrifice their means to accomplish such a great task. The members of the church were students of the Scriptures, and with the understanding that the Lord desired a place where the Saints could gather to worship and perform ordinances in His name, built temples for this purpose."

The events leading up to the building of the St. George Temple, Church of Jesus Christ of Latter Day Saints, all center in the fire and determination of the leader, Brigham Young. There was little time to pause and rest after the emigrant band reached the Salt Lake Valley. The far-seeing leader had already formed plans for an empire where his followers could live and work and expand without the harassment they suffered in the mid-West.

Only a few months after arrival in "The Place," Young sent forth an expedition under Captain Jefferson Hunt to take a sampling of the country west of Salt Lake. Hunt's party reached the coast via what became known as the "Mormon Trail." Two years later, armed with information gained, a company of nearly fifty men set out under the leadership of Parley Pratt to explore the southern section of Utah with plans for founding sustaining settlements. They followed the trails blazed by Escalante and Smith from the rim of Salt Lake Basin to the banks of the Virgin River.

The first reports were discouraging. "The country southward for eighty miles shows no signs of fertility . . . only a wide expanse of chaotic wasteland presents itself, sandy deserts, grassless plains, perpendicular cliffs, inconceivable confusion." But when the explorers reached the place where Santa Clara Creek joined the Virgin River, they painted a different picture. Here were broad,

fertile bottom lands and, as the report noted with gross understatement, "perhaps subject to overflows." Here were grassy meadows for stock forage and although true forest was lacking, cottonwoods along the river would provide temporary building material and much firewood. The men made another discovery. "The Indians are well armed with bows and poisoned arrows. . . . We fed them . . . sung for them. The chief made a speech welcoming us to their country." Here the party had touched on the second factor that, along with severe damage from recurring floods, would menace later founded establishments. All in all, prospects for settlement of the valleys of the Virgin and its tributaries seemed favorable and were so reported to the leader on return to Salt Lake.

In the fall of 1851 a party, headed by John D. Lee, headed south to establish a beachhead in the land so slightly explored. Lee and his men organized several small settlements, including Harmony, where he found February weather as warm as May. Yet it was not until the outbreak of the Civil War that large scale efforts were made to settle the new land. The determining factor was Brigham Young's thought that the war would cut off the country's supplies of cotton and that in the warm southern sections of Utah his people could raise an ample supply of the valuable crop. So a general call was issued for settlers in the new "Dixie."

The "call" was on a voluntary basis. Most of the Saints were hardly settled after flight from persecution in Illinois, were weary of forced travel. Young, well aware that few would volunteer, read in church the list of settlers he had pre-selected. Men and women on hearing their names took the blow calmly, at least in public. Privately there were tears and protests, but all realized that there was no alternative. Accordingly, a month later three hundred families again took the hard trail, eventually arriving in the new promised land.

Brigham Young made a wise choice of settlers, selecting men skilled in all trades needed. Town-

ord Desired

St. George Temple was built in 1877 and town still lacked water system. Cistern was dug in block adjoining church, catching ground water and roof drainage. Water was then pumped to tank in town, dropping by gravity for use in baptismal font and lavatories.

Ingenious system served for 25 years when George Woodward, an original pioneer, donated $4,000 for installation of modern water supply from city system. Building was erected for future, one room 99x78 feet with 27 foot ceiling (photo courtesy Church of Jesus Christ of Latter Day Saints).

sites were surveyed quickly. Lot numbers were put in a hat, names of each man in another. A slip was drawn from each and the two passed to the man selected. Not all were thoroughly satisfied but most adjustments were made by swapping. Once a man knew which spot along the river would be his homesite, he built a shelter of willows cut from the banks, then set about readying his land. Later better homes were erected and with the city organized, plans made for a place of gathering and worship.

The first temporary structure in St. George, a "Bowery," was erected on lot 8, block 25. At projected corners four stout posts were placed, then a matting of woven willow wands was hung on the supports, this forming both roof and walls. The flimsy structure served very well during the long dry season in Dixie and sufficed for an amazing ten years.

Then, in October of 1862, came the order from Salt Lake that a more permanent structure must be built. Local plans were laid in December of the same year and the Tabernacle finished in 1876, in spite of hundreds of difficulties for the builders.

One of them was the securing of 2244 sheets of glass for windows so extravagantly planned for. These had to be hauled by wagon all the way from the nearest shipping point, Wilmington, California. There was not enough money available for this expense, so more pressure had to be put on the brethren. One man, Peter Neilson, a native of Denmark, had accumulated $600 as his life's savings, and after a sleepless night he made his decision. Up at dawn he walked the several miles to St. George to offer the money toward purchase and freighting of the glass.

The total cost of the Tabernacle was in excess of $110,000. While the bottom of the barrel was being scraped for these funds, and with completion date still four years distant, there came a letter of stunning impact—an order from Brigham Young saying, in effect, "It is time to build a Temple in Dixie and St. George is the selected place." Many of the men already building the Tabernacle were hard pressed to spare the time from their farms. Those same ranches had already been several times ravaged by spring floods and were in need of rehabilitation. Indian troubles were ravaging nearby settlements. Yet a Temple must be built.

Two factors worked for the Saints to accomplish what would have been impossible under ordinary circumstances. Most of the materials needed were available at hand, such as black volcanic rock for the foundation. The same red rock used for construction of the Tabernacle was still abundant in the quarry. This material would not be dressed but covered by a thick coat of mortar. All labor, of course, was to be donated to the Church.

Breaking of the ground was set for November 6, 1871, but a hard storm delayed it until the 9th. At the ceremonies were many Mormon dignitaries, including Brigham Young, Erastus Snow and George Smith, who officially started the work by lifting shovelsful of earth. The men doing the initial excavating soon ran into excessive ground water and the builders appealed to Brigham Young to select another location. But the leader said, "This spot has been consecrated to the building of a Temple, so let the work proceed in spite of such troubles."

Builders then took over the vacant adjoining block, constructing a deep cistern, into which drained all interfering ground water. After completion of the building, roof downspouts were also directed to the cistern to be used in commodious baptismal font and the lavatories.

The font was built oval in shape, nine feet wide on the top, six on the bottom, and 46 inches deep. It was cast in six sections, two forming the bottom, two the curved sides and two the ends. Seventeen year old George E. Howe was given the job of machining the six font sections. He did his job so well that when the pieces were bolted together they were water tight.

While work was still progressing on the upper floor an accident occurred. Young John Burt fell from the top scaffolding, dropping seventy feet to the ground. His body struck the puglocks bracing the scaffold, and he was picked up for dead. Some of the other workmen laid their hands upon him, annointing him with oil, promising him that he would recover. And he did, complaining only of some aches and sore spots.

Five years after the start of work, the Temple still lacked outside stucco, but Brigham Young, who was ailing, wished to dedicate, ready or not. On January 1, 1876, he was carried to a spot before the baptismal font. Here he sat, as other dignitaries stood around him, while Wilford Woodruff conducted dedicatory services from the upper steps of the font. Before Young left to return to Salt Lake City he remarked that he did not like the looks of the tower. "It is much too low to have grace," he said. Since the structure was so nearly completed the tower was left as it was, but five years later a fierce wind storm all but demolished it. The rebuilt tower was then brought up to the height the leader desired. But Brigham Young never returned to St. George, never saw the actual completion of the Temple.

Baptismal font, first plans for which were sternly criticized by and rejected by Brigham Young. "The oxen are bad," he said. Committee scoured Utah and Idaho for "perfect" ox which was quartered in special stable while artist Amos Howe measured and studied anatomy, plans then receiving Young's approval. Entire font with accessories weighing 18,000 pounds was cast in Salt Lake City, transported to St. George by real ox teams (photo copyright by Church of Jesus Christ of Latter Day Saints).

MONTANA

Bad men and good

Last remaining relics of one of Granite's four churches, presumably the Presbyterian. After town was abandoned church pews were taken down to Philipsburg to be used in new church building there. Stone foundations stand secure, now enclosing small and large pine trees.

Four Churches . . . Eight Saloons

THE TOP of Granite Mountain is shaped something like a dumbbell. After a severely steep climb one emerged upon a sort of landing where many buildings, including the Bi-Metallic Mine, hospital and Miners' Union Hall were built. The main street continues along the connecting bar with barely room for buildings on both sides, their fronts resting on the edge, rear ends supported on stilts. Of Granite's four churches one was built in this fashion. It is said a new preacher in it, one known for vehemence, was cautioned, "Please don't pound too hard on the pulpit, parson. There are only two props at that end."

On the propped-up line of Granite's buildings was a section of cribs termed "Silk Stocking Lane," the residence of the mine manager and three other churches. Two have completely disappeared, and of the third, almost surely the Episcopal, some traces remain scattered inside a solid granite foundation.

Any man with a thirst could find solace in one of Granite's eighteen saloons. In accordance with usual mining camp proportions, the houses of worship numbered four—Episcopal, Catholic, Presbyterian and Methodist—serving a peak population of 3,000.

Muriel Sybell Wolle in her definitive book *Montana Pay Dirt* reports that the Presbyterian Church was built in 1887 under Bishop Breer's supervision and that among chief contributors were the Charles Clarks, the McLures and other St. Louis people, as well as Mrs. John Plummer of Granite.

The ruined and deserted city of Granite crowns the actual summit of Granite Mountain. It was one of the highest mining camps, ranking with Animas Forks, Colorado and Skidoo, California, and legend gives the finding of silver here by a deer as "more truth than poetry."

Eli Hamilton was hunting on the mountain top when he shot at a deer and wounded it. The animal fell, lay still for a moment, then kicked violently, scuffing the surface patina from a rock, then regained its feet and bounded away. On reaching the spot Hamilton discovered an exposed area of shining silver. Colored or not, the facts are, Hamilton was the discoverer and the date July 6, 1875.

Hamilton teamed up with two partners and started work on the claim. They hired one McIntyre to drill a fifty-foot shaft on the ledge as a beginning, McIntyre to receive one-fourth share as pay. Each day "Mac" walked up the steep hill from Phillipsburg to oversee the work. When the shaft was finished Hamilton complained the hole did not look fifty feet deep and, when measured, the depth proved to be forty-nine feet. McIntyre was so informed and retorted, "Finish it yourselves. I wouldn't walk up that damned hill again for all the silver in the world." When put into operation in 1889, the mine returned $200,000 to $250,000 each month, none of which ever went to McIntyre.

The silver crash and resulting panic of 1893 ended a period of glory for silver mining camps. Included in a lengthy list of casualties was Granite. For the town on top of a mountain "the letter edged in black" was a telegram advising the mill foreman to close the plant. He pulled down the lever for the steam whistle, tied it in place and slowly walked home to pack. The whistle blew shrilly for a long time, then lowered in pitch and volume, some who listened weeping with the mournful tones.

Hangings Hastened Hallelujahs

Methodist Church in Bannack—one of its first frame structures, with pale blue plastering on interior walls. During the 30-year period following dedication in 1870 little church was more or less regularly used for services. Gold seekers being ever fickle, it fell empty and dusty when population drained off to new discoveries at Alder Gulch and Last Chance then was again refurbished and put to use as the wave returned. Around the turn of the century, with cessation of most mining and dredging, church was empty most Sundays, finally being abandoned entirely.

THE SUMMARY EXECUTIONS of Henry Plummer and two highwaymen had a salutory effect on crime in Bannack and the camp, slowing to normalcy, began tending to business and moral uplift. Catholics and Methodists held services in various homes until 1870, when a community church was erected on the west side of the one main street. It was intended to be completely interdenominational, but present at the dedication ceremonies was well-beloved Brother W. W. Van Orsdel, itinerant Methodist preacher. Thereafter the church was always regarded as Methodist, although other sects occasionally did hold services there.

Early in 1804 President Jefferson called Meriwether Lewis and William Clark for a final briefing before sending them on their epic journey to the Pacific Ocean. He told them to observe and record details of all plants, wild life, geography and ways of the natives. Perhaps fortunately there was nothing said about panning for gold or the course of empire might have been changed.

The explorers followed the Beaverhead River almost to its headwaters, naming a small tributary Willard Creek, but not noting that its sands were loaded with gold nuggets. They went over Lemhi Pass into present Idaho, and it was fifty-seven years before anyone found the gold.

Prospectors John White and John McGavin found plenty of it in the bed of the same creek, which they called Grasshopper because of the swarms of them in the area. It was late summer, the weather still warm, and they threw up makeshift shelters, wasting no time before getting at the gold. When the bitter cold Montana winter set in they built log cabins, and so began the town named for nearby Indians of the Bannack tribe.

During the first two years all trails and prairie tracks leading to Bannack were traveled by miners and long wagon trains, swelling the population to three thousand people of all sorts. Many were honest and hard working, but in all too big a proportion were the assorted rascals, male and female. Most of the latter were prostitutes, some with a specialty of rolling patrons passed out in drunken stupors. Lawless males were gamblers, thieves and murderers. While many of these who died have been forgotten, at least three remain etched in infamy—double-lived Henry Plummer and his bloodiest agents, Ned Ray and Buck Stinson.

Under an effective front as sheriff of the community, Plummer led a band of highwaymen, and during the first week in January, 1864, he made a fatal slip, inadvertently exposing his real identity during a holdup. On January 9 Vigilantes from nearby Virginia City took him from his office and the next day hanged him from the gallows he as sheriff had ordered constructed for the execution of a horse thief. Also hanged on the same day were Ray and Stinson, all three being buried near the gallows behind Skinner's Saloon which had served as their rendezvous.

Graves of Henry Plummer and henchmen are well removed from cemetery for more respected citizens. Unmarked except by pile of stones for years, Plummer's remains were disturbed on at least two occasions. His skull was said to have ornamented local bar for years until fire destroyed it.

House of Prayer on the Prairie

THE LATE 1830s marked the beginning of successful conversion to Christianity of aboriginal Indians in Montana. Most of them were overwhelmingly hostile but some actually requested the word of God. Hearing of the "word" from employees of the North-West Company, the Flathead and Nez Perce sent four representatives to St. Louis in 1831 with the request that missionaries be sent to their tribes to teach them how to worship the white man's God. Two of the Indian envoys died in St. Louis and were given burial in the cathedral.

Filled with enthusiasm by the story of savages awaiting conversion, Father Pierre Jean de Smet, Belgian Jesuit, traveled to the Rocky Mountains in 1840 by way of the Platte River.

He was met by a Flathead delegation on the Green River in Wyoming, baptizing many and celebrating Mass on July 5. Then he accompanied his new converts to their Gallatin Valley and there left them.

The following spring Father de Smet with two priests and four lay brothers returned to the mountains, founding St. Mary's Mission in Bitter Root Valley. As always, construction of any kind in a raw country required the utmost in ingenuity. The church was built of planks produced by whipsaw, which involved an elevated platform on which was placed a log. One man stood here to operate the upper end of the long saw; another in a pit below worked the lower end, at the same time receiving a shower of sawdust at every

Original St. Mary's Mission Church at Stevensville was forced to close in 1850 because of attacks by Indians stirred to rebellion by wintering traders and encroachment of newly established Fort Owen. Father Ravalli returned to Mission in 1866 and found much improved atmosphere, largely because of mitigating influence of Major Owen's soldiers. He then built a new church which still stands, constructed mainly of logs with finishing touches of lumber on facade (photo courtesy Byron Larson, Portland, Ore.).

stroke. Wooden pegs were fashioned to take the place of nails in the construction work. It is said that near the end of this work an Indian laborer told of a prophecy made earlier by a 13-year-old girl named Mary. "Listen to the Blackrobes," she said. "On this very spot they will build the house of prayer on the place where I am dying."

The next spring Father De Smet secured potatoes, wheat and oats from Colville, Washington, to plant the first garden in Montana and, shortly after, left for the mission at St. Paul. He also procured a pair of mill stones at Fort Vancouver where they had been dropped off by a ship from Antwerp, Belgium. When Father Ravalli came to the mission in 1845 he joined the industrious workers in building a mill that would grind grain or raw lumber, the saw fashioned from the iron tire of a wagon wheel.

Five years later, Father De Smet, who was undoubtedly one of the most traveled of all early missionaries, dropped in on Father Ravalli to see how he was getting along and later wrote that he was "most agreeably surprised. The flour mill grinds ten or twelve bushels a day, and the saw mill provides an ample supply of planks, posts, etc., for the public and private building of the nation settled here."

Father Ravalli had the courage and stamina of his predecessor. Sitting in his cabin one night he looked up to see two Indians at the window holding a wavering gun on him. Although the weapon was fired, the priest was not harmed, for once thankful his assailants were drunk. A man of many talents, he was responsible for the beautifully carved and painted wooden statues in the church. As a physician he treated his fellow workers and the Indians for wounds and diseases.

After a period of success at St. Mary's it became evident that more and more trappers and traders were taking advantage of the comparatively mild climate of the Bitterroot Valley. At first they were made welcome by the mission priests, but the men returned the hospitality by debauching the Indian converts. When the priests remonstrated the traders incited the natives against them, and in 1850 the priests were forced to close up the mission, selling the buildings to Major Owen who was establishing a fort at the site. The old mission building was incorporated in it.

In the fall of 1844, Father DeSmet assisted by Father Hoecken established the first mission to be called St. Ignatius. The location on a great bend in the Pend Oreille River about forty miles above its junction with the Columbia. By the following spring the willing and cooperative Indians of the area had constructed fourteen log houses and a large barn. Some 300 acres were then planted to grain.

Succeeding springs brought devastating floods severely damaging the buildings and farm crops. This fact, plus the temporary closure of St. Mary's forced the selection of a new site for St. Ignatius. In the rugged area since termed Mission Valley, the Fathers located a spot that was centrally located to serve three tribes, the Kalispels, Flatheads and Kutenais and was safely above any possible flood levels. The year was 1854.

By the spring of 1857, staff personnel consisted of Father Hoeken, his assistant Father Memetry and three lay brothers. In 1864 four Sisters of Providence traveled the difficult and dangerous miles from Montreal to establish a school for the Indian girls.

In the same year that saw the advent of the courageous sisters a church was erected. Built of lumber cut on a primitive whipsaw, the structure was surmounted by a belfry more than 100 feet high and was a marvel to see in that primitive wilderness. In 1891 it was replaced by the present edifice of brick.

St. Ignatius is the oldest active mission of those established in Montana Territory in mid 19th century. Shown here is the original home of the Jesuit priests who founded school, hospital and church in vast, remote wilderness of valley named for Mission Range towering above.

BRITISH COLUMBIA
Ministers and Mounties

Anglican church of St. Michael's and All Angels' in Ymir, resembling country school except for Gothic windows in front, did serve as school during week. Regular heating plant proving defective or inadequate with age, additional stove was installed with chimney emerging from window. Arrangement, meant only to be temporary, remained unaltered with cessation of church services and modern bussing of children. Surrounding trees are all 'second growth," original timber having long ago been cut for lumber, fuel and shoring in mines.

Christianity

St. Saviour's Anglican Church retains simple lines ascribed to it in Barkerville *Sentinel* in 1870. It lacks much exterior ornament, even barge boards ordinarily subject to elaboration, being quite simple. Nave is 30x20 feet, walls 18 feet high, ceiling 23 feet above floor. Brass cross, once surmounting cupola, was stolen by vandals in 1961.

Although anything but robust, enthusiastic Rev. Reynard aided in construction work, standing in dusty pit, handling lower end of whipsaw, making daily rounds of mines to gather discarded scraps of metal, taking them to blacksmith shop where he helped make nails. In carpenter's apron minister drove many nails into rough planks.

178

n the Cariboo

NLIKE THE DISCOVERY of gold in the Cariboo which came from a lucky dip of the pan, it took a bitter struggle to get an Anglican church in Barkerville.

This camp and a smaller one near it did develop a population sufficient to support churches of several denominations—Roman Catholic, Wesleyan, Presbyterian, Welsh and Anglican. All faiths built and supported church buildings but only one remains, St. Saviour's Anglican. And that church is no fading ruin but one of the most substantial relics remaining from the Cariboo rush.

It was a fantastic strike and sparked a mass migration into the British Columbia bush. Prospectors on their way to the rumored rich fields on the Thompson River farther north stopped to eat, then took one more panful of gravel from the river before pushing on. It came up nuggets. Later the place was known as Hill's Bar, but in the meantime the rush began and soon filled most of the Fraser River canyon, spreading up to the Cariboo and reaching New Caledonia.

The gold in the California Sierra was running thin. Thousands had either exhausted their claims or failed to strike any gold, and when the finds on the Fraser were news in San Francisco, the footloose adventurers were the first to board steamers for the north country, or set out overland through Oregon, Washington and British Columbia. In May, June and July of the Fraser discovery year, 23,000 left San Francisco by boat, 8,000 on foot or horse (see *Ghost Town Trails*). By the spring of 1861 the rising tide had reached the small creek called Williams, some sixty miles east of Quesnel Forks. Along the stream rose several thriving gold camps, the most important one Barkerville.

The establishing of the Anglican Church and getting a building followed the classic pattern of privation and dedication of ministers. The struggle began with the coming of Rev. R. Lundin

Church holds prominent position at end of main thoroughfare. This photo made about 1874 shows herd of beef cattle being driven into town. Except for doomed beasts, church and street still look about the same (photo courtesy B.C. Provincial Archives).

179

Brown in 1861, who made a desperate effort to clean out the "dens of iniquity" at Barkerville and neighboring camps, Cameronton and Richfield. Promoters of gambling and prostitution fought the cleanup successfully, and another missionary, Rev. C. Knipe, was sent to his aid. In spite of their gallant drive, vice in the Cariboo still proved triumphant and the missionaries left in despair.

Two others—Rev. John Sheepshanks and Rev. R. J. Dundas—picked up the trail, found the opposition of saloon keepers still strong but yet a few chinks in the miners' armor. Sheepshanks brought in with him a library of 250 books, no mean accomplishment in a country where even food was scarce. He and Dundas selected a site for a church but could not raise the necessary $1,200 and left in discouragement, the mission remaining closed for the next two years.

Next to march in the forlorn parade was a Methodist preacher from Yorkshire, Rev. James M. Reynard. With great enthusiasm, unwilling to wait for what might be the uncertain erection of a church, Reynard bought a small saloon which he promptly emptied, holding services on Sundays and teaching school on weekdays. Hardly two weeks later, on September 16, 1868, Barkerville was destroyed by a disastrous fire. The holocaust, having its origin a playful struggle between a miner and a prostitute in her crib, incinerated ev-

Chancel of St. Saviour's is set in distinct apse, 16' high, 12' wide. Centrally placed is old "bishop's chair," accurately fitted together without nails. Special services are still held infrequently in old church. Natural finish of wood in pews has become satiny through use.

erything Rev. Reynard had worked for. "My lamps, benches, robes and books are gone without a trace," he later lamented.

By this time a church was partially built at the older camp of Richfield, but it was unusable as winter had arrived and no window glass could be found in the entire area nor any trails open. "Most people," wrote Reynard, "advise me to leave, but this I cannot do, dare not and will not think of."

The winter was one of extreme hardship. There was little food available and Reynard lacked funds to purchase much of what there was. He did manage potatoes on Sunday, very likely averting scurvy, and on Christmas he indulged in a veritable "feast" of that luxury item, cabbage.

The minister's lack of funds was greatly caused by his putting almost all of his tiny stipend into a church building fund. It was a lonely effort, the Barkerville merchants showing little or no interest in the project. Finally, in a mellow mood, one of them contributed a generous sum, the act sparking further contributions, and by the spring of 1870 a church seemed assured. The exultant Reynard was quoted in the local newspaper, the *Sentinel,* as saying, "My task will be to erect a church which shall prove that men working underground still have some hopes which go upward and heavenward."

During the summer the *Sentinel* had this item: "The new church promises to be an elegant structure. It is being built from designs by the Rev. J. Reynard, which are being ably carried out by Messrs. Bruce and Mann. The style is 'Early English' in which the architectural effect is attained by due proportion of parts, bold and simple forms rather than by elaborate ornament. . . . A schoolroom and vestry complete the building. We congratulate the friends of the Anglican Church on possessing a church so appropriate to their worship. Certainly those who wish to pray as their fathers did before them here in a church which in form if not in material will remind them of the village churches of their 'fatherland.' " On Sunday, September 24, 1870, Rev. Reynard had the great joy of holding services in his own church.

Though spiritually as strong as ever, rigors of the Cariboo had weakened the pastor physically. Continued hunger and exposure drained Reynard's religious zeal, and soon after dedication of the new church he collapsed. He was forced to move to Nanaimo for medical attention but died soon afterwards, still a young man.

Venerable St. John the Divine, affectionately termed "Miners Church," Yale on Fraser River, still contains much original material after being used for more than century. Little bell was bought by popular subscription among well-wishers in England. Original cross, rotted off at base, is now in Provincial Museum, Victoria (more about Yale in *Ghost Town Trails*).

Early day view of Yale, from Provincial Archives, Victoria, was originally in collection of Rear Admiral George Fowler, Hastings, B.C., who was commander in chief of Pacific Station. Yale was originally simple stockade post and soon abandoned. Revival as town came with gold rush in late 1850s. Front Street, facing Fraser River, was lined with saloons, dance halls, gambling houses. Many victims of "rolling" were drugged or knocked out, then dumped into fast-running Fraser to be seen no more. Gold rush to Cariboo made Yale important as upper limits of navigation, stampede continued by land, route lying along precipitous, rocky canyon walls.

St. John's Indian Church was built on Lillooet Indian Reservation, on banks of Bonaparte River, at Carquille, few miles above junction with Thompson River which later joins with turbulent Fraser. Early day church was until 1955 jointly used by Indian congregations and white Catholics of Ashcroft Manor, Thompson River. When Indian population grew too large for joint use, white Ashcroft section adopted old building in town as church, later built new one. Oldest portion of Ashcroft is original building now called Ashcroft Manor, situated on hill and across Thompson. Here was early Anglican Church, later moved to brow of hill facing more modern town.

The Priest Got Rich

URING THE BRIEF PERIOD Fort Steele was "occupied" by North West Mounties, commanding officer Major Sam Steele was able to conciliate the Indians of the Kootenay to the point where whites were no longer considered in danger of a general uprising. The truce however was an uneasy one so far as native leader Chief Isadore was concerned.

Father Coccola and other priests from the mission established a short distance north in Mary's Valley had been working hand in hand with Major Steele in efforts to bring general peace with the natives. Since the Indians were suspicious of the strong combination, departure of the Mounties actually helped smooth relations with the tribes, only Isadore remaining implacable. When Father Coccola tried to move him to the mission he replied, "No. You can even threaten me with attack by soldiers, but next spring I will plow my land as usual, as I would rather die of bullets than by starvation." But by the fall of 1888 Isadore too was persuaded and total peace was established.

It was true that government funds did help sustain the mission school, that parents grudgingly

St. Peter's Catholic Church, along with buildings at St. Eugene's Mission, was built with aid of funds from silver mine originally located by Indian Peter. Church is kept in original condition, says Fr. Casey of St. Eugene's Mission. "There are two beautiful gas lighting chandeliers near the front, just above the first pews. We have had many tempting offers for them, one of $200, but we regard the church as a historical relic. Everything is the same, the carved wood reredos, elaborate, French style altar and Stations of the Cross." Fr. Casey says Mass at St. Peter's twice monthly and on special feast days. "Our congregation is tiny now, only about 15 or 20, but these are faithful. There are indications that Moyie may cease being a near ghost town, as people come to live near the beautiful Moyie Lake."

acknowledged their children attending it were "fat and healthy," not all adult Indians so well looked after. To further drain meager operating funds, out-of-luck or injured white miners dropped in for food, lodging or hospitalization. When a hungry group of Indians came to Coccola for help one day the desperate priest made a suggestion.

"Until we get enough money to help your people more fully, why don't your men go out in the hills to see if you can find a silver mine as some white men have been doing."

The several Indians did exactly that. After a lapse of a few weeks a single native named Indian Pete returned to the mission and asked to see Father Coccola, insisting the audience be completely private. When he was alone with the priest he opened a little rawhide bag and from it took a chunk of almost solid silver the size of an egg. The dazzled Coccola sent for James Cronin, a mining expert visiting at the mission.

A small party was organized to go to the spot where the galena was found, Indian Pete leading the way. The vein ultimately became the famous St. Eugene silver mine at Moyie, at its height the largest producer in the country, in ten years yielding over $10 million.

The location was immediately developed under the direction of a man who knew how to do it, technician James Cronin. One claim was staked out to Indian Pete, the next one to Father Coccola. When work began it was discovered the St. Eugene (Coccola) vein dipped into Pete's, all agreeing the two properties be worked as a unit. Deeper penetration in 1895 exposed a vein of silver-lead eight feet wide, and it was obvious the mine was bigger than the priest could manage with the small funds available. He sold out to financier John A. Finch of Spokane for $120,000, dividing it with Indian Pete and returning to his mission.

The Indian bought a plot of good farm land, had a home and barn erected on it and stocked it with cattle, horses and sheep. Coccola spent his share to build a fine new church, St. Eugene, at the mission, and finished paying for the hospital built earlier on hope. There was enough left to feed and care for his parishioners for some time.

As more money became available Fr. Coccola built a church at Moyie, a few blocks north of the St. Eugene mine. When ordering its bell from Troy, N. Y., he specified that his name be cast on the side. Fr. Casey of St. Eugene's Mission Church says, "It is considered that this was a 'trademark' of Fr. Coccola, our bell here has the same inscription as do several others built by him." The church, dedicated in 1904, was called St. Peter's, some saying that Fr. Coccola had in mind Indian Pete.

Finch retained Cronin as manager, then took him as partner. The two later acquired several more recently found claims at Moyie, by 1898 owning the Lake Shore and Moyie locations. In a few years they sold out two-thirds of their accumulated holdings, transactions from there on becoming complicated in the extreme. In 1899 a Toronto concern bought in and put $150,000 worth of equipment into the mine. In 1901 prices and general status of silver had become very unsatisfactory and the mine and concentrator were shut down, having already produced hundreds of thousands of dollars. At least the company was clear of debt, silver and lead produced having paid for all equipment recently purchased, with $200,000 ahead for a fresh start when conditions might improve. Aid came in 1904 from an unexpected source, the Canadian government, which offered a bonus of $15 per ton for silver produced in Canada by Canadians.

The next difficulty encountered was a very long, hot summer without rain, when the stream supplying necessarily huge amounts of water to the concentrating mills dried to a trickle. Then pumps were installed with lines to the almost inexhaustible Lake Moyie, fortunately close by. As time went on, trouble piled on trouble, the mine alternately opening and closing, with huge amounts of concentrate being produced whenever conditions warranted operation.

Eventually shafts grew so deep as to make lifting difficult and over-expensive. Since the tunnels ran horizontally out under the lake, one company, the Cambrian, undertook to sink a caisson of fir timbers to bedrock out in the lake, planning to pump out the water so as to drill directly down to the lode. This worked until water leakage stopped operations. All mines then closed down for twenty years.

Then a new outfit, the Consolidated Company, made large investments at the site to rework the old sumps still holding much metal wasted in older methods. Processed ore finally considered exhausted was run on a conveyor over the railroad to the lake and there dumped. Newspaper accounts at that time (1907) seemed optimistic, but the spurt of activity again proved only temporary. The St. Eugene, Society Girl across the lake, and other smaller mines have been idle a long time now.

"*Christianity's Onward March*"

ADIES AND GENTLEMEN, it would seem particularly appropriate that on this anniversary day of Most Gracious Majesty the Queen, ruling over the destinies of the greatest Christian nation and people on all earth, that we should be permitted to participate in the laying of this cornerstone of the edifice that will mark another milestone in the progress of Christianity and civilization." On and on flowed flowery rhetoric, at last ending with "Years hence as man passes through these natural gateways to the North, possibly we may all have passed away, may this edifice stand as a monument of the pioneers who have gone before, the pioneers of Christianity in this wilderness of mountain, lake and stream."

Thus spake Capt. John Irving, famous Fraser River skipper and coastal steamboat man as quoted in the *Bennett* as he addressed the faithful at the dedication of the Miners' Church in Lake Bennett, B. C. on May 24, 1899. And so Presby-terians had a "house of God" in the Yukon.

No one wanted a church in 1897 when the word was out that there was gold in the Yukon. The only thing the thousands that rushed northward wanted was gold. They left a general despression in the United States and wanted to get away from it as well as go hell-bent into some adventure. And now, after Skagway, White Pass or Chilkoot Trail, all they wanted was more food, more rest—and that gold.

At Lake Bennett boats must be built to get to the Yukon and Klondike Rivers, 550 miles downstream. Trees were cut and whipsawed into planks, the vessels put together and the seams caulked with pitch from the same spruce trees that supplied the lumber. With all the traffic the lakes became a pair of huge bottlenecks, particularly Bennett where most of the boat builders were. It was said there was a swarm of 10,000 men there during the rush.

A sizeable city was formed, the shelters mostly

Rear view of miners' church shows construction mainly of bark slabs from logs. Until break-up in late May this vista is one of ice and snow. This photo taken in June shows some snow remaining on mountain sides.

Against spectacular backdrop of snowy peaks old Miners' Church stands isolated on knoll once swarming with boat builders. Only other building now is way-station of White Pass and Yukon Railroad, out of photo at left. Little narrow gauge train still runs between Skagway, Alaska and Whitehorse, Yukon Territory. Stopping here at noontime, passengers may detrain long enough to enjoy bounteous, family-style lunch. Main course is roast moose meat. This may explain origin of stacks of immense antlers stored in otherwise empty church.

Scene at Lake Bennett in old photo before church was constructed on knoll at left center.

tents or tent houses. On this scene, in late 1898 arrived the Presbyterian minister and church builder, Rev. Andrew Grant with his coworker Rev. A. J. Sinclair. These hardy pastors had been entrusted with the job of bringing Presbyterianism to the Yukon.

The pair had come thus far in the same fashion as did the miners. Arriving in Skagway, Alaska, they were just in time to witness the historic clash between famed bad man Soapy Smith and law man Frank Reid. Neither contender survived, Smith dying on the spot and Reid succumbing shortly. There being no other ministers in Skagway at the time, Rev. Andrew Grant obliged by conducting the funerals. He and Sinclair found other tragedies along the way, including the deaths of several men who had died from accidents. For these they also performed final obsequies. At Bennett City, at the lake head, the ministers agreed a church was badly needed there

and that the Yukon could wait a little longer.

Selecting a site on the knoll, with a view surely unequaled anywhere, Grant and Sinclair set about collecting materials and help from the boat builders. They got bark slabs, discarded when logs were squared for whipsawing, and some lumber. Work progressed all winter with temperatures often dropping far below zero, and at last the church was finished in May.

All this time a railroad was building up the pass from Skagway, and was completed that same year. Grant and Sinclair had failed to realize what would happen once the narrow-gauge was completed through Bennett to White Horse. There would be no need to stop at the city by the lake. And so when the line came through shortly after completion of the church, erstwhile boat builders folded up their tents and silently stole away on the train. The church so enthusiastically constructed of slab wood was left to decay in isolated splendor.

YUKON
Under the Midnight Sun

St. Andrews Presbyterian Church, erected in 1901, was built near Yukon River. First St. Andrews in Dawson was log structure built by Rev. Andrew Grant who had arrived by same route from Skagway, Alaska, followed by argonauts of gold rush, sometime in 1897. Rev. Grant, locally called "Doctor" because of his medical training, was called upon to serve in extra-curricular capacity when pneumonia epidemic ravaged Dawson in fall of 1900. Appointed director of Good Samaritan Hospital, he organized staff of several nurses including a Miss Smith as matron. Though sketchily equipped, pastor-doctor and nurses saved many who would have died in privations of freezing, drafty shelters, poor diet lacking in essential nutrients.

Called east in 1900, Rev. Grant was replaced in Dawson by Rev. J. J. Wright who had been serving in Whitehorse. During following year Rev. Wright obtained hall and reading room for church. In 1901 Rev. Grant was recalled to Dawson and for succeeding seven years continued as minister and hospital superintendent. During 1901 with generous support of members and adherents he erected this structure, said to seat congregation of 600 besides choir. Soon after finishing of church, a pipe organ was installed and manse added (photo courtesy John Gould, Dawson, Y.T.).

Monument to Courage

STANDING ON THE BANK of the darkly rushing Yukon River in Canada is a simple white monument marking the grave of a tragic figure of the great gold rush of 1897. The inscription on the face, translated from the Latin reads, "Here lies the body of Father William H. Judge, S. J., a man of charity, who with the cooperation of all here, first erected a house for the sick and a temple for God; a man who, being mourned by all, died piously in the Lord, the 16th of January, 1899." Resting in this vast land of lonely spaces are the remains of a saintly man who, in the middle of a madness for gold that obsessed thousands of ordinary mortals, never panned out a shovelful of gravel. Father Judge, little known outside of the Far North, would surely be unique anywhere in his singleness of purpose, that of saving the souls of men.

Preceding the discoveries of vaster amounts of gold in the tributaries of the Klondike (then called the Troandik), the yellow stuff had been located at Fortymile, about half way between Klondike and the Alaskan border. Here in 1896 Father Judge set up a small church for the miners. Hardly had the temporary structure been completed when news of the strike on Bonanza Creek reached Fortymile. Following the usual pattern, the population of Fortymile soon began to filter away, departing for the new location farther up the Yukon.

A man of clear perception, Father Judge saw that his duties would be far more important in the camp that would soon eclipse the settlement at Fortymile. It was typical of him that, while he saw to it that a medical kit was placed on his sled, food was almost forgotten. Before the week on the trail was ended he nearly starved and his death was reported. Two days later Dawson's newspaper, the *Klondike Nugget* carried the news, "The stampeders from Fortymile to the Klondike in the winter of 96-97 remember overtaking a solitary and feeble old man with a single rope over his shoulders, and a single dog helping the lead along. This was the Father hastening to a field where he was conscious his ministering services would be most required."

First gold strikes were along Bonanza Creek. The stream flows into the Klondike, in turn emptying into the mainstream, the mighty Yukon. At the latter junction there is a nearly level area, a sort of delta formed by debris deposited by a regularly rampaging Klondike slightly spreading and slowing at this point. Here Father Judge found an already established city of tents. A few log cabins were being erected, the timbers having been rafted down the Yukon.

Noting many sick and injured men going without attention Father Judge first saw to it that a rude hospital was built of some of these logs and rough material. This structure measuring 20 by 50 feet, two stories high, was ready for use on August 20, 1897. Still not quite dry was the white lead-sized muslin that disguised the rough logs inside.

It had been planned that the Sisters of St. Ann would arrive from Seattle in time for the opening but the boat ran aground in unseasonal low water. They were forced to return as far downstream as Holy Cross where they spent the winter. In early July when the ice-bound river had opened, the Sisters resumed their journey, arriving to meet a joyful mob of Dawson residents.

As soon as construction was under way for the hospital Father Judge turned to his church. By this time another batch of logs arrived by raft and dog sled. With the willing and able help of miners, shell of the structure was soon erected and chunks filled with mud. It was built just south of the hospital and parallel to it, an imposing 50 by 24 feet with a small tower, steeple and little bell.

Yukon's rigorous winter arrived before final completion but services were held in the rough barnlike building, worshippers, clad in full outdoor clothing, huddling around two huge stoves while observing Mass. Just before Easter Sunday of 1898 glass windows were put in place, a little hand organ brought up from an abandoned mission downriver, for Easter services the homely little instrument augmented by a "fiddler" who did his best at sacred music. The congregation of about 200 miners, gamblers and dancehall girls was seated on rough planks laid on stove-length sections of logs. This particular Easter Sunday was doubtless the happiest day in the life of the little priest who worked so hard for its celebration.

Finished August 20, 1897, edifice served Catholics, many Protestants in camp until next June when it was destroyed by fire. Adjoining structure shown in this post card view is St. Mary's Hospital which escaped destruction by efforts of volunteer fire fighting residents. Behind is seen part of Moosehide Dome. In Dawson's heyday summit of butte was scene of annual celebration when gay crowds assembled to view Midnight Sun which rolled along summits of Ogilvie Mountain Range near Arctic Circle, then rising to begin another day (more photos, story in *Western Ghost Town Shadows*).

But on Sunday, June 5th the church lay in blackened ruins. Two weeks later Father Judge later wrote sadly, "My nice church in which I took so much pride, all the altar furniture, vestment, lace curtains, flowers and everything for Mass and benediction, were burned."

He could blame only himself. He worked late and was saying his nightly prayers when a miner rushed in to tell him a friend was badly hurt and wanted the priest. Father Judge rushed to the bedside of the injured man, forgetting the candle which continued to burn until the flame reached the base of the wooden sconce, then ignited the muslin on the wall.

To a man the population of the camp joined in a heroic effort, not so much to save the obviously doomed church as to evacuate patients from the nearly filled hospital close by. A bucket brigade formed a line to the Yukon, the first man splashing pails of water on each blaze.

In the meantime religious authorities realized the growing town of Dawson would very soon require more than one lonely missionary so four priests and one secular priest were dispatched to the Far North. First to arrive was Father Lefebvre O.M.I. carrying a portable altar for use in planning outlying missions. He and Father Judge set up a large tent at the foot of the "dome," a small mountain backing the town, and here services were held until a new church could be built.

Most of the eager men who rushed to the Klondike were doomed to failure and bitter disappointment but some lucky few made fortunes. One was "King" Alex McDonald, the first load of gold from his locations to arrive in Dawson weighing 750 pounds, valued at about $150,000. Always handsomely dressed and more than six feet tall, McDonald walked into the tiny tent housing Father Judge soon after the fire and said to him "Father, I'm very sorry you have lost your church, but I'm sure we can do something about it. I will undertake to provide all the money necessary to build a new one immediately." With almost unlimited funds, the new church, three times the size of the first, went up in record time. Again Father Judge records, happily this time, "The new church is very fine for this part of the world and would do credit to a much older town. It has cost $25,000 and is the gift of one good man, Alexander McDonald. I said the first Mass in it on August 21, 1898 and blessed and then turned it over to the Obiates of Mary who have charge of the parish now . . . I think we shall have about 15,000 people in Dawson this winter. I fear there will be much suffering; there are thousands without money, without work and trying to live in tents with winter already upon us."

It was characteristic of the man that he did not mention the fact it was his health, never good and now failing, that forced him to withdraw from active participation in heading the new church, only voicing his concern for others.

The only official duties now for Father Judge were as hospital chaplain. He had a new chapel built to adjoin the building, said the first prayers there and a few days later went to his bed where he died, Jan. 16, 1899. He was 49 years old.

Records of the funeral state that "A great concourse of people composed of the most respectable people in town, without respect to nationality or creed" assembled for the funeral. He was burried "under the Gospel side of the altar." So many people expressed a wish to leave some sort of record of what Father Judge had meant to them that a simple statement was prepared to this effect. The short document carries the signatures of 231 citizens ranging from the mayor to a dancehall girl.

Dawson's second Catholic Church, erected through the generosity of Alexander McDonald and dedicated August 21, 1898, received a general refurbishing in 1900. At the same time a pipe organ was placed in the edifice. Shortly after all this a bell weighing 1,150 pounds and bearing in bronze the names of donors was hung in the belfry. The official blessing of the bell was celebrated by Bishop Langevy, June 23, 1901.

The big church was built almost on the bank of the Yukon and at the extreme north end of the then sprawling town. In a few short years it became painfully apparent that the big days of Dawson were fading, the first fantastic rush from the outside lessening, the town shrinking. Already the business center had moved south, two blocks from the waterfront and when the religious authorities decided to build a school they did so with caution and foresight. In 1904 a two-story structure was placed in a more central location, lower floor dedicated as a school, upper with a sparsely furnished chapel.

Dawson at its height held some 30,000 people counting those living along nearby creeks, the "suburbs." By 1910 the glittering gold that had been so abundant in the Klondike was reduced to a fine powder, available only to huge dredging operations. Individual miners and families moved to the outside or other fields and the big church on the river bank was often empty excepting in summer and on such special days as Christmas and Easter. In 1923 Father Rivet was at last forced to pull down the church. With the help of a Mr. Trembly, he did so gradually and sadly.

Most of the furnishings, such as the sanctuary lamp, communion rail and statues were removed to the chapel in the newer building. Also transferred were the bell, tall cross over the altar and finally the altar itself. Before the latter was touched Father Rivet carefully marked the exact spot of Father Judge's resting place. When all evidence of the once proud church was gone a monument was placed on the grave, now exposed to open skies, surrounding hills and darkly rushing river.

Old log rectory, Whitehorse, Y.T., completed in 1901 (photo courtesy George Kellett, Whitehorse).

Pastor Brought Accordion

THE FIRST ANGLICAN SERVICE to be held in Whitehorse was conducted by the Rev. R. J. Bowen who came up to the Yukon by one of the steamships. One of the interesting sidelights to this is that he bought an accordion before starting on his way as he knew there were no facilities for music. Apparently he was threatened with the same fate of Jonah as he practiced on the journey.

The Rev. R. J. Bowen with the assistance of the people in Whitehorse started to build the Old Log Church in 1900, and had it completed very quickly, by October of thear year.

Robert W. Service was the secretary to the Vestry, and his minutes can be seen in the church museum. Queen Elizabeth's signature is also there, and a record of the visit of Prince Philip.

There were additions to the church at various times, and in 1963 the building was raised and repairs done to the foundations. The floor and sides are now in excellent condition, but some work is required on the roof.

It was the Cathedral church of the Diocese of the Yukon after 1953, when the Right Reverend Tom Greenwood transferred his see from Dawson City to Whitehorse. In 1960 the church was replaced as a place of worship by a new Cathedral, and is now a church museum for the Yukon. It holds relics from all denominations.

The Rectory was built immediately after the completion of the church and was finished in 1901. It was originally a square structure, with two rooms up and two down. It had electricity installed right from the beginning, but not plumbing. This was put in at a later date. It has always been heated by wood, although at one time there was an oil cook stove. It takes about 14 cords of wood all the year round.

Like the church, it has been added to at various times, and the alterations made to the heating and other facilities. There are now ten rooms, but not all can be used during the winter. At one time the kitchen was a school for Indians.

In 1964 the Rector moved to a new building, Mr. and Mrs. George Kellett acting as caretakers for the house and grounds around the church. It is a very comfortable home and a source of interest to the many visitors.

Old log church, Whitehorse, Y.T., built in 1900 (photo courtesy George Kellett, Whitehorse).

INDEX
to Churches and Denominations

BIBLIOGRAPHY

The Saga of the Comstock Lode—George B. Lyman
Baptists and the Oregon Frontier—Clifford R. Miller
History of the State of Idaho—Cornelius J. Brosnan
God Goes West—Muriel Sibell Wolle in *Colorado Quarterly*
Stampeded to Timberline—Muriel Sibell Wolle
Montana Pay Dirt—Muriel Sibell Wolle
Ghost Towns of British Columia—Bruce Ramsey
Indian Shakers—H. G. Barnett
Barkersville—Bruce Ramsey
Writers' Project Guide to the Western States
Here Rolled the Covered Wagons—Albert and Jane Salisbury
Temple Square and other publications, Church of Jesus Christ of Latter Day Saints
Pioneer History of Oregon—Emma Gene Miller
Tumacacori's Yesterdays—Earl Jackson
The Ghost Town of Bodie—Russ and Annie Johnston
Story of Bodie—Ella Cain

Story of Early Mono County—Ella Cain
The California Missions—Lane Books
Historic Spots in California—Hoover and Rensch
Ghosts of the Adobe Walls—Nell Murbarger
Ghosts of the Glory Trail—Nell Murbarger
Nevada's Turbulent Yesterdays—Don Ashbaugh
The History of the State of Nevada—Thompson and West
History of Milwaukie (Oregon)—Charles Oluf Olson

ACKNOWLEDGEMENTS

SPECIAL THANKS to David Anderson, Ferndale, Calif.; Andrew Genzoli, Eureka, Calif.; Rev. Albert Shadrick, Trinidad, Colo.; Dean C. Mabry, Municipal Judge, Trinidad, Colo., and many ministers, priests, rabbis and other religious leaders for their help, information and use of historic photos.